HOW TO
HELP YOUR CHILD
OVERCOME
YOUR DIVORCE

For separated, divorcing, and divorced parents with children ages twelve and under

HOW TO
HELP YOUR CHILD
OVERCOME
YOUR DIVORCE

Elissa P. Benedek, M.D.
Catherine F. Brown

Newmarket Press
New York

First Newmarket Press paperback edition 1998.
Copyright © 1995 by American Psychiatric Press, Inc. All rights reserved.

Previously published in hardcover by American Psychiatric Press, Inc. Books published by the American Psychiatric Press, Inc., represent the views and opinions of the individual authors and do not necessarily represent the policies and opinions of the Press or the American Psychiatric Association.

This book is published in the United States of America and in Canada.

10 9 8 7 6 5 4 3 2 1

LIBRARY OF CONGRESS CATOLOGING-IN-PUBLICATION DATA
Benedek, Elissa P.
How to help your child overcome your divorce / Elissa P. Benedek and Catherine F. Brown.
— 1st Newmarket Press paperback ed.
p. cm.
Originally published: Washington, D.C. : American Psychiatric Press, c1995.
Includes bibliographical references and index.
ISBN 1-55704-329-9 (pbk.)
1. Children of divorced parents—Psychology. 2. Children of divorced parents—Family relationships. 3. Divorced parents—Psychology. 4. Divorced parents—Family relationships. 5. Divorce—Psychological aspects. I. Brown, Catherine F., 1954–. II. Title.
HQ777.5.B45 1998
306.89—dc21   98-5011
                                                                                        CIP

BRITISH LIBRARY CATALOGING IN PUBLICATION DATA
A CIP record is available from the British Library.

QUANTITY PURCHASES
Companies, professional groups, clubs, and other organizations may qualify for special terms when ordering quantities of this title. For information, write Special Sales, Newmarket Press, 18 East 48th Street, New York, New York 10017, or call (212) 832-3575, or fax (212) 832-3629.

Manufactured in the United States of America.

NOTE: The authors have worked to ensure that all information in this book is accurate at the time of publication and consistent with general psychiatric and medical standards. As medical research and practice continue to advance, however, therapeutic standards may change. Moreover, specific situations may require a specific therapeutic response not included in this book. For these reasons, and because human and mechanical errors sometimes occur, we recommend that readers follow the advice of physicians and therapists directly involved in their care or the care of a member of their family.

Contents

**Minimizing the Effects
of the Legal Process on
Your Children**

Impact of Divorce on Children

CHAPTER 8 141

**Special Parenting
Issues**

CHAPTER 9 155

**Parenting Techniques
to Build Your Child's
Self-Esteem**

*The names of people and
identifying circumstances of cases
cited in this book have been
changed to ensure confidentiality.*

Introduction

One evening not long ago I[1] was having dinner with a friend of mine who has two children, Natalie, nine, and Max, twelve. As we waited for our food, she heatedly told me about what had happened to her children at school a few days earlier.

"You wouldn't believe it!" said my friend, Edith. "The other day I had to run into the school office for a few minutes after I picked the kids up. They waited for me by the car in the parking lot. I wasn't in the office long when next thing I know, Nat comes running in to tell me that some boy is hitting Max!"

She took a deep breath and went on with her tale. "I left the office and ran out to the car, but by that time, the boy was gone. Max had a cut on his face where the boy had hit him. Nat said that she tried to stop the boy from hitting Max, but the boy pushed her away."

"Was Max all right?" I asked.

"Yes, he was OK, but I think Nat was the one who was really upset," said Edith. "This wasn't the first time the boy had attacked Max, so I felt I should tell the principal what had happened so she would discipline him or take some other suitable action."

"Did she?" I prompted.

"Well, no," said Edith, by now her expression hardening.

---

[1] "I" throughout this book refers to Dr. Elissa P. Benedek.

"I went to talk to her the day after this happened. I had Max come with me so he could tell her exactly what the boy had done and how Max had responded. She looked at the cut on his face, and then sent him back to his classroom. I couldn't believe what she said next." By now Edith was angry. "The principal said, 'Well, the boy's parents are divorced. In these kinds of cases I don't think there's much we can do. We just have to have extra understanding.'"

Edith paused for a moment. "I don't see what having divorced parents has to do with anything. The principal has essentially given this boy permission to keep on terrorizing other kids."

Edith was right. The principal in this case did a huge disservice to the boy on a number of counts. First, the principal's attitude reflected her assumption that children whose parents are divorced are somehow different from children in traditional two-parent families—that perhaps they can be expected to get into more trouble, have more difficulties with other kids. Second, she failed to hold him accountable for his actions, making excuses for his irresponsibility and dangerous behavior. And third, she ignored information suggesting that the boy needed help in learning how to express his emotions in a safe and effective way. Perhaps in the back of her mind was the notion that such instruction would have little effect on a child from a "broken" home.

Unfortunately, this principal is not alone—many people hold similarly erroneous assumptions and attitudes about children whose parents are divorced, including the parents themselves.

Divorce is probably one of the most traumatic events that children can experience, and it usually sets off a series of transitions in children's lives that have the potential to seriously affect their development. Notice I used the word *potential*. Living in a divorced family is not inevitably harmful to children—it's how the parents handle the dissolution of their marriage, conduct their lives and their relationship after the divorce, and continue to care for the children that counts. Thus, as a parent who is divorced or contemplating divorce, you should know that you have the power to approach this time in your life in such a way that your children will adjust successfully to the family's changed circumstances and grow into well-adjusted and competent adults.

One of the biggest challenges faced by divorcing parents is being able to provide extra attention and strong, consistent guidance to their children at a time when they may feel incapable of doing so. Not surprisingly, many divorcing parents are consumed by their own problems and expend most of their energy in trying to handle them. Not much may be left over for the children. And families in which there is a long history of abuse— physical, emotional, or drug related—are at an even greater disadvantage, since these children may have had inadequate parenting for quite some time. With confidence and determination, however, you can overcome these types of problems and achieve success in parenting your children at this time. Although occasionally it may be difficult, and even lonely, your commitment is important to your children's future.

The first step toward helping your children adjust to your divorce is being aware of the primary tasks facing you at this time:

➢ To help your children understand what separation and divorce mean in your family's particular situation.

➢ To tell your children about how the divorce will affect them in concrete terms, appropriate to each child's age.

➢ To reassure your children that they will continue to be loved and well cared for and then follow through on that promise.

➢ To encourage your children to have a happy, close relationship with their other parent and then do everything you can to make that possible.

➢ To keep your relationship with your ex-spouse as free of conflict as possible. If there is conflict between the two of you, you must shield your children from it.

➢ To cooperate with your ex-spouse on matters pertaining to the children.

➢ To help your children feel good about themselves as unique and valued individuals.

➢ To help your children obtain help and guidance from other people in their lives and professional sources as necessary.

This book is the product of my years of experience as a child psychiatrist who has dealt extensively with divorced and divorcing families in treatment and in the judicial system, and it will give you the information you need to help you fulfill these obligations. Although this book is not a surefire guide for avoiding all childrearing problems related to divorce, it explains certain principles to follow so that, at the least, you know you are doing your best to raise your children to be emotionally healthy, happy, and secure and to create a stable home in which they feel supported and safe. Making the effort to focus on your children's needs during this difficult transition not only benefits them now but also builds a strong foundation for their future well-being as they mature into adults.

You and the children's other parent will always remain the most important figures in your children's lives. The greatest tragedy that can befall your children right now is the feeling that they have lost both of their parents. The best feeling is that they have two loving parents and a dependable network of supportive family members and friends.

Chapter 1

It's a Different World Now

If you grew up in the 1950s or '60s, you're probably familiar with the television sitcom *Leave It to Beaver*. In this popular series still in reruns, June and Ward Cleaver were the parents of what appeared to be the picture-perfect family. Living in a settled, handsome neighborhood, they had two rambunctious but lovable boys. The typical episode revolved around the boys' escapades and their owning up to some relatively minor misdeed just before the closing credits.

June reminds me of many of the mothers I knew when I was growing up. Like her peers, she was a stay-at-home mom, on call whenever the family needed her. In her cheerful willingness to serve, she was a nearly invisible, but essential, backdrop in her children's and husband's busy lives. Ward, too, was the epitome of the perfect '50s parent. While June kept the domestic front purring smoothly along, Ward left their nicely appointed colonial each morning for his white-collar job. When he returned home in the evening, he was always ready with just the right lecture for his errant sons, delivered with the appropriate balance of firmness, understanding, and humor.

Now it's the 1990s, and it looks as though June and Ward and Wally and the Beaver have left the neighborhood, never to return. Indeed, if the Cleavers lived in today's fast-paced, demanding, and sometimes scary world, their lives would be far different: most likely, June would be working full time, and the young Beaver would be in a day care program at the end of his school day. Wally might be over at his girlfriend's house, unsupervised by adults because *her* mother would be at work as well. Ward might stop for a few groceries on the way home and start dinner after he cleaned up the leftover breakfast mess. After dinner, June might run the washer while Ward checked over the kids' homework.

Although it's regrettable that family life in this decade is typified for many of us by having to work so hard to keep up with the high cost of living, and never having enough time to do all the things we must or would like to do, there are many positive aspects to the way American society has evolved in the past 30 to 40 years. Today, women have many more choices to make about the course of their lives, and they have gained many kinds of freedom. Perhaps the most important is economic: now earning their own paychecks and making their own decisions about how they want to live their lives, women no longer must depend on a man—be it father or husband—for food, clothing, and shelter. Women also have reproductive freedom; they are in full control of the decision when or whether to have children. Men have been challenged as well as a result of these changes: they are learning to express their feelings openly, share childrearing responsibilities, and accept women as their equals.

It's no coincidence that the divorce rate, relatively low in the 1950s, soared in the '60s and '70s. In the evolving, freer climate, and with the emphasis on the happiness of the individual as opposed to the good of society, both men and women have felt more open to questioning social and religious strictures about the permanence of marriage. Along with this has come acceptance of no-fault divorce and the notion that a marriage can be ended because the parties have stopped getting along or loving each other. No longer is it necessary to prove mental cruelty or conduct a smear campaign against a spouse to have a marriage legally dissolved.

Although most of these changes are for the better—in fact, as a woman practicing in a traditionally male-dominated field, I have benefited from many of them—we, as Americans, have not yet taken the appropriate steps to reshape our society in such a way that most of these changes work more successfully. For example, although about 40 percent of the mothers in this country are now in the labor force—and 18 percent of these women have children under the age of six—government has taken little action to make day care more available, affordable, and safe. Even mothers and fathers in higher income brackets often cannot find acceptable or reliable care. And although no-fault divorce has certainly made it easier to escape a failed relationship, many custodial mothers are having a difficult time collecting adequate child support. The time has come to address these and related problems that undermine the future of children in this country.

What Price Freedom?

Tragically, one of the prices we are now paying for the gain in personal growth and expansion of life choices is the disintegration of the traditional family and the repercussions of divorce. Consider these statistics:

➢ Since 1974 the number of divorces has exceeded a million a year.
➢ One of two marriages contracted today will end in divorce.

➢ More than a million children each year experience their parents' divorce.

➢ Forty-five percent of the children born in 1983 will experience parental divorce, 35 percent will experience their parents' remarriage, and 20 percent will experience a parent's second divorce.

➢ About half of all marriages end within seven years of the marriage. This means that many children—about a third of those born in the 1980s—will spend some time in a single-parent household before the age of 18.

➢ Forty-three percent of divorced mothers have annual incomes of less than $10,000.

➢ Visitation disputes occur in 44 percent of families undergoing divorce with children who are age five or younger.

➢ Diagnosable psychological problems occur in 30 percent to 40 percent of individuals whose parents divorce. This rate is three times higher than that for individuals growing up in families that remain together.

These statistics leave no doubt that divorce is a serious social problem, but it is simplistic to think of divorce in good versus bad terms (a topic that is discussed further in Chapter 2). Attitudes toward divorce have changed over time, depending on the needs of society. The first written divorce regulations appeared in the ancient Babylonian Code of Hammurabi. In many ancient societies, only the husband had the power to divorce his wife. When Christianity was established, its early teachers eliminated divorce, believing that marriage should be permanent until death. The result was not only family unity (regardless of the happiness of each family member) but also community stability. Today most Christian sects recognize divorce. One exception is the Catholic Church, which continues to maintain strict teachings against divorce and complicated guidelines on granting annulments. In many areas, however, the church sponsors outreach efforts aimed at divorced Catholics and their families.

We can now say that, for the most part, the pendulum has

swung to the point where the good of each individual is an important and worthy consideration. And, albeit much too slowly, this trend has begun to include children. It's surprising to us in late twentieth-century America to realize that it wasn't all that long ago when children were valued primarily in economic terms, an asset on the ledger sheet for the work they could perform to help support the family. If the family lived in a rural area, the children picked cotton or worked in mines. If the family lived in the city, the children were hired out to work long hours in factories and shops for a pittance. Many children were abused or injured until a new federal labor law was passed in 1938 placing strict limits on the use of child labor.

Perhaps today, some cynics would argue, children are being used in different, perhaps no less harmful, ways by divorcing parents who become pitted against each other, either by their own intentions or by the nature of this country's adversarial legal system. Thus trapped in a tug-of-war between their parents, children have oftentimes been treated much the same as the family's washer and dryer: Who gets to keep them? Mom or Dad?

Chapter 2

THE DECISION TO DIVORCE: PUTTING THE CHILDREN FIRST

Given the sobering facts associated with divorce and the accumulating data showing that children whose parents are divorced are at a higher risk for a variety of developmental and psychological problems, many parents may find themselves questioning the wisdom of splitting up the family. Some may wonder whether they should put aside their personal wishes and stick with their marriage, at least until the children leave home. Those who never wanted the divorce in the first place but whose spouses demanded it may feel tempted to throw the statistics at them in an attempt to create feelings of guilt or bring about a change of mind.

Research findings and my own clinical experience have demonstrated repeatedly that staying together just for the sake of the children is rarely successful. Depending on the particular family's circumstances, staying together may harm the children more than had the couple divorced when their problems became irreconcilable. Children who witness parental conflict—ranging from studied silences to constant shouting and threatening to actually hitting each other and worse—are less well adjusted than children from divorced families. Such verbal and physical abuse is not uncommon among divorcing couples. It has been estimated that almost half of all divorces involve some degree of physical violence. In these cases, the children may welcome a parental separation as a respite from the fighting, a chance for the home to evolve into what it should have been all along: a protected haven. In short, sometimes the only way to fix a marriage is to end it.

"My dad used to threaten my mom that he was going to leave her," twenty-year-old Carl told me one day. "Then he'd act like he was going to hit her until she'd break down and cry. When she finally did, he seemed almost happy. Then he'd grab the car keys, drive off, and wouldn't return until he was good and drunk. I hated him. I often wished he'd never come back."

Carl was in therapy because, in his words, he had no friends. He learned through our sessions together that his lack of friendships was partially caused by his difficulty in trusting people. In his formative years, he had learned that words could never be taken at face value and that he could rely on no one to protect him and give him support, not even the two people responsible for bringing him into this world. Not incidentally, he also learned intimidating ways to relate to other people.

In cases like these, divorce can indeed be a rational solution. The first few years of fifteen-year-old Sarah's life were much like Carl's, but her mother divorced her father when Sarah was six. I saw both Sarah and her mother in therapy as they made the adjustment to their new circumstances, and although there were the inevitable ups and downs, their lives returned largely to normal within a few years. When I ran into them ten years later, mother and daughter were happily shopping for a prom dress. The lesson Sarah learned was far different from the one Carl absorbed: Sarah's role model was a strong, capable woman who was able to take control of her life and come up with workable solutions to her problems.

Having divorced parents or being part of a divorced family is not harmful in itself. Far more important is the quality of the relationships between family members and their home life. This is not to argue that in all cases divorce is the answer. In this post–Me Decade era, many individuals feel they have a right to put their own needs ahead of everyone else's regardless of the consequences. People may turn to divorce instead of to a marriage counselor or therapist, because they don't believe they should have to work hard to make a relationship successful and satisfying.

Each person's situation must be analyzed according to its own unique circumstances, and trained professionals are available for doing just that (see Chapter 12 on how to choose a therapist). When parents are certain that in their case the right course of action is divorce, however, my message is unequivocal: their primary goal must be to minimize the impact of the divorce on their children.

Children Know Something's Wrong

Because marital breakups are not uncommon today, most children, except for the very youngest, are familiar with the word *divorce* and have some understanding that it refers to families in which "the mommy and daddy don't live together anymore," as one five-year-old once told me. Most children have at least one friend whose parents are divorced or have cousins or other relatives living in families of divorce. Such is the pervasiveness of divorce that even children who live in a happy home often worry that their mom and dad might get a divorce, too—just like their best friend's mom and dad did. This is a powerful fear in children's lives, extending to the very heart of their sense of identity and security.

If your marriage has been strained or unhappy for some time, there's a good chance that your children are already aware that something is amiss. In fact, in homes where there is a lot of conflict—especially physical violence or alcoholism—children learn to read their parents' moods without even realizing they are doing so. They pick up even the most subtle of clues as to when it is safe to approach an angry or upset parent or wise to stay out of the way. To misjudge that parent, they know all too well, can elicit a barrage of angry words or a swipe to the head.

Having a rudimentary knowledge of divorce and living with parental battling, however, don't prepare most children for the announcement that their parents are separating and divorcing. When the rupture in the family occurs, as made evident by one of the parents moving out of the family home, many children are genuinely shocked. Of course, the shock is even more marked in those relatively few children who have been shielded from their parents' disagreements.

The reactions of most children to their parents' divorce are deeply rooted in a child's self-centered perception of the world. In their few years of life, they have had ample evidence to support that view: Mom's and Dad's lives appear to revolve mainly around the kids and their needs. A different world order is impossible for them to imagine, as they have known nothing else.

The Importance of Attachment

From early life, children form attachments to their primary care-takers, usually the mother and father. This is a sign of healthy development. Without secure attachments, and the loving physical contact from which they spring, children fail to mature normally. As these children grow up, they feel insecure and un-sure of themselves, have difficulty forming relationships with other people, and are at risk for developing a variety of behavioral and personality problems.

That humans need nurture from other humans is a biologically programmed feature. Research in infant development shows that children's earliest abilities are instinctively directed at getting responses from the most important adults around them. In the early days and weeks of their lives, infants gurgle and smile, respond to their parents' voices, stare intently at familiar faces, and track the movements of the people around them. Few adults can resist this seduction, and they fall completely in love. As time goes on, the parent-child attachment intensifies; in essence, the children's survival depends on it.

You're probably familiar with the term *separation anxiety*. This is part of a normal developmental phase. Being apart from a parent (even an abusive one) probably gives rise to the most terrified feelings children can have; even very young children— well before their first birthday—can experience such feelings. When parents decide to divorce and one of them leaves the family, the children's sense of security—their very sense of survival—is shaken. That Mom and Dad will no longer be together is a disaster on the same scale as an earthquake that eats up the ground on which their home sits.

The renowned child development expert John Bowlby, M.D., noted that children experience a three-stage *acute distress syndrome* when they are neglected by or separated from a parent for a long time: first they are upset and protest what has happened. Next they become withdrawn and sad; they may become depressed, lose weight, or experience sleep problems. Finally they become detached. They may deny interest in the absent or departed parent. In seeking out attachments to other adults, they may become overneedy or demanding.

It is natural for children to long for the parent who has left the family. Even seeing that parent regularly through a generous visitation schedule leaves many children dissatisfied and unhappy. Although the parent has left, the children's feelings of attachment are not extinguished. These feelings are poignantly conveyed in a letter I received from a mother whose ex-husband had been out of touch with their son for four years and now contacts him only sporadically:

"My ex-husband has never seemed to understand that what he does or doesn't do has an impact on our son, Peter. I had to tell my ex-husband to sign his letters 'Dad' and to not tell Peter to take care of me—after all, we're the adults, and we're supposed to take care of him. All the time that my ex-husband's been gone from Peter's life, my brother couldn't understand how Peter could miss him. 'How could he miss someone he doesn't even know?' my brother would ask me. Well, you miss your dad because he *is* your dad, because you have to live with the knowledge that there is one person, and only one person in the whole world, who is your dad, and he's out there somewhere, and he doesn't care enough to come see you or write or call. Peter could, I think, have dealt with the fact of the divorce much more easily if his dad had visited him regularly. It was the abandonment that was so painful and probably will be to some degree or another all his life."

Children Need *Both* Their Parents

Most children with divorced parents live with their mothers; only 11 percent of divorced fathers have physical custody of their children. That divorced mothers have custody of their children—by either choice or decree—is not necessarily the best policy in all families, but it is the one that has evolved in this country over the years. Only in the past decade have fathers increasingly sought and been awarded custody of their children, but judges' bias in most cases still tilts toward mothers.

Most mothers who do not have physical custody of the children stay in close contact with their children to a far greater degree than noncustodial fathers. One national study found that 50 percent of children in the custody of their mothers had not seen their fathers in the past year, and only 16.4 percent saw them once a week or more. In contrast, only 13 percent of the children in the custody of their fathers had not seen their mothers in the past year, and 31 percent saw their mothers once a week or more. According to the U.S. Census Bureau, 38 percent of fathers who were not living with their children in 1990 had neither visitation privileges nor joint custody arrangements with their children. These data indicate that fathers are more likely to drop out of a child's life than are mothers. A mother and a father, however, are not interchangeable in a child's life. Their roles are complementary, and children benefit in different ways from exposure to each.

Most fathers are a positive, loving influence on their children's development. When fathers leave home, they rob their children of a strong day-to-day model of masculinity. Moreover, sons lose probably their most reliable source for learning powerful lessons about appropriate male behavior in a variety of areas—responsibility, achievement, fatherhood, getting along with others, relating to the opposite sex, and handling aggressive feelings.

Studies have found that boys in homes in which the father is absent may be less competitive, less interested in sports, more dependent on others, and more aggressive. They may perform less well in school and be more difficult to discipline. If fathers leave when the boys are preschoolers, the boys may become even more confused about their gender identity.

Girls with absent fathers tend to have difficulty learning how to relate to the opposite sex. Some girls are sexually forward because of their lack of experience in getting male attention in the kinds of nonsexual ways they would have practiced with their fathers. Younger girls may create a fantasy father—someone for whom they make excuses to comfort themselves and avoid the pain of reality. Sadly, many daughters who are neglected by their fathers grow into women who define happiness in terms of how successful they are with men. Some women spend years in relationships with men unconsciously trying to rework their preadolescent or adolescent years, in which they felt neglected or rejected by their fathers. Most of these relationships are unworkable and eventually end. One study linked the girls' sense of neglect and rejection with their poor psychological adjustment as young adults years after the divorce.

Fathers who do not maintain contact with their families are hurting their children in other ways, too. Studies show that one of the best predictors of children's adjustment to divorce is the mother's ability to handle stress and continue nurturing the children. Mothers who receive little help and support from their ex-husbands in caring for the children can be expected to have a more difficult time keeping their lives on an even keel. These mothers must shoulder a wide variety of responsibilities that were once handled, at least to some degree, by two people—from child care to household chores to financial matters. Fathers who remain connected with their children lighten the mothers' emotional load and, during children's visits, give them badly needed time to themselves. It also provides children with an important role-modeling opportunity to observe a man and a woman cooperate in a give-and-take relationship. This is especially important if the parents' divorce was full of animosity and conflict.

Children's development of a healthy self-image and the ability to form stable, loving relationships with others as they grow up depend on having continued access to the most important attachment figures in their lives—their mother and father. As you will see in the course of this book, divorce does not have to interfere with this process if the parents are able to put the children's best interests first. Admittedly, this is no easy task. The dissolution of a marriage is a drama in which the two leading actors are playing out an ending they had not anticipated, and the children seem almost like bit players. Understandably, it is difficult to turn the spotlight away from the variety of emotions common at this time—be they hurt, anger, humiliation, relief, or guilt—but committed parents must make every effort to do so. If the parent-child relationship withers after a divorce, it's because the adults have failed to live up to their parental responsibilities.

Chapter 3

How to Tell Your Children

S ome parents think that it is not necessary to tell the children about their intent to separate and divorce. After all, they reason, such decisions are made by adults, and therefore they are none of the children's business. If the children are especially young—under age five—they won't understand anyway, parents assume. And in cases where one parent wants a divorce but the other doesn't, they believe that telling the children would only cause an awful scene, replete with unfair accusations and tears. Better for the departing parent to leave quietly and let the remaining parent explain, they think.

Rationalizations like these are a mistake: no child should awake one morning and find that Daddy has gone, toothbrush and all, or return home from school someday to find a note from Mom that she has left for good. Not only do such thoughtless actions feed the child's feelings of rejection, but they also unleash the children's imaginations to try to make some sense out of the void. Faced with the unexplained departure of his mother, three-year-old Tom asked his dad whether the police had taken her away. Just the week before he had watched a man being arrested in the neighborhood convenience store and taken away in a police car.

How you tell your children about your separation and divorce will help establish the mood for adapting to the many changes of this new stage of family life. Keep in mind that separation and divorce aren't themselves harmful to youngsters. Your children's welfare directly hinges on how you and your spouse behave individually and jointly, as well as on the decisions you make from here on out. To cope successfully with the events following your separation and divorce, your children need to feel that you are proceeding with careful and reasoned consideration for all concerned.

Take a moment to think of marital breakup from your children's perspective. Although your marriage may be ending, in all truth your world is not. You have the chance to take control of your life, to start over in other circumstances that hold out some hope of contentment or eventual fulfillment. In contrast, your children are at the mercy of you and your spouse. Their fate is intertwined with yours; they lack the capacity to control the outcome. The resulting jumble of feeling sad, helpless, rejected, and angry leaves them upset and confused. It is up to you and your spouse to replace the family unit as the children knew it with a new matrix in which stability and routine can be maintained. Within this matrix, they need to have a nurturing relationship with both their parents, presumably in the same way they had all along.

Preparation Is Necessary

In the real world, it is a rare couple who is capable of planning one spouse's departure from the family home to minimize its

impact on the children. In many families, one spouse leaves before telling even the other spouse, let alone the children, or de-
parts right after making a sudden announcement. Little thought
is given to the children's reactions. If you are still in the stage of
contemplating a separation or divorce, you and your spouse
need to think through how you are going to break the news to
your children. The better prepared you are to answer the children's inevitable questions, the more successful you will be at
helping them handle their reactions.

As you talk to them, one of the most important points to get
across is that they are not to blame for the problems between
you and your spouse and for your decision to split. Children,
particularly the younger ones, often assume that they have
caused mom and dad's breakup for any number of reasons,
some logical and some not: they got a bad report card, they had
a fight with the parent who's leaving, they broke the VCR, they
stole money from the parent's wallet, and so on. Five-year-old
Josh tearfully informed me after his parents separated that he
knew it was all his fault: "I told my daddy to go away and never
come back because he wouldn't buy me a new bike." Thus, you
need to emphasize—and reemphasize—that the children did
nothing to cause the separation and divorce and should not
blame themselves in any way.

Sometimes when the conflict between the spouses has been
going on for quite some time, the children do cause more tension between them and may be the subject of many arguments.
Other people abandon their families precisely because they feel
overburdened by the responsibilities of childrearing. Even under these conditions, however, *the children are not to blame when
a marriage breaks up.* Spouses who cite their children as the reason for their constant arguments are using the children as a
handy excuse to continue their fighting. And people not willing
to learn how to become good parents when they "don't like" the
demands being made on them are compounding their immatur-
ity by running away.

Here are some of the most common questions that children

ask when they learn of their parents' impending separation or divorce.

➤ **Who is going to move out of the family home?**
Explain which parent is moving out of the family home and with whom the children are going to live.

➤ **Why is that parent leaving?**
A variety of reasons are appropriate, depending on the child's age, but be aware that what you <u>say</u> is just as important as what you <u>don't</u> say. Supplying your children with too much information in this opening conversation will only overwhelm them and confuse them further; they cannot possibly digest it all right away. For example, you can explain that Mom and Dad don't get along as well as most parents should or that you don't love each other anymore. But you should not start by saying that, for example, Dad has a girlfriend and is going to live with her or that Mom drinks too much. Such explanations may be appropriate later but should not be the focus of the initial discussion. The point here is that whatever specific problems exist between you and your spouse, they should not be foisted on your children.

You should also avoid the temptation to create such a negative picture of the other parent that the children's relationship with that parent can be severely injured, or that they are forced to choose sides. Children love and identify with both their parents. If parents make their children feel there is something wrong with loving their other parent, the children inevitably feel something is wrong with their judgment—and thus them. They may eventually lose their ability to trust their own feelings.

In addition to this question, your children will probably ask a number of uncomfortable or embarrassing questions about the breakup. Keen observers of their surroundings, children are quite sensitive to parental behavior that is out of the ordinary. If they question you on the specifics of your breakup, respond as honestly as possible. Sooner or later, the truth will come out, and covering up or lying will most likely backfire on you and undermine your future credibility. Of course, you should not supply them with all kinds of details, but a general acknowledgment of the situation is appropriate.

For example, if your ten-year-old son asks, "Are you leaving Mom because you have a girlfriend?" frame your response in a way that doesn't tear down your spouse and that shows you are still part of a team when it comes to the kids. One response might be, "I am leaving because your mother and I no longer get along. I am sure you've noticed that we've been fighting a lot lately, and we agree that this is not a good way for us, and for you, to live. So I am moving out, but I will see you and talk to you as often as possible." If you are pressed about the existence of the girlfriend, or if you will be living with this person, tell the truth: "Yes, I have a new friend, but I am still your dad. I love you and always will."

Questions dealing with a parent's dangerous behavior can be handled more directly. If you are separating because of physical or emotional abuse, you should acknowledge that from the start. The children obviously know what's been going on, and your promise of protection is the first step toward their recovery and feeling safe again. "I am leaving your father and taking you with me because he sometimes gets very angry and hits us. I cannot permit us to live in a home where any of us is afraid of being hurt. It is not a good way to live. I want a chance to make a happy home for us." This answer emphasizes the positive outcome of your action and plays down the conflict between you and your spouse. You should not respond, "Yes, we are getting a divorce because your father is a bad, hateful man, and he likes to hurt people. He doesn't love you very much or he wouldn't act that way toward you." Although some of this may be true, such a diatribe may lead children to feel they must defend their father or question their loyalty to him.

➢ **Why will we be living with the one parent and not the other?**
Regardless of which parent the children will live with, you should emphasize that the children's welfare and comfort motivated the decision. Do not say, for example, that one parent loves them more than the other. Also, don't suggest that one parent is more fit than the

other. An exception is families where such problems as violence, alcoholism, sexual abuse, and so on have been obvious to the children for some time, not just alleged by one of the spouses.

Here's one possible response: "I wish we could all continue to live together, but we can't. So Mom and I decided that the next best thing is for you to remain here with her at home. That way, you can still go to your same school and keep your same friends. But you can still spend a lot of time with me."

➤ Where is the parent leaving home going to live?

Be as specific as possible without sharing details that the children don't need to know. If, for example, Dad is going to live with his girlfriend, the children need only be told initially that Dad will be living with a friend. (Dad would be better advised to move to his own place, for his sake as well as his children's, but this is off the subject here.) The children can be told additional circumstances later, as they become relevant.

Since small children think in concrete terms, they may want to know such mundane information as whether the new residence has a stove, refrigerator, and bed. Also, they need to have some understanding about exactly where the parent is; otherwise, they'll fill in the blanks themselves. One four-year-old told me that her daddy was in heaven—a comforting thought, since to her heaven was a happy, safe place where he could receive the ultimate in care.

If it's possible, you might want to show the children the parent's new residence and reassure them that the parent will be fine.

➤ Will we ever see that parent again?

This also is a question often asked by preschool children. Their ability to think beyond what they know and experience firsthand is limited. The children should be told that they can call or visit the departing parent whenever they like (if that's true). If the parent is moving far away from the family home, children older than six should be told how the move will affect their seeing that parent. Children younger than six don't have a clear understanding of distance; they are not able to discriminate between the town down the road and a city halfway across the country. All they know is that the parent isn't there with them.

The departing parent should be clear about plans to call the children and visit them. A time and date for the first call or visit should be made—ideally for as soon as possible.

➤ What will happen to us?

School-age children in particular want to know in specific terms how their lives are going to be affected by their parents' decision. Where will we live? What school will I go to? Can I still see my friends? Grandma and Grandpa? Can I still belong to my Girl Scout troop (or other activities they are involved in)? Can we take the dog? and so on.

If the separation and divorce do not entail a move for the children, all the better for them. Their adjustment to the news will be eased by the stability in their living situation at a time in their lives when the emotional environment is unstable. But if you don't know the answers to some of these questions, be honest and say so. Better that the children see that you have thought about these important matters—which will show them that you are in control of the situation—than to have to keep changing your story every few days or weeks.

Preschool children should also be told how the separation or divorce will affect their lives, but in terms that emphasize the continuing relationship of the departing parent with that child. Keep it simple and to the point.

Most important, regardless of their age, both parents should reassure the children that they still love them and will continue to take good care of them.

➤ Won't the parent who is leaving home be sad and lonely?

It is natural for children to worry about the parent who is out of sight. They are projecting their feelings onto the parent in much the same way they react when they misplace a beloved doll or stuffed animal: "She'll cry if I don't find her right away!" Of course, it is the child who is shedding the tears.

You should acknowledge that the parent will indeed be sad and lonely, but that those feelings will be eased through frequent phone calls and visits with them. Don't deny such feelings in an attempt to alleviate the children's fears, since they also need to feel that they are important enough to the parent that they likewise will be missed sorely.

➢ When is the parent leaving home?

There is no right or wrong time for the parent who intends to move out of the family home to actually depart. Even under the best of circumstances, when the time finally comes, those who are left behind will be upset. I have seen all kinds of arrangements: the parents agree to separate bedrooms until they determine that the children are ready for the break; the departing parent agrees to remain for a specified time, say a week to a month—sometimes as long as six months; the parents announce the divorce to the kids while the departing parent's bags sit by the front door.

Ideally, the children should be given about a week to two weeks to adjust to the news of the separation and divorce. In that time, both parents should encourage the children to discuss their questions and concerns. Letting more time elapse may raise false hopes that the parents are remaining together.

➢ Will the parent ever come back?

Not all separations lead to divorce. Sometimes couples separate so that they can sort out their problems and decide what course of action to take. Sometimes a separation may be undertaken with the understanding that a spouse who is alcoholic or abusive may return if he or she gets counseling and straightens up. Such separations are undertaken in good faith and are less complicated when no children are involved. When there are children, however, a parent's moving in and out of the family home keeps everyone living on pins and needles, keeps the parents' relationship on everyone's minds, and prevents the family from getting on with their lives. All of this has the potential to feed the children's insecurity and cause them to lose trust in the adults supposedly taking care of them.

If your separation is meant to be conditional or trial, tell your children that there is a chance the departing parent may come back at some unspecified time. But don't hold out false hope, since sometimes such separations do lead to divorce. Try to establish a routine (if safety is not an issue) in which the parent who is no longer at home visits regularly with the children. Don't live each day waiting for the prodigal parent to return.

Although it is hoped that parents can work out their differences during a separation, they should not permit the family home to be used like a hotel with a revolving front door. Some spouses use leaving home as a means to intimidate or scare the other spouse; others come and go as they please because they cannot make the hard decision to commit themselves to the marriage or to separating and divorcing once and for all. Regardless of the reason, people whose bags are never unpacked are no longer acting in good faith but only out of self-interest, and people who permit such behavior need to take a good look at themselves: Why are they letting themselves be used in this way? Why do they let their lives be constantly disrupted by someone who is too immature to take control of his or her life? If they believe that they are motivated by the hope of putting their marriage back together for the sake of the youngsters, they are only kidding themselves. This revolving door syndrome only serves to keep conflict alive and shows the children that their parents cannot handle their lives. Such people need professional counseling, because they clearly cannot solve their problems on their own.

Telling the Children: With or Without Your Spouse

Once you and ideally your spouse have thought through your responses to the various issues I've discussed above, you're ready to talk to your children. You and your spouse should both lead the discussion and take turns talking. One parent should not present a monologue while the other parent appears to be part of the audience; children whose parents share the responsibility for the divorce are better adjusted in the long run.

Choose a time when the two of you are calm and when the family has plenty of time to talk without being rushed or interrupted. Although it may be difficult, try to avoid appearing extremely upset or out of control. Children often become very distressed at the sight of a parent's crying, and they may be far less likely to ask questions or express their feelings in an attempt to end the conversation and thereby the parent's tears as quickly as possible. Remember, the emotions displayed by the parents largely determine the children's reaction to the news. If one parent is shaken and upset, so will the kids be. If both parents are reasonably confident and secure in the information they are providing, even though they are understandably upset, the children will react with greater trust.

If the divorce is one-sided, the parent who prefers to keep the marriage intact should not act like a martyr or long-suffering soul in front of the kids by making such remarks as "Your father is leaving home. I don't know why he is doing this to us." "Your mother has another friend now. She doesn't need us anymore." Admittedly, this may be difficult when the parent feels that he or she has been terribly wronged, but again, this attitude unfairly burdens the children to take sides. And no matter whose side they take, they'll feel guilty and torn.

If your spouse refuses to join you in the discussion, the same advice holds: You should try to remain composed, sure of yourself, and open to questions. Don't tell your youngsters that your spouse or anyone else is to blame for the family's breakup—the issue of blame is an adult concern and should not be made the children's burden. This may be particularly hard if your spouse suddenly moves out, leaving you to explain why. Nonetheless, your goal is to provide the children with the information they need to know now, to reassure them about the future, and to leave the door open for them to communicate with you, their other parent, and other appropriate people.

Here are a few additional points to consider that take children's ages into account. If your children fall into more than one age group, you can tailor an explanation to each child's level of understanding.

Under Age Five

Young children don't need a long, involved explanation of their parents' breakup. You should use the word *divorce* (if you are indeed getting a divorce and not just separating on a trial basis); the child will probably not understand it initially, but will over time. Also, children in this age group tend to think of their parents as a unit, not a separate Mom and Dad. Thus, you should explain that nothing bad is going to happen to the parent who is leaving home. Since young children in particular may think that they are driving the parent away, you should take care to assure them that the breakup is not their fault.

Describe the departing parent's new living arrangements in simple terms: "Angela, I'll be living nearby in my own apartment, and Mommy and you are going to stay here. Tomorrow I am going to take you to see where I'm living, and you can come visit as often as possible. I would like to keep some of your toys in my new house, if that's OK with you."

The tone of your voice, perhaps even more than the actual words you use, will help reassure your children no one is disappearing from their lives.

Ages Five Through Eight

Most five- to eight-year-olds will be able to grasp the implications of what you are telling them, and they will want information from the perspective of "What about me?" Since they are just beginning to separate from parental ties and identify more with their peers, you should emphasize the ways in which their lives will *not* be affected by one parent's leaving home. For example, "You'll still be going to the same school and have the same teacher." "Even though Mom and Dad won't be living in the same house anymore, we'll still be working together as your parents. You can count on us."

As with smaller children, you need to emphasize that the separation and divorce are not the children's fault—or anyone else's, for that matter. Since children of this age are still trying to learn how to control their behavior, you can show them that you are in control by explaining the separation and divorce as a mature, mutually agreed-on decision—even when it's not.

Ages Nine Through Twelve

Many of the issues that concern five- to eight-year-olds are important to children in this age group as well. But you can expect these older children to react more passionately, more angrily, to your news—if not now, then later. Children in this age group have more fully formed, but still immature, consciences. They tend to think in terms of right and wrong, good and bad; they may feel that they must take sides. Thus, a child who suspects that a parent is leaving home because of a new lover may ask very pointed, angry questions about that new relationship and be vocal in blaming the family's breakup on the parent who is having the affair. Also, their comments and questions may reflect their growing awareness of their own sexuality.

You should explain that the separation and divorce are best for all concerned and that the relationship between the children and the departing parent will continue, even though the parents' marriage is ending. Because it is at this age that boys are forming a particular attachment to their father and developing a stronger gender identity, boys remaining with their mother may need greater reassurance that they will continue to see their father.

Ending the Discussion

If it hasn't come up before, you may want to end your discussion by telling the children they will still be able to see all the relatives they normally do, regardless of which side of the family they are on. Explain that divorce is something that takes place only between the two people who are married, not between the relatives in that family.

Although seeing your spouse's relatives at this time may be painful or make you uncomfortable, you should not cut off your children from people they love. (In some states, you may not have a choice, since relatives such as grandparents have a legal right to continue seeing the children.) Your children are already experiencing enough losses in their lives; they need all the reassurances of love, security, and stability they can get. In fact, relying on relatives may help lessen your burden by not only providing babysitters in emergencies but also giving the children additional outlets for working through their feelings about the separation and divorce.

Furthermore, invite the children to discuss their reactions with you, now as well as later. If their immediate reaction is one of silence, don't assume that they have understood and accepted your announcement. Sometimes children won't talk or will try to change the subject in an attempt to block out what they've heard and pretend nothing has changed. These are signs of denial. If they react angrily, try to deal with the situation without losing your temper, crying, threatening punishment, or resorting to such behavior as blaming your spouse for the scene as an outlet for your distress. Regardless of their initial reaction, tell the children that you (and it is hoped their other parent) are always available to answer their questions when they feel like talking further.

Here are some questions to ask the children to get them to open up and let you know whether they understand what you are telling them. You can use these and similar questions after the initial discussion as well as in the coming months as more changes come into your lives:

➢ Do you have any questions about what I've/we've told you?
➢ How do you feel about what I've/we've told you?
➢ What is it about the divorce that makes you sad? afraid? happy? excited? relieved? (Choose the reactio child appears to be showing.)

> ➤ What do you think will happen to Dad/Mom when he/she moves out?
> ➤ What do you think will happen to you?

You might want to end the conversation by asking your children whether they would like an opportunity to talk with someone outside the family. Close family members, such as a favorite aunt or grandparent, are good choices. If you can afford it, or your health insurance provides it, a mental health professional specializing in children and adolescents is another option. Also check with your local school system to see whether it offers programs for children from divorced families or can recommend other community resources.

Keeping the Lines of Communication Open

From the time the announcement about the separation or divorce is made, you should continue to reassure the children that they will not be abandoned and invite them to share their feelings with you. When they ask you questions, even if it's in the middle of a traffic jam, make every attempt to answer in some way; you can always provide more information later if necessary. Don't become impatient if you are asked the same question over and over again. Also, keep in mind that young children have not mastered the language yet and can't express what's on their minds very well. Sometimes questions may have a hidden meaning that you have to ferret out.

For example, one day five-year-old Duncan approached his father, who did not have custody of him, and asked, "Why does John come over to our house so much and sleep in Mommy's bed with her, like you used to do?" A father's first reaction might be to pump the child for more information or fly into a rage about the mother's seeming lack of morality. Neither reaction is ever appropriate. Children should never be used as spies, nor should they be the audience of a tirade in which one parent vilifies the other. These kinds of reactions reflect the parent's feelings; they are not directed at the kernel of the child's question.

Duncan's father realized that his son didn't want to know about his mother's love life. What he really wanted to know was: Does Mommy still love me? If she is paying so much attention to her new friend, will she continue to take care of me? If she was able to replace you, will she replace me, too? Some parents in this situation, even if they are able to perceive the real worry, may still be tempted to attack the former spouse in some way. Don't do it! Children need to feel that they are supported in their love for their other parent.

Don't keep news of the impending divorce to yourself. For your children's sake, it is vital that you tell the other important people in your children's lives about the divorce and other pertinent facts they need to know to deal with your children and answer any questions they might have. Such people include grandparents and other close relatives, family friends, teachers, coaches, day-care workers, babysitters, housekeepers, and doctors. You also should ask them to be sensitive to behavioral changes or other problems in your children and tell you about them. For example, your child may act aggressively at school toward other youngsters, even though at home he may remain compliant and cooperative. Although he is upset enough to be acting out at school, he may be trying hard not to misbehave at home because he is afraid that he will drive you away, just as (in his ego-centered world) he drove his other parent away.

Chapter 4

Minimizing the Effects of the Legal Process on Your Children

If you are contemplating divorce or are in the early stages of divorce proceedings, you have an opportunity to establish an open, cooperative atmosphere for discussion and negotiation with your spouse in which the best interests of every member of your family can be taken into consideration. This chapter will help you accomplish this task. It also includes advice on avoiding hateful and destructive conflict and on resolving disputes that divorced parents may encounter down the road.

Getting Off on the Right Foot

As I've said earlier, living in a divorced family is not necessarily harmful for children; it is the conflict and other problems arising from the divorce that can cause long-lasting damage. Parents who want to prevent the divorce proceedings from deteriorating into a messy, ugly, finger-pointing battle have the power to do so. They can set a tone for communication and cooperation that will help shape their relationship for future dealings. It may be tempting, for example, to fight mercilessly for a huge settlement—the house, the car, the furniture, the whole works—to get even with a spouse who left a marriage to be with someone else. But such a fight will create so much acrimony and resentment between the former spouses (and in the process consume such enormous financial resources) that communication and cooperation in matters relating to the children will be nearly impossible. Such people may win the battle, but they—and their children—will certainly lose the war.

If there is conflict between you and your spouse—and you can expect that there will be—save it for the things that really matter. Don't waste time and energy fighting over the little things, such as who will store the kids' bikes or get the family computer. It's often small matters like these that take up much more time and energy to settle than they deserve. Their symbolic meaning in the ending of a marriage makes them seem much more important than they really are, or should be, at this difficult time.

As you make the decision to go forward with a legal separation or divorce, it's a good idea to start by educating yourself on the relevant laws and procedures in your state. Your local library or government center should have on hand helpful pamphlets or books or be able to tell you where you can get such information. Next, you should consult with a lawyer to protect your interests and those of your children. Your spouse should do likewise. It is best that both of you seek your own attorney to make sure that the final settlement is fair to all the parties involved. People who don't care whether the final settlement is fair to their spouse are already on a course headed for trouble for themselves and their children.

Be sure to engage an attorney experienced in divorce and matters related to divorce, such as custody, visitation, and child support. This seems an obvious point, but many people simply turn to the Yellow Pages or call the lawyer who handled some matter for their next-door neighbors. Among the best referral sources are the local bar association and people whose divorces were handled well.

Some families may already have an attorney and may naturally turn to him or her to handle the divorce. One advantage of doing so is that this attorney is already familiar with the family on both a personal basis and a business or financial basis. However, the family attorney should be used only in the most amicable divorces. Since in most cases the family attorney has a closer relationship with one spouse than the other, the attorney's judgment may be biased in that person's favor. Under these circumstances, the attorney should refuse to handle the divorce, citing conflict of interest. If the family attorney does handle the divorce, another attorney should review the terms of the settlement before it is made final.

It's helpful to realize from the start that there is probably going to be some disappointment associated with whatever legal arrangement you and your spouse finally agree on. Given the variety of options and the particular situation and problems of every family, it is rare indeed to craft a settlement in which all parties are equally satisfied. Accepting this fact early in the legal process will help you be open to compromise and avoid getting stuck when negotiating minor matters. Nonetheless, it is possible to achieve a situation in which both parents have a great deal of access to the children. The children's emotional stability and long-term well-being depend on having a nurturing, stable relationship with both parents, regardless of who has custody of them.

As I emphasized in the last chapter, it is important that you and your spouse be open and honest with your children throughout the process of separation and divorce. The more you talk with your children, the better. Keep them informed of what's going on—again, tailoring the message to their level of maturity.

In addition, keeping family life as stable as possible should be one of your highest priorities right now. The period of transition from marriage to divorce is obviously a stressful, demanding time. You are being forced to make a lot of difficult decisions, and your life is undergoing fundamental changes. Similarly, great demands are being placed on your children, often more than the experience of their tender years permits them to handle. Tensions run high; tempers run short. You need to fight impulses to be impatient with your children and say or do hurtful things (for instance, spanking) that under happier circumstances might not even enter your mind. You should be especially careful not to say anything that might cause your children to assume that *they* are the reason for the family's breakup.

One mother I know became exasperated at her four-year-old daughter when she failed to put away her things after repeated reminders. Worn out at last, the mother barked, "You know how Dad always got mad when you'd leave your toys in the yard!" The mother was surprised when the child remarked a few days later, "Mommy, if I clean up the yard, will Daddy come back?"

Your parenting skills are probably undergoing their greatest test ever. Although you may be overburdened right now—and understandably so—try to keep daily routines and family traditions going. Continue to hold birthday parties and plan trips to the circus and the zoo. If you always ate a large Sunday dinner at a formally set table, don't stop now. This is also a good time to start some new traditions. Put yourself in your children's shoes: What would *you* appreciate the most? Reassuring words, a bedtime story, making dinner together, a quiet walk to the store—simple activities that you can do together but that demonstrate to your children that you remain available to them. Show them that there are some things in their lives that they can always count on.

Getting Off on the Right Foot

As you begin divorce proceedings, here are some points to keep in mind:

- Make every effort to keep the level of tension in the home as low as possible and not to fight with your spouse in front of the children. They will adjust better to the divorce if you and your spouse can learn to put aside your differences and communicate so that their welfare comes first. Be aware that children's threshold for tension is lower than adults'.
- Both spouses should have their own lawyers, to protect both their individual interests and those of the children.
- Keep your children informed about the divorce proceedings and continue to encourage them to talk to you about it. Also, don't keep news of the divorce to yourself. People who play a major role in your children's lives should be informed as well—grandparents, close family friends, teachers, coaches, and so on—so that your children will have other people who can look out for them and to whom they can turn as necessary.
- Try to keep up the normal routines of everyday life. Children need stability and predictability in their lives.

Methods of Dispute Resolution

Divorce is the legal recognition of the end of a marriage. As such, the court system must be used to some degree. Just how much will depend on the ability of the parting spouses to cooperate in reaching a divorce settlement that attempts to address the needs of all family members: the more they cooperate, the faster and less traumatic the process will be. That's really what counts.

To help you make the decisions commonly faced by divorcing parents, you need to understand the basic legal terms pertaining to such matters as methods of devising a divorce settlement, child custody, visitation, and child support. Most of these terms are probably familiar to you already. However, when you first meet with an attorney (or some other relevant professional, such as a mediator), you should ask that person to review these terms with you to avoid any confusion.

You also need to know how these options impact on children. Depending on your family's situation, some have the potential of working out just fine, whereas others could be devastating.

Litigation and the Adversarial System

The legal system in the United States is an "adversarial" system. The term *adversarial* is derived from the Latin word for *opponent.* The term *litigation* means legal action or process. Simply put, court cases involve two principal parties; the positions or arguments of these parties are presented to a judge or jury in such a way that the disparities in their positions help arrive at the "truth." Both parties must follow strict procedural rules that ensure that the process is conducted fairly.

Under the adversarial system, for example, a person charged with murder by the state is presumed innocent until proven guilty. In such a criminal case, the alleged murderer is the *defendant*, and the state is the *prosecutor.* The burden is on the prosecutor to prove the defendant's guilt beyond a reasonable doubt. In a civil suit, the party bringing suit is the *plaintiff,* and the sued party is the *defendant.* Both parties together are the *litigants,* that is, involved in a lawsuit. In the United States, one person can sue another for virtually any reason.

In these types of cases, the adversarial system appears to work better than other judicial systems devised and tested over time. Families are better served, however, by avoiding a situation where one spouse is pitted against the other. Often caught in the middle are the children, torn by their loyalty to both parents. This situation is harmful to all family members. The irony is that, in the end, the fate of such families is in the hands of a judge who, after hearing a litany of statements by attorneys, experts, and other witnesses, may hand down a decision that makes neither side happy.

One particularly touching situation I remember is one of a child who not only remained loyal to her parents but also tried in her own way to attain a truce between them by using a technique far beyond her years. When her mother would condemn her father for some misdeed, imagined or real, six-year-old Rebecca would remind her, "But Mommy, Daddy does a lot of good things, too." She would do the same when she was with her father. Clearly, the attachment she felt to both her parents was something to be supported, not destroyed.

Divorcing parents often complain that "the lawyers caused all the fighting" between them. Certainly, lawyers can promote fighting in their zeal to obtain the best possible settlement for their clients. Thinking in terms of winning and losing is part of their job. Many clients, however, seem to forget that their lawyer is their employee. Many years as a forensic psychiatrist have shown me that the client sets the tone in divorce negotiations. If the client appears to be reasonable, the lawyer will be, too; if the client is combative and irrationally demanding, so, too, is the lawyer. Such stubborn people often end up in expensive, emotionally exhausting litigation. Clients who want to reach a settlement through compromise and reason should make that known to the lawyer in the initial interview, with periodic reminders. This course best serves the children by helping to keep parental conflict to a minimum.

Sometimes conflict is unavoidable. For example, if the parent demanding custody has physically or sexually abused the children or is mentally unstable, the other parent may have no choice but to take steps to reduce or end the children's contact with that parent. When the conflict is of a far less serious nature, however, there are options for avoiding debilitating courtroom drama. Prime among them are mediation and arbitration.

Mediation

Mediation is far less expensive in terms of emotion and money than is litigation. In mediation, both spouses discuss and negotiate their own terms of divorce through the guidance of an impartial third party. This third party, known as a mediator, is usually a lawyer but can be a mental health professional or a person from a related discipline. Some states require that all divorcing couples enter mediation; if it fails, only then may they proceed to litigation.

Since this is a relatively new field (it burgeoned only in the last decade), the credentials and experience of the mediator should be thoroughly checked out. Prospective clients also need to ask the mediator whether he or she has any preconceived values or ideas about divorce and related issues that may affect the mediation process. Some sample questions: Do you think divorce is bad or wrong? Do you think that it is better to grant custody to mothers instead of to fathers? Do you always recommend joint custody? sole custody? Would you ever support one parent's request to limit the other parent's access to the children? A mediator should exhibit impartiality and nonjudgmental attitudes on the issues such questions raise.

Furthermore, it is important that the mediator not have any previous ties with one of the spouses that might result in bias.

By using mediation to arrive at a divorce settlement, both spouses make the decisions and assume the responsibility for solving their own problems. Since the solutions are their own, they are far more likely to abide by the agreement in the long run. In addition, mediation permits both parties to try out an arrangement to see how it works before signing the final agreement. The only limitation is that the final agreement must conform to state law. It's an easy matter to return to mediation if a new problem develops or if an old solution no longer works.

An extremely useful byproduct of mediation is that it can teach the divorcing couple how to communicate effectively and reach consensus. They will need to have these skills to be good parents and cooperate in matters relating to their children.

Unless there are compelling reasons to the contrary, the spouses' individual attorneys should support their decision to try mediation. (Sometimes a couple elects to seek out a mediator even before they have hired their own attorneys.) Attorneys who oppose mediation or try to discourage it are not serving their clients or their clients' families well. I'd consider finding another attorney.

There are different ways to proceed when a couple agrees to mediation, but I prefer this procedure: Together the spouses select a mediator, someone whom they have never met before and have no ties to. No fixed number of sessions is necessary, but it usually varies from six to ten. Good mediators insist on both spouses being present. Meeting individually with the husband or wife undermines the mediation process; the idea is for both spouses to work together to achieve an agreement. It also can create (or deepen) feelings of mistrust, since one spouse may think that the mediator is siding with the other spouse or that he or she is being left out of something.

In the initial session, the mediator should explain how mediation works and its advantages over litigation. The mediator will probably require each spouse to sign a statement spelling out the rules of the game and terms of payment. In brief, both spouses must agree to be honest and forthcoming with all information (financial, medical, and so on) that the mediator deems pertinent to arrive at a fair agreement. Outside consultants, such as accountants and mental health professionals, may be hired as well, if the mediator thinks they are needed.

During the sessions, the mediator's job is to keep the participants on track and moving forward. The mediator makes sure that the couple addresses all the necessary issues, and he or she explains the options for each issue. This includes explaining the effects of the options on each spouse, to ensure that both are treated fairly and understand what they are agreeing to. If the two begin to attack each other or raise irrelevant points (which inevitably happens, because it would be impossible for them to leave their emotional baggage at the door), the mediator intervenes and returns them to the matter at hand.

The mediator needs to be sensitive to a variety of interpersonal problems, such as spouses who talk too much versus those who don't talk at all, or spouses who are aggressive or domineering versus those who are afraid to disagree in any way. The mediator must intervene to be certain that each spouse expresses what's on his or her mind and does not feel railroaded. Some people are quiet or unassertive precisely because they want to shorten the process; their discomfort at being in the presence of the other spouse may be so high that any agreement may appear to be the better alternative.

After an agreement is reached, it is prepared as a legal contract and reviewed by both parties. Each spouse should have his or her attorney study the document to be sure that the agreement is in that person's best interests. If both parties find the contract acceptable, they may be asked to sign it. The contract is then made part of the final divorce decree, which must be granted by a judge.

Some mediators believe that the divorcing couple's children should be included in the process at some point. I do not advise this when the children are younger than fourteen (and sometimes even older, depending on the children's maturity). The decisions reached through mediation should be made by adults; children do not have the insight, experience, or emotional capability to make these decisions. Forcing them to do so unfairly burdens them.

Jeffrey, a bright, particularly mature eleven-year-old, was included in his parents' mediation. He described to me what it felt like to "sit on the hot seat" as the mediator asked him, in the presence of his mom and dad, which parent he preferred to live with.

"What could I say?" he asked me with distress. "If I had chosen my mom, my dad might have thought that I didn't want to be with him anymore. If I had chosen my dad, then my mom might have thought I didn't love her anymore, and she would have been left alone in our big house. Well, I didn't want to choose, so I didn't," he said defiantly. "I just want my mom and dad and me to live together again."

Jeffrey's response was to run out of the room. After that episode, he began to lose weight and had difficulty sleeping. His parents finally brought him to me for psychiatric help. It didn't take much digging to get to the root of his problem. I subsequently explained to his parents that it was their responsibility, guided by the mediator, to decide Jeffrey's custodial arrangement. They needed to understand that the important goal was to agree on an arrangement in which Jeffrey had as much access as possible to both parents, regardless of whom he lived with.

Jeffrey was a lucky child; his parents were motivated by a sincere desire to make him happy. But the case of nine-year-old Bobby demonstrates another reason that parents should remain in charge. Bobby was asked the same question as Jeffrey, for ostensibly the same reason, but the outcome was far different: Bobby chose his mother, and his father never let him forget it. "You mustn't love me very much, or you would have picked me." "I can't afford to get you that tennis racket. If you had lived with me, we'd have more money, since I wouldn't have to support two households." And on and on. By the time Bobby entered high school, he needed therapy to deal with his overpowering feelings of guilt that he had somehow let his father down.

Although mediation is a sound way to resolve disputes, it is not always successful, and there are cases in which it should not be used (unless state law requires it). Some parents are not good candidates for mediation, and some situations are better handled through the adversarial system. Mediation may not be successful or appropriate for the following people:

➤ Those who are unwilling to divulge all pertinent information needed to arrive at a fair settlement. A frequent sticking point is the area of finances and property settlement, particularly in families with substantial assets.

➤ Those who communicate only through their lawyers.

➤ Those who seem determined to "win," believe their position is the only right one, are unwilling to give in to the other spouse, and so on. Whether they realize it or not, such people do not want to put an end to the fighting and so are incapable of compromise. Successful mediation is based on compromise; there are no winners or losers. Furthermore, parents who think this way often use the children, unwittingly or not, as a weapon or bargaining chip to hurt the other spouse. In the end, the children are treated as little more than part of the "winning" parent's bounty.

➤ Those who feel so guilty over the divorce that they are, in effect, willing to give the other spouse anything he or she wants, including the children. One particularly unfortunate effect of their guilt is that often they shy away from or eventually cut off all contact with their children to avoid being reminded of the suffering and harm they have caused by splitting up the family.

➤ Those who feel they deserve nothing. Unlike the guilty person described above, these individuals often do not want the divorce. Their self-esteem is so low that they are behaving self-destructively. Mediation is usually futile for such a person without a mental health professional's help.

➤ Those who have an emotional problem or are mentally ill to the degree that the impairment prevents reaching a fair or informed agreement. However, sometimes during the mediation process, the mediator realizes that one or both of the spouses need psychological or psychiatric help to make the mediation productive. At this point, further sessions are suspended until the spouse or spouses are capable of continuing.

➤ Those who are suspected of physically or sexually abusing the children or behaving in other ways that could harm the children, such as criminal activity, verbal abuse of the children, and substance abuse (alcohol and/or other drugs). I discuss these further in Chapters 8 and 12.

Arbitration

Another alternative for resolving disputes between divorcing couples is arbitration. It is somewhat similar to mediation in that both spouses select and work with an independent third party to help them resolve their differences. However, an arbitrator takes a more active role in the process by offering specific recommendations based on the information the arbitrator has collected from the couple.

As you may know from business, labor, or sports disputes, there are two kinds of arbitration: binding and nonbinding. In binding arbitration, the parties must accept the arbitrator's recommendations; in nonbinding arbitration, the parties can either accept or reject the recommendations.

On the basis of even this short explanation, you probably recognize mediation's major advantage over arbitration: the divorcing spouses are responsible for solving their differences themselves (under the mediator's gently guiding hand) and controlling the outcome of the final agreement.

Couples who have not been successful at mediation may want to try arbitration before turning to adversarial litigation, which I consider the last resort in most divorce cases. Litigation thrives on conflict; its nature demands that there be a winner and a loser. Yet in most cases no one truly emerges the victor—certainly not the children. The only winners are the attorneys, who have done their job by hammering home their clients' opposing positions, and the judge, who believes he or she has handed down a decision whose wisdom only Solomon could surpass.

Custodial Arrangements

Regardless of which method of conflict resolution divorcing parents choose, their most weighty decision concerns the custodial arrangement for their children. Should they live with Mom? Dad? Should Mom and Dad share custody? Should the children be split up, one with Mom, one with Dad? Are both parents capable of sharing the responsibility for making decisions affecting the children's welfare, or should this power be relegated to only one parent?

These are difficult and heart-wrenching questions. As you and your former spouse try to tackle them, the children's best interests should come first. Sometimes this is easier said than done. Although your marriage is ending, the two of you are still, and will remain, the children's parents.

If you are the rejected partner (even if the divorce was your idea), you must resist any temptation to punish or get even with your spouse for leaving you and the children in a devastating predicament. Try not to think in terms of "abandonment," even though it may well be accurate. It is much more emotionally loaded.

If you are the rejecting partner, your inclination to get away from the unpleasant repercussions of your actions must be resisted. Don't burn any bridges between you and your children in your desire to move on with your life.

Sole Custody

In sole custody, the traditional custodial arrangement in this country, complete legal responsibility is given to one of the divorcing parents, and the children live with that parent most of the time. If the parents are able to agree which of them is to assume sole custody of the children (and if there is no state law mandating joint custody), the judge will generally accept that decision and make it part of the final divorce settlement. When the parents can't agree, a custody lawsuit is inevitable.

In deciding which parent should be awarded custody, judges generally use the "best interests of the child" criterion. They weigh each parent's ability to care physically and emotionally for the children, health and mental health status, and history of gross immorality and physical or sexual abuse of the children. The children's gender, race, and religion may also be taken into consideration. The information is usually revealed through testimony and reports provided by the parents themselves, mental health professionals, and others (such as grandparents). Sometimes the children are questioned as well; depending on their ages, they may be asked which parent they prefer to live with.

Although in recent years judges have increased their sensitivity to fathers' rights and their ability to parent, judges are still much more likely to grant sole custody to mothers. In contrast, up until the beginning of the twentieth century, fathers were routinely given custody of their children. Divorced women were not considered capable of taking care of their children, since many were not educated, had few legal rights, and had no prospects for decent employment. Also, as discussed in Chapter 1, children were a valuable economic commodity that fathers wanted to retain. When women began to demand their rights and gain entrance into educational institutions, and societal attitudes toward children shifted, the states changed their laws, and the trend toward granting divorced mothers custody of their children began.

Joint Custody

Another arrangement for divorcing couples has now spread like wildfire: joint custody. Two variations are now in common use: joint legal custody and joint physical custody. The most common joint custody arrangement is sharing legal custody of the children, but in many families, parents have both legal and physical joint custody.

Under joint legal custody, both parents share the legal responsibility for making decisions affecting the children, although they live most of the time with one of the parents. The parents make all the decisions affecting each child together; neither parent's rights are superior to the other's.

Children in joint physical custody alternate living in the home of each parent for an agreed-on interval (or they remain in one home while the parents alternate at the agreed-on interval). There is no correct interval; it varies from days to months depending on the family's particular needs. For example, the children might spend three days with the mother, then four days with the father. Or they might make the switch every week or month.

Sole or Joint: Which Is Better?

In the past few decades, the enthusiasm for joint custody (physical and/or legal) has grown to the point that many states have passed laws mandating it. Thus, depending on the state in which you live, you may have no other choice of custodial arrangement unless there are good reasons against it.

Today, many child experts agree that under certain conditions, joint custody is often the best arrangement for children whose parents are divorced. Its outstanding feature is that it permits a great amount of access to both parents on a predictable basis. Furthermore, when it works, the children are exposed to strong role models who, despite having failed at their marriage, are competent at parenting. The children's insecurities over having their family torn apart are diminished when they see that their parents are reliable, capable of taking care of them, and able to cooperate with each other.

Secondarily, joint custody avoids many of the undesirable side effects of sole custody, especially if the sole-custody decision was made by the court. Parents who lose their bid for custody often feel that they were judged the less adequate or capable parent. Their self-esteem suffers, as does their sense of value to the children. Furthermore, they experience a very real loss: that of seeing their children regularly. They may fear—and with some justification—that stilted visits on weekends or holidays can never replace the joy of being needed to kiss away a hurt or scare monsters out of closets, of sharing the incidental triumphs or sorrows that a child may not even recall the next day—in short, of simply just "hanging out" together, for no apparent reason other than that they love each other.

For joint custody to work well, however, it requires a huge commitment from both parents. Ideally, if parents share physical custody of the children, they should live within walking distance of each other so that the children (if they are old enough) can come and go as they please and enjoy the same set of friends regardless of which parent they are living with. If the children are school age, the parents must live within the same school district to ensure continuity in the children's schooling. Joint legal custody demands that both parents be capable of cooperating on matters related to the children and communicating without fighting and hostility. They also need to have similar attitudes toward parenting, though not necessarily similar parenting styles. Children are generally flexible and can adapt to a situation where, for example, the mother is the disciplinarian and the father is a softie.

Parents interested in pursuing joint custody in whichever variation need to be clear about their motives. Some parents who say they want joint custody may not have pure intentions. They may be embarrassed to admit that they don't want sole custody and view joint custody as a face-saving way out of their dilemma. Other people think of joint custody as a convenient babysitting option, giving them license to dump the children on the other parent's doorstep whenever they wish. Many parents feel caught between the realization that they are incapable of handling parenting responsibilities fifty fifty with their former spouses and the fear that their children will think less of them if they don't agree to joint custody. Probably the worst transgressors I've seen in my clinical practice are people like Jill. Jill knew that a judge would never place her two children completely in her custody. She was driven by so much bitterness toward her husband, however, that she was determined to win joint custody simply to deprive him of sole custody. She got her way, but when she couldn't handle the responsibilities, she and her ex-husband ended up back in court.

Even when joint custody is based on the best motivations and goes smoothly initially, people and situations change over time so that it may stop working. A parent may be offered a job opportunity that requires an out-of-state move. Another parent may remarry, reawakening feelings of hostility in the ex-spouse to such a degree that cooperation is no longer possible. Stepchildren may complicate living arrangements. Sometimes the constant interaction that joint custody requires of the parents encourages the children to fantasize that Mom and Dad will eventually get back together.

Clearly, joint custody is not for every family, and judges who force a joint custody arrangement on most families may be doing a serious disservice to children. In fact, joint custody may be precisely the wrong solution for many families who end up before a judge to determine custody. These families are already ensnared by both parents' resolution to fight and win their case. When families are not capable of the kind of commitment described above, the children will inevitably suffer from the disruption as they make the transition to yet another new arrangement.

With all the pressure on parents to enter into joint custody agreements, sole custody is gaining an unfair reputation as being somehow bad or far less desirable. Oftentimes it provides the only practical solution for families of divorce. Regardless of terms or legal agreements, what matters to the children is that they have access to both parents. Don't let labels interfere with that goal.

The Role of Mental Health Professionals in Custody Disputes

In too many custody disputes, each parent is determined to convince the judge that he or she is a far better parent than the other. Rather than stopping at making their own case, however, they try to prove why the other parent is grossly incompetent and would turn the youngsters into juvenile delinquents—or worse. How can the judge decide, when, playing fairly or not, both parents may be making compelling cases?

One way is for the judge to turn to mental health professionals to provide information about the family. Generally, these professionals are psychiatrists, psychologists, and social workers who are child or family experts and have experience evaluating families for legal, or *forensic,* purposes. In most cases, these professionals are involved in custody cases in one of two ways: they are asked to do the evaluation by a parent's attorney or by the court. In either case they are impartial and report their findings and recommendations to the court in written and/or oral testimony.

In recent years particularly, expert witnesses have come under attack for being hired guns—experts who are paid by the client to testify. The payment is thought to contaminate the experts' testimony, because the assumption is that the fee influences them to say what clients or their attorneys wish. Undoubtedly this may be true in some cases. But I believe the court—and the children involved in custody disputes—can be served well by the use of expert witnesses who follow rigorous ethical standards. These practitioners state up front that they cannot ensure that their testimony will support the client's position; their job is to arrive at an honest evaluation of the client's ability to be a good parent.

In collecting the information they need to make a determination, expert witnesses interview the client, the client's children, the children's other parent, and others they believe can provide information. They present the information in the form of a report and are prepared to answer questions posed by the judge and both parties' attorneys in court. After all the testimony has been entered, the judge decides which parent the children will live with.

Court-appointed examiners are usually asked by the court to evaluate both parties in the dispute—most often the mother and the father—and the children. They conduct the same kind of investigation as expert witnesses, but the goal of their evaluation is to determine which is the better parent for the children to live with. The judge, however, still makes the final decision.

Occasionally therapists are asked by patients to testify on

their behalf in custody disputes. Therapists who agree should make it clear that they will answer questions only about the patient, and no one else, including the patient's spouse. Testifying about people whom they have not examined is unethical and constitutes hearsay and conjecture. When the patient is a child, the child's agreement to the therapist's testifying, as well as the permission of both parents, should be obtained.

Many parents who need mental health help are often reluctant to enter therapy if they anticipate or are in the middle of a custody battle. They fear that if the opposing attorney finds out, their case will be weakened because the information could be used to prove, for example, mental instability or inability to cope under stress. This fear is sometimes well founded, but it can be countered by calling on the treating therapist to explain that people who recognize when they need help and then seek it are actually showing great insight and strength. Much more destructive are people who need help but are too proud or stubborn to admit it.

Visitation

When parents don't have joint custody of the children, they must spell out the terms for visitation in their divorce agreement. Here again, the agreement should be based on the goal of giving the children as much access to the parents as possible, regardless of the custodial arrangements. But parental responsibility doesn't end there: the children should be encouraged to spend as much time as possible with both parents.

This is a taller order than it sounds. Some parents, without even realizing it, give cues to the children about their distress whenever the children spend time with or show their love for the other parent. For example, seven-year-old Matthew returned home after spending a happy afternoon at the zoo with his mother. As he eagerly showed off a collection of animals his mother had gotten him as a reminder of their day together, his father sighed, "Are those cheap plastic things all she bought you?" Over time, such remarks, intended or not, will blunt a child's happiness and make him question his own judgment of his mother.

There is no right or preferred visitation schedule. Permitting the children to spend weekends and holidays with the noncustodial parent may be a popular schedule, but it is not the only one. Ideally, the schedule should fit the parents' as well as the children's needs. Visitation schedules for preschoolers are often easier to devise, because they don't have to take into account the myriad activities in which school-age children are usually involved. Thus, parents can be more flexible about midweek overnight visits and other unusual times.

There is some disagreement over whether overnight visitation should be permitted when the child is an infant and the mother is the custodial parent. In most cases, however, I believe that it should be not only permitted but encouraged. Today it is a rare father who is not able to care adequately for an infant, and few mothers, particularly if they work, rely solely on breast feeding. If the baby is taking only breast milk, the milk can be expressed and stored for later use.

Visitation issues are discussed in greater depth in Chapter 7.

Child Support

When parents bring a child into the world, from that moment on they are *both* responsible for its care. That means financially as well as emotionally, even when the parents are divorced. Many parents who have agreed or are ordered to pay child support, however, shirk that commitment.

In the past decade, the government has become acutely aware of the link between mothers on welfare and other kinds of public assistance and the failure of fathers not living in the family home to pay child support. In 1984, Congress passed legislation requiring state governments to help custodial parents collect the court-ordered child support they were due. The states were to order employers to withhold the payments from the wages of parents who were at least one month delinquent. The state would then pass on the payments to the parents.

In 1992 the U.S. General Accounting Office reported to Congress that the legislation was not working. In 1990, for example, state agencies reported that support payments were being collected in only 17.9 percent of the twelve million cases they were handling. Congress planned to use the GAO report to improve the law and collection procedures. Legislation was signed into law in late 1992 making it a federal crime to flee across state lines to avoid paying child support. To persuade more parents to pay up, some jurisdictions now publish the names of delinquent parents in local newspapers or arrest and jail them. Other jurisdictions are giving unemployed deadbeat parents suspended jail sentences in return for participating in job training and placement services. Many custodial parents, frustrated at the government's inability to force noncustodial parents to pay up, have turned to private collection agencies. These agencies, now proliferating in many parts of the country, keep a percentage of the money they collect from delinquent parents.

Nina's parents divorced when she was three. Her father, a businessman, bitterly contested the divorce and fought hard for custody of his little "princess." When he lost, he was devastated. He felt as if he had nothing but his business left, and he poured all his energies into making it successful. His efforts paid off handsomely. Since he could now afford bigger child support payments, Nina's mother took him back to court. Although she won the increase, he never paid it. Nina, now age ten, couldn't stand the ongoing conflict between her parents and told her mother that she really didn't care about the money. Nina told me, however, that in addition to being tired of the fighting, she was deeply hurt that her father did not want to share his good fortune with her voluntarily. Wouldn't he want to get her piano lessons? Wouldn't he want to see her live in a house instead of an apartment? Would it be so terrible if her mom could work fewer hours and spend more time with her?

In a society such as ours, where money has so many loaded

meanings, it's useless to think that children won't feel hurt or cheated to some extent when a parent refuses to pay his or her fair share. The children are bound, at some point, to interpret the failure to pay child support as a lack of love or interest in their well-being.

Aside from looking at the issue as a financial and legal responsibility, I'd like to make another point. All parents have the responsibility to take care of their children to the best of their ability, whether or not they live with them. They should not cast aside that responsibility when they are angry at their children's other parent. By withholding child support, they think that they are punishing their former spouse, but they lose sight of the fact that they are really punishing their children. Here's an acid test for such parents: If they were still married to the children's other parent, would they refuse to support them or make certain opportunities available to them?

Handling Disputes
After Your Divorce Is Final

Even if a divorce is relatively amicable, most couples can count on one thing when children are involved: there's still some degree of conflict ahead. And there probably always will be. Remember when you and your former spouse were happily married? You had your disagreements even then, but your reaction to the fighting was different: because you loved your spouse, it was in both your best interests to resolve your disagreements and kiss and make up. That incentive is now gone, but in its place should be another one: because you love your children, you should want to keep peace with their other parent (your former spouse) for their benefit and yours, too. Keeping anger and hostility alive interferes with your ability to move on with your life, could cause you and your children serious psychological harm, and undermines the children's right to a healthy, nurturing relationship with both parents. Furthermore, you can be sure that people who are using up a lot of energy fighting with someone else probably don't have a lot of energy left over for parenting their children properly.

So what should you do when your former spouse refuses to pay child support? Or demands more visitation with the children than you think is reasonable? Or wants to fight you for sole custody of the children? Should you simply give in? Sometimes yes, sometimes no; it depends on the circumstances. Ways to deal with a former spouse over such disputes are addressed in Chapter 14, but two points are important here. First, parents should shield their children from their disagreements as best they can. Second, parents should turn to litigation to resolve their differences only when all other options have been exhausted (assuming that sexual or physical abuse is not involved). Admittedly, avoiding litigation may be difficult; competing interests—from grandparents to friends to attorneys—may push one or both former spouses toward the courtroom. But the price exacted by going to court can be too high. It often pulls the scabs off emotional wounds that have finally begun to heal since the divorce. Both parties may be brought to the brink of financial ruin. And litigation may not solve the problem anyway because months, even years, may pass before the court makes a final judgment or payment is collected.

When Dorothy came to see me for treatment, she was very angry at her ex-husband. The two of them were locked in battle on various fronts—visitation with the children, financial matters, even medical decisions. She constantly complained that her husband refused to cooperate in any way to resolve their problems. Eventually Dorothy permitted me to talk to her husband, who welcomed the opportunity to discuss their problems. He turned out to be a kind, reasonable man at a loss about how to deal with her. It was clear that Dorothy had exaggerated the situation and that she was a major part of the problem.

There are a variety of morals to be drawn from this case. The first is that almost every spouse—particularly the one who didn't seek or want the divorce in the first place—believes that his or her spouse is uncooperative. This is not surprising, nor is it abnormal. Part of the initial animosity that results when someone is asked for a divorce translates itself into different defensive reactions.

For example, a husband who didn't want the marriage to end may find that he and his wife can't agree on a visitation schedule. In frustration he charges that she is totally uncooperative and inflexible, yet a look at the facts reveals that it is he who insists that the children be returned to her at a time when they would have normally been asleep in their beds. Although he does not realize it, his behavior is saying, "Why should I cooperate when I didn't want this divorce anyway?" In effect, he is sabotaging efforts to arrive at some kind of a mutually agreeable schedule with his wife. Although such behavior helps him deny the reality of the divorce, it can't change what has happened. And it only leads to more hurt and anger, to which the children will certainly react.

Another possibility this scenario suggests is that sometimes both spouses are guilty of being uncooperative. They are so busy blaming each other that they fail to grasp that they themselves are contributing to the stalemate. Here are some questions to ask yourself when you encounter conflict with your ex-spouse about the children:

➤ **What compromise can *I* make on this issue?**
In the above visitation dispute, the mother could have agreed to permit the father to have the children late every other weekend and see what happens.

➤ **Am I contributing to the problem by not recognizing the motives behind my behavior?**
Some people attempt to forbid the children to be with the other parent when that parent will be with someone he or she is seriously dating. The ostensible reason is to prevent the children from being exposed to sexual activity. The real reason, however, is that they are jealous of the former spouse's new love interest.

it possible that if I offer a compromise on one issue, my spouse will compromise on another?

Some issues are bound to be more important to one parent than to the other, making it possible to make a trade. Maybe Mom hates taking seven-year-old Mary for her skating lessons on Saturday morning, and Dad feels out of his element at the pediatrician's office. A tradeoff may solve both their problems.

➤ When we fail to reach agreement, am I thinking through the options, or am I just digging in my heels as a matter of principle?

Your former spouse asks that instead of picking up the children for their weekends together on Saturday morning, he'd prefer picking them up after school on Friday afternoon. You say no. When he asks why, the best answer you can muster is, "It's not in our agreement, and I see no reason to change." Many problems can be avoided simply by keeping an open mind to your former spouse's requests and taking the time to think through a response.

➤ Do I find that I am doing most of the talking and little of the listening?

People who are less assertive or seek peace at any cost are unusually compliant in the negotiating process. The more assertive spouse should not take advantage of the situation, since agreements reached in this way may not serve the best interests of the family. These agreements also have a higher likelihood of unraveling, because the less assertive spouse was merely giving in, not really arriving at an agreement.

➤ When I don't give in to a request because I think my children will be harmed by what my ex-spouse wants, have I taken the time to find out whether this is true?

Say that your former spouse wants to take your eleven- and thirteen-year-old kids on a white-water rafting vacation. You are right to be concerned about their safety, but talking to the owners of the operation and obtaining additional information from the library or local outing groups will provide you with the information you need to make a reasoned decision. Again, the idea is to avoid knee-jerk responses that further entrench the two of you as opponents.

➤ **When the children make a request that would hurt the other parent, could I be the cause?**
At first glance, this may seem impossible: How could you cause the children to hurt their other parent? But consider this situation: Your children say that they don't want to spend time with their other parent anymore. Your first reaction is probably to empathize with them or resolve to protect them from suspected harm. Surely they wouldn't make such a request if there wasn't something awful going on. However, there are many reasons children may make such demands. For one, children are adept at playing one parent against the other. They may be trying to gang up on one parent to solidify their relationship with the other. Another reason is that one parent may be making them feel so guilty over their joy in spending time with the other parent that they look for ways to avoid their feelings of discomfort, even at the cost of cutting one parent out of their lives.

If the children say they don't want to spend time with their other parent, don't jump to conclusions. Instead, ask them why. (If they cite physical or sexual abuse, see Chapter 12.) It is not enough for divorced parents to set up a visitation schedule; they also need to do all they can to encourage and support the children's interaction with both of them. This is true regardless of which parent has custody. Parents who place obstacles in the children's way—whether physical or psychological—without denying access outright may be sticking to the letter of this responsibility, but not to its intent.

When a spouse is truly uncooperative, it's helpful to remember that people and circumstances change over time. Don't give up. (I have often seen uncooperative spouses suddenly become very cooperative when they begin to date someone and contemplate remarriage.) You can expect cooperation to be the most difficult to achieve in the initial stages of negotiation because this is when the hardest and biggest issues are usually discussed.

Of course, if conflict continues, professional help becomes a necessity. In the case of Dorothy and her husband, they engaged a mediator and (even to my surprise) were finally able to reach an agreement. A therapist is another good choice, depending on the nature of the problem and how it is manifested.

Again, let me emphasize that the primary responsibility of divorcing parents is to place their children's welfare first and make every effort to cooperate to serve the children's best interests. As long as former spouses share offspring (expectably, until one of them dies), they will have an ongoing relationship. Fighting it is futile and causes children to become resentful. Eventually they will be old enough to judge the behavior of both their parents for themselves.

When There Is No Conflict

Of course, there is always the possibility that you will not encounter serious conflict as you and your spouse devise a workable divorce settlement. Consider yourself lucky, for you are in the minority. Remember, however, that although you may be pleased, you still have a responsibility to view the settlement in terms of the children's needs and best interests.

Perhaps the most common example of this situation is the area of visitation. If your noncustodial spouse does not seem interested in a generous visitation schedule, you need to find out why. Remember that children benefit from consistent, supportive contact with both parents after a divorce. Although you might welcome a situation in which you will not have to face your ex-spouse very often, it will not serve the best interests of your children. You need to do all you can to make sure your children maintain a relationship with their other parent.

Chapter 5

IMPACT OF
DIVORCE ON CHILDREN

From the moment of their birth, children are mastering new skills and gaining new knowledge—absorbing an almost incomprehensible amount of information on their way to becoming adults. On that long journey, most children without serious physical or mental disabilities pass through predictable stages of physical, emotional, and intellectual development. Although each child progresses at his or her own pace, for the most part children of similar ages share many characteristics.

Experiencing a severe trauma—such as the divorce or death of a parent—may interrupt a child's development. The child may become stuck at the stage in which the trauma occurred or regress to a stage that had already been mastered. When parents say that they want to help their children overcome a trauma, in psychological terms this translates into ensuring that their children continue to develop normally and maintain a positive out-look. Children's energies cannot afford to be diverted by parental battling, an unstable home life, difficulties with friends, and neglect of their needs. If such stresses continue, even the most resilient child may develop problems.

As I emphasized earlier in this book, how intensely children respond to separation and divorce is linked to the amount of turmoil in their lives and ongoing conflict between their parents. If parents can maintain a stable environment for the children and communicate reasonably well, the children will fare better in the long run. Nonetheless, children can be expected to have difficulty coming to grips with the fact that their family, as they've known it all their lives, is no longer the same and they are powerless to put a stop to it. The fear of the unknown consumes their imaginations. Even when there have been open violence and years of fighting, most children are still shaken by the collapse of their family and prefer that the family had remained together.

Reactions Common to Most Children

Just like adults, children experience a wide range of emotions in response to the breakup of their family. Children may experience and reexperience these feelings at different stages of their lives. Some feelings may be more prominent at one age; others may recede then and revive at a later age.

Children must let their emotions surface so that they can work through and resolve them, and parents must help them with this task. If children are not allowed to come to grips with their feelings, these feelings may emerge later as other problems, such as depression, anxiousness, separation anxiety, personality problems, or lack of concentration. Moreover, these children will be more needy and demand more attention from the adults in their lives. As they grow older, they may not be able to set and achieve goals, feel at ease when they are alone, or show empathy to others, because they never received it themselves.

Permitting children the emotional space to work out their feelings and offering them a ready ear may be difficult at a time when parents are having trouble handling their own emotions. LaWanda, for example, felt helpless when her son would cry himself to sleep at night after she and her husband had separated. As her son sobbed softly into his pillow, all she could think about was how much she, too, missed her ex-husband.

"I just didn't know how to go about comforting Zac when I couldn't comfort myself," she told me. "I was afraid that if he saw me crying too, he'd only feel worse." Once LaWanda made up her mind to deal with her own pain, she found that she was in a stronger position to help Zac. The more she made herself available to Zac, the less comforting he needed. "I've learned to say to him, 'We are both feeling a little sad now,'" said LaWanda.

Here are some of the reactions most commonly experienced by children immediately after separation or divorce. By knowing what to expect, you'll be better equipped to help your children deal with the ones they experience. Techniques for helping your children express their feelings are described in Chapter 8 under "Active Listening." Reactions that are more troublesome or go on for long periods are discussed in greater detail in Chapter 12.

Fear

Almost all children express fear over their parents' breakup and the collapse of their family; precisely what they are afraid of is related to their age. Preschool children are more likely to suffer from such basic fears as being abandoned by the parent with whom they now live, left without food or a place to live, and replaced in the departed parent's affections. Such fears may surface in the form of crying and clinging when the parent must leave the child with someone else and by not wanting to let the parent out of sight. Another sign is taking up a beloved object they had already outgrown, like a Teddy or blanket. Although older children may also fear abandonment by the custodial parent, their fears are more along the lines of how the divorce will change or interfere with their lives.

To help your children feel less at the mercy of the unknown, ask them to describe to you what they are afraid of. Some questions: What do you think will happen to you when I go to work today? What do you think happens to Daddy when you aren't with him? Do you think that Mommy doesn't love you anymore because she isn't with you all the time?

Further, you and your ex-spouse should behave consistently and reliably toward the children, reassure them that neither one of you will abandon them, and make yourselves available to discuss their fears with them.

Sadness

Probably children's most pervasive reaction to the family's breakup is sadness. It is almost impossible to capture in words the degree to which this emotion consumes them.

After watching *Bambi* at home on the VCR one evening, five-year-old Yaphet burst into tears. "Now he has no one to take care of him!" he told his mother. At the time this happened, the boy hadn't seen his father for a year and a half.

The absence of one parent from children's daily lives and missing the family as it once was produce grief reactions not unlike those that arise when a loved one dies. A parent is irreplaceable in a child's life, and, quite simply, will be greatly missed, even if the parent was abusive. Thus, it is normal for children to cry for an extended period about a parent's departure, mourn for the way their lives used to be, and long to return to the time when the family was together.

Crying and looking sad are just a few ways children express sadness. Other signs are wanting to be alone, being less talkative and friendly than normal, drawing pictures that suggest sadness (tears coming down a child's face, a heart broken in two), constant daydreaming, and showing little or no interest in activities that were once enjoyed. Boys in particular may express their sadness as anger and aggression.

Like LaWanda, many parents fear that if they talk to their

children about feeling sad, it will make the children focus on it more and thus make them feel worse. This is not true. The best way to help children handle their sadness is to give them permission to express it and talk about it on their terms. Don't ignore their sadness or hope that it will eventually fade away on its own. Also, don't deny their right to their feelings by making such belittling remarks as "Crying won't do any good; it won't bring your mother back." "I don't understand what you are crying for. You should be glad your dad left."

Boys may need extra encouragement and support to express their sadness. From an early age, boys in our society are given the message that it is somehow "bad" or "weak" for them to be sad or cry. In my own office I've heard many parents say to a boy on the verge of tears, "Big boys don't cry" or "You're acting like a girl. Come on, be a man. Don't cry."

Once you have acknowledged your children's feelings and comforted them, try to redirect them to an activity they enjoy. Also, as I discuss later in this chapter, it's a good idea to share *your* feelings with your children, too. Although it might scare them initially to see the depth of your emotion, it conveys the message that such feelings are appropriate: "You know, there are times when I am very sad, too. I really miss the way our family once was, and thinking about the past sometimes makes me cry. I bet you feel that way, too."

Very much in touch with her feelings, seven-year-old Dana didn't try to hide her sadness. Doing her own rendition of the children's song "If you're happy and you know it, clap your hands," Dana sang to me, "If you're sad and you know it, wipe your tears." She had the right idea.

Anger

There are many ways in which children express anger at the breakup of their parents' marriage, depending on their age, temperament, and family's circumstances. Many children, especially boys, may act out their feelings by getting into fights; yelling at their parents, teachers, and other handy people; and being destructive. Because older children have a greater ability to understand the details of their parents' breakup, they may direct their anger at the parent they believe is responsible for the divorce. Anger is not all bad news, however: it signals that the children are beginning to accept the situation. Otherwise, they wouldn't feel the need to fight against it.

In the short run, the best antidote to anger is permitting your children to express their feelings in acceptable ways. This validates their right to be angry and shows them that someone is willing to listen. Even little ones will feel calmer knowing they can count on you to help them contain what are oftentimes overwhelming emotions. Also point them toward physical activities that provide an outlet for their jumbled feelings, such as punching a pillow, running, swimming, or playing on a jungle gym.

In contrast, some children react by withdrawing from others and isolating themselves. They should be encouraged to express their feelings as well.

What you *don't* want to do is to deny their anger, tell them it is wrong or bad, or force them to keep it bottled up. Children who are not allowed to show their anger are more likely to become depressed. Also, don't bait your children with such comments as, "You're pretty mad at your dad for leaving us, aren't you?" Rather than demonstrate empathy, such questions are more likely to reinforce their hostility toward their other parent or put them on the defensive. Helping your children learn how to express anger in a positive, appropriate manner is a lesson from which they can benefit throughout their entire lives.

A few years ago I treated an attractive young woman named Helen who had great difficulty in expressing her feelings, especially anger. When Helen was about seven, her parents announced they were getting a divorce. This was a great shock to her—she had never even heard her parents fight; there had been no angry words, no threats, no nothing. In Helen's family, the prevailing "culture" had been for family members to keep their anger to themselves. Only a few years later did Helen learn that her father had been having an affair with a neighbor woman.

After her parents separated, Helen and her younger brother remained with their mother. Whenever the two siblings would fight, Helen's mother would say, "You shouldn't be angry with your brother. You're his older sister and you should know better." Unfortunately, Helen internalized two lessons: to turn her anger inward and to bend over backward to make excuses for people who had hurt her or let her down. No matter what people did to her, she could always turn it around to its somehow being her fault. Through therapy Helen learned, among other things, to express her anger and disappointment and hold people responsible for their behavior toward her.

For most children, anger has a way of working itself out when parents are patient and empathic. About a year after their divorce, Lettie's former husband suddenly and completely dropped out of sight; no one knew where he had gone, only that he'd left the area. One day it got to be too much for their son, Wayne, who was nine at the time. He took one of his dad's old shirts and ripped it to pieces. When Lettie found Wayne, she could see that he was angry and upset. But at the time, all he'd admit to was that he was making rags for cleaning his bike. Later, Lettie was able to encourage him to open up and discuss how he felt about his dad's absence.

"Are you still angry with your dad?" she asked Wayne about two years after this scene.

"No, not anymore," he replied. "But I am angry at you."

Surprised, Lettie said, "Why on earth are you mad at *me*?"

"Because you're here!" Wayne started to laugh. "Who else am I going to get mad at?"

Guilt

Children have no control over their parents' decision to go their separate ways. One emotion that returns some of that control to them is guilt. It stems from children's belief that they are the center of the world and as such must either be the cause or the target of everything that goes on around them. If only they had behaved better, had earned higher grades in school, hadn't secretly wished that Dad would go away, hadn't talked back to Mom the other night—any number of things—then Mom and Dad would still be together, they think. Many also think that it is their duty to do whatever they can to get their parents to reunite.

Children, of course, can't tell a parent in so many words that they feel guilty about the breakup. But one indication is showing a willingness—almost an eagerness—to step forward and take the blame for all kinds of things: "I broke the lamp." "I took the cookies out of the cupboard." "I hit your car with my ball and broke the antenna."

Guilt feelings are often so strong that it's hard to convince children that they are not to blame for the divorce. This is why I emphasize in Chapter 3 that from the time parents separate, they need to be clear with the children that they are not the cause. Children also need to understand that the divorce is permanent and there is nothing they can do to get the family back together again. These messages should be repeated over and over again, especially during the initial period of adjustment.

Parents should never make such remarks as "Maybe Dad wouldn't have left if you hadn't gotten into trouble at school" or simply "It's all your fault this happened"—they confirm the children's darkest suspicions and tell them that their guilt is appropriate. Even well-intentioned remarks can subtly suggest to children that they are the root of the parents' problems: "Having four kids was simply too much for your mother—she just couldn't take it anymore" or "We thought that the divorce was the best thing we could do for you kids right now." Because of children's guilt, it's important to choose words with care and sensitivity.

Loneliness

When a family loses the daily presence of a member, a huge hole is left in its fabric. The family is changed now; it will never be what it once was. The children will be lonely for the parent who left the family home, whether that parent was close to the children or not. Furthermore, the new living situation brings on loneliness in other ways. The custodial parent, particularly if it's the mother, may have less time to spend with the children; she may be working full time now or holding down two or three jobs to make ends meet. She also has to assume the everyday chores once shared by two people. As a result, the children are by themselves more often. Younger children may create pretend playmates to keep them company. Older children may become latchkey kids, forced to fend for themselves and handle their fears and apprehensions in the lonely hours before Mom or Dad returns from work. Their minds have more time to contemplate their sadness and their fantasies about making their family whole again.

   Loneliness is not the same as being *alone*, however. Although children may indeed spend less time with their parents now, they can use this time to grow intellectually and learn more about themselves. They need to feel comfortable spending some time alone, perhaps to pursue some favorite or soothing activity, such as reading, drawing, shooting baskets in the backyard, writing a letter to their other parent, or just sitting and thinking.

   You'll notice this list does not include such activities as watching television and playing video games. These are passive entertainments and do not encourage children to use their imagination and learn how to structure their time. Unmonitored television watching presents other dangers as well. Television viewing has been linked to increased aggressiveness and tolerance of violence in children, and it may expose them to sexual images not suitable to their age and understanding.

Rejection

It is difficult for children to understand that a marriage occurs between two adults, not between the adults and any children they may have. Unfortunately, children may believe that because their parents have rejected each other, they are now rejecting them, too, as part and parcel of the whole deal. Since the family breaks up when a marriage breaks up, their confusion is understandable. A withdrawn 8-year-old once tried to explain to me, "I don't fit in anywhere. I feel like my insides are missing."

In explaining the separation and divorce, you and your ex-spouse should state unequivocally that your relationship has no bearing on the relationship between each of you and the children. Further, the parent no longer living with the children bears the greater part of the responsibility for keeping the relationship with the children alive.

Regression

Many children respond to their parents' separation and divorce by regressing to an earlier stage in their development. In the short term (up to a few months), this is a normal reaction; it permits children to take a breather from events too overwhelming for them and to retreat mentally to a safe, comforting place in which they had greater control.

Some common regressive behaviors are thumb sucking, bed-wetting, temper tantrums, hitting, clinging to parents, and resurrecting an old security object, such as a blanket or a doll. Although such behaviors can try your patience or disappoint you, do not respond with punishments. Not only are they ineffective, but they are also the opposite of what the child needs right now: your support and gentle reassurance. It might help to remember that the child is not trying to get back at you or demand your attention by being "bad"; the child simply is not ready to handle his or her emotions.

Sleep Problems

Many children experience sleep-related problems, such as difficulty in going to bed, insomnia, anxiety, and nightmares. Sleep represents another potential occasion for loss and abandonment—a venture into the dark unknown. Bedtime may be even more loaded for the children who woke up one morning to discover that a parent had left home the night before.

Sleep-related reactions should also pass in a few months, but in the meantime you might want to pay special attention to evening and bedtime rituals. This will help ease the transition from a busy day to a peaceful, soothing night. You may especially want to keep alive the rituals that were observed before the separation. If your children were accustomed to a bedtime story or an evening walk before the separation, don't stop now, even though you may be bone tired or feel there's no time. Such activities are important not only for their content but also for the closeness and memories they engender. Also, take time to talk about your children's school day and review homework so you can stay informed about each child's activities and progress.

You might also try keeping activities similar from evening to evening, so that each child knows what he or she is supposed to do and when. This will keep fussing, nagging, and further disruption to a minimum. One family uses this simple after-school routine: snack, homework, dinner and related chores, finish homework, and get ready and go to bed. Following a schedule the family draws up together and posts on the refrigerator, the children take turns doing such chores as setting the table and cleaning up after dinner, taking out the garbage, and changing the cat's litter. Playing with friends or watching television is permitted on school nights if homework and chores are completed early. The father always makes it a point to spend a few minutes with each child at bedtime.

Young children especially may cry and cling when it's time to say good night to a parent. Therefore, you should reassure the child that you'll be only steps away and will check on the child before going to bed yourself. Don't give in to the temptation to stay in the room until the child falls asleep—not only will you become resentful over the child's demands on you when you find you must do this night after night, but also you are ultimately causing harm by not giving the child an opportunity to learn how to comfort herself.

The case of four-year-old Molly illustrates the long-term repercussions of such behavior: After her parents' separation, Molly was allowed to sleep on her mother's bedroom floor when Molly couldn't sleep at night. By the time she was ten, Molly still couldn't or wouldn't sleep anywhere else most nights unless she was visiting her father.

Although her mother's intentions were good-hearted, she fostered overdependency in her daughter and interfered with Molly's normal childhood development. The lesson: Don't get into bed with your child or allow your child to sleep with you. If you come across information in the popular media promoting the family's sleeping together, don't fall for it.

Here's a proven way to help children learn to fall asleep by themselves:

1. When the child first gets out of bed, the parent should firmly return the child to the bedroom and spend a few minutes reassuring him or her. Some children hate having the door shut so much that shutting the door as you leave will persuade them to stay put after one or two repetitions. Older children can be given a book and permitted to read until they fall asleep.
2. If the child cries, the parent should allow 20 minutes to pass before returning to the room and repeating step 1.
3. If the child still continues to cry, allow longer intervals to pass before returning to the room. No need to panic or feel guilty—you are not harming the child in any way. The child will learn eventually, usually within two or three nights, that you mean business.

Masturbation

From an early age, children explore their bodies and discover what feels good to them. This is a natural part of growing up and learning about their sexuality; it does not mean that a child has been sexually abused. If you detect a marked increase in masturbation or notice that your child is constantly touching his or her genitals or masturbating absentmindedly in public, however, professional help may be needed.

School Problems

Children often express the upset they feel over separation and divorce through increased aggression and declining school performance. The more successful you are at helping your children handle the feelings discussed above, the less likely it is that their schoolwork and relationships with friends will suffer. As I've said before, it's a good idea to meet regularly with your children's teachers. They can tell you whether your child has recently developed trouble concentrating on schoolwork, getting along with classmates, and so on. It is not unusual for children to develop problems in school but not at home.

In my practice I've come across many parents who keep their children home from school to stave off their own loneliness and comfort the children. This is clearly not appropriate and sets up a harmful pattern of dependency for parents and children alike. Eventually such children may feel that if they do return to school, something awful will happen to the parent. Further, the children are being deprived of their education and social relationships. Parents must be responsible for their own well-being and not in effect become their children's children.

Physical Problems

Some children react to stress by developing physical problems, such as stomachaches, headaches, chest pains, and cramps. Children may also develop such problems when they cannot or are not allowed to acknowledge, express, or deal with their feelings openly. These aches and pains are usually real and may require a doctor's care.

Children rarely use these complaints intentionally as a way to get a parent's attention, at least initially. Sometimes, however, children claim they have a physical problem that only a parent can minister to. The parent whose attention they are seeking may be either the custodial or the noncustodial parent.

Keep in mind that children, particularly preschoolers, seem to catch almost every bug that comes their way. Thus, when children complain of not feeling well, it probably has nothing at all to do with the divorce. Let your pediatrician make the determination. One of my neighbor's children, for example, seemed to suddenly develop an earache the night before his mother was scheduled to go on a business trip. The mother thought that the child was faking because he didn't want her to go away. A few days later the aunt who was caring for him noticed fluid dripping from the boy's left ear. On taking him to his pediatrician, the aunt learned that the boy had not been faking at all. The delay in getting treatment had resulted in a ruptured eardrum.

Eating Problems

Eating problems are more common in girls than boys, but every child should be watched for signs that eating habits have become unhealthy or have significantly changed. In the past few years, anorexia nervosa (undereating or refusing to eat altogether) and bulimia (gorging on food and then vomiting it) have received much attention in women's magazines and television, but they are not the only types of eating problems that children may have. They also may overeat, hoard food in their rooms or school lockers, or eat only one or two types of food. Eating problems sometimes indicate that a child has an emotional problem or is locked in a power struggle with one or both parents.

Some change in eating habits may be a normal reaction to the family's breakup. Don't be surprised if (much like you) your children lose interest in food or have an increased appetite. However, if you notice that a child is gaining or losing more than a few pounds, or showing too much or too little interest in food, you should visit your pediatrician immediately.

Wish for Reconciliation

Years after their parents have divorced and even married a second time, many children still hold on to their fantasy that someday, somehow, their parents will reconcile. Although this a

normal reaction, you should not encourage their wishful thinking, even if you yourself share that wish.

Ted, the thirty-three-year-old father of two girls, six and nine,
used his children as messengers to his former wife in the hope
that she would consider a reconciliation. Through poignant
notes to their mother, the girls pointed out how lonely and sad
Dad was without her and that they prayed every night for her
return home. Not only did Ted prevent himself from moving on
with his life, but he also cruelly set up the girls for more disappointment when his plan didn't work. The girls, of course,
blamed their mother for being so "mean and stubborn." This
family made progress only when Ted could admit to himself that
the marriage was over and explain that fact to the girls.

Sometimes, however, parents send children unintended signals that raise their hopes falsely. After the parents separate, a
truce may set in, in which the parents put aside their differences
and collaborate for the good of their children. When the children notice that the fighting and tension have stopped, they assume that their parents are getting along better, making the
divorce unnecessary. If you suspect your children are thinking
along these lines, you may want to say something like "Mom and
Dad are not married to each other anymore, and we can never
live together again. But we want you to know that we will continue to work together to make sure that we raise you in the best
possible way. We will always be your parents, and that means
talking or getting together once in a while to discuss what's best
for you."

Your Own Reactions
Have an Impact, Too

Children's reactions to separation and divorce are greatly influ-
enced by parental reactions. Studies have shown that the psychological adjustment of the custodial parent is a crucial factor
in the long-term adjustment of the children. The better parents

are able to handle their lives after the divorce, the calmer their children will be. The more they allow stress to overcome their lives and spill over into the children's, the slower and more difficult the children's adjustment will be.

If you are unhappy and resentful about the separation and divorce, there's a good chance you'll relay those feelings to your children in not only obvious but also subconscious ways. For example, by now you know not to belittle your spouse in front of the children through such remarks as "What a louse your father is. He left us in quite a fix, and I don't know what we're going to do," or "Your mother didn't know how to take good care of you kids. All she cared about was getting drunk. I'll do a much better job without her." But don't forget the wallop an endless succession of these kinds of remarks can deliver to your children as well: "The neighbors are probably relieved that it's much quieter here now." "I'm so glad that I don't have to get anyone's permission before I buy something new anymore." "Your *mother* is on the phone." "Now we're free to do exactly as we please, without anyone's interference." And so on. Remarks like these carry an unspoken message: that you have not yet reached any peace with the past and your ex-spouse. You can be sure that sooner or later the children will react to the implication that their other parent is somehow bad or unworthy of their loyalty and love. They will feel unhappy and confused.

It's not necessary to shield all your feelings about the divorce from your children. On the one hand, you don't want to appear constantly depressed or angry over what has happened; this will feed the children's upset. On the other hand, you don't want to create the impression that your marriage meant nothing to you. How can you strike just the right balance? You'll know you are doing a good job if you can rationally explain your feelings without resorting to anger, name-calling, or blaming or unreasonably losing control. In other words, the focus of your explanation should be on *your* feelings and end on a positive note whenever possible.

The emotion that probably presents the biggest challenge to most people is anger. How else can one parent feel when the other parent hasn't contacted the kids for months? or is behind on a child support payments? or is fighting over visitation privileges?

Think about how you would handle this situation: One evening your kids come in from playing outside; they take one look at your agitated face and ask you what's wrong. It's all you can do to prevent yourself from throwing the dinner dishes on the floor and screaming obscenities. Should you "share" your feelings?

The answer is yes—but selectively. Responding to the children in a manner that reflects your boiling insides might permit you to let off some steam, but that's about all it will accomplish. It won't solve your problems, and the children gain nothing—in fact, they will be hurt—by observing the depth of your anger toward their other parent and getting worried about matters that don't concern them. In these kinds of situations, it is best to wait until you regain your composure and then talk to them: "Kids, right now I'm pretty upset, and I don't think now's the time to go into it. But thanks for asking. It's good to know you care. Tell you what—let me finish making dinner, and then we'll talk after we eat." When later comes, you can say, "I was really angry today, but I feel much better now. Sometimes I get frustrated when things don't go just the way I'd like them to, but taking some time to think things through really helped. Did you ever feel that way?"

This approach invites them to share their feelings and let them know that it's all right for them to feel strong emotions. Had you instead answered "nothing" when they first asked you what was wrong, they would begin to have difficulty in reconciling their perception with your words. Eventually they might lose faith in their judgment and trust in you. They also might come to believe that if you must hide your feelings, they should hide theirs, too. Communication will break down.

As you share your thoughts with your children, be aware of the distinction between feelings and the personal problems that give rise to the feelings. Your children are not the proper audience for personal problems. When you feel the need to talk about your problems, turn instead to trusted friends or relatives or a therapist. They can provide a safe sounding board for you, as well as give you adult insights into your problems, which is what you need anyway.

Keep an Open Mind

When a child appears upset, don't automatically assume that it is related to the divorce or to something you or the other parent has done (or not done) regarding the child. Choosing to focus on only these kinds of explanations will not help you get to the root of the child's problem; it merely ends the possibility for fruitful discussion. Even if you know beyond a doubt that the other parent is the reason for the distress, you should refrain from saying so. To do so puts your child in an impossible situation, testing his loyalty to both parents. (An exception is sexual, emotional, or physical abuse, discussed in Chapters 8 and 12.)

Say you see your child crying a few hours after a visit with his other parent. Your first impulse might be to demand, "What did your father do to you to make you so upset?" The child's immediate reaction might be to defend his other parent—"He didn't do anything"—and the conversation, such as it is, hits a dead end. If you challenge the child further, he may give you more details, but not willingly, for now he thinks that the two of you have become adversaries, operating on opposite sides: your goal is to prove your spouse's guilt, the child's goal is to protect his other parent. Whatever happened to the child's problem? Much more productive is to frame questions in an emotionally neutral way, such as "I can see that something's wrong, Timmy. Can we talk about it?"

Special Considerations Based on Age

Preschool Years

Children under the age of five are in the midst of an exciting expedition in what is to them a nonsensical world. Their main preoccupation at this age is mastering certain skills—chief among them language and movement—as they try to sort things out within their very limited intellectual framework. Children who experience their parents' separation and divorce at this age are more likely to regress and have sleep difficulties than are older children. One of the first abilities to regress or appear abnormal in a stressed youngster is often language. Increased aggression is common in children who were exposed to fighting, whether physical or verbal.

During this stage, youngsters' attempts at reasoning are characterized by fantasy and magical thinking. Because they believe that events in nature are focused around them, they may think that they caused their parent to leave home and may feel guilty and sad about it. They also may create fantasies in which they pretend that the separation never happened or spin elaborate explanations to make sense out of their feelings of rejection and loss.

Four-year-old Jerilynn was sitting on the couch one morning with her teddy bear propped beside her. She had taken an expensive atlas and was drawing lines with a black crayon on one of the maps. On finding Jerilynn and the ruined book, her mother demanded, "Who told you you could take this book and draw in it?" Jerilynn calmly replied, "Teddy told me to do it. He said that we should draw a line from our house to Daddy's so we'd know how to get there. Daddy's waiting for us to come." Jerilynn was not trying to lie to avoid punishment; she wanted very badly to be with her father, who had moved recently to a faraway state.

Creating imaginary companions and having conversations with them are normal at this stage and help stressed children work through their feelings. Such activities do not indicate multiple personality or other serious psychiatric disorders.

Fear is the flip side of fantasy. With their increasing—but still limited—sense of time, young children can appreciate that "bad things" may have happened in the past or be just around the corner. It's important to realize two things about children's fears: in moderate doses, they are necessary for healthy emotional and intellectual development, and they appear at predictable ages in most children.

At two years old, for example, Kyle was afraid of nothing. He could climb higher than his older brother on the jungle gym, never asked for a night-light, and made friends easily. By the age of three and a half, he developed what his mother thought was a bizarre fear of the moon. As darkness approached, Kyle would cry and cling to her. "The moon's going to come in my room and take me away," Kyle would sob. On nights he suspected the moon would be out, bedtime became a battle between mother and child as he refused to stay in his room. His mother suspected that something had made him afraid of the moon; what is just as likely, however, is that Kyle had developed a fear normal for his age. In his magical, egocentric way of thinking—typical for his age—the moon was alive and plotting a way to steal him from his mother.

Children's fears cannot be approached rationally or explained away with fact. Since they are not based in reality, such an approach often makes children feel that a parent doesn't understand. Kyle's mother learned that she was able to calm him faster when she said this simple incantation as she looked out his bedroom window: "Oogie, woogie, boogie-ay, Mr. Moon please go away! Don't take Kyle for a ride. He'd much rather stay inside!" What could make Kyle happier than knowing his mom could chase the moon away! (Incidentally, she also empowered him by teaching him to say some of the magic words by himself whenever he was afraid.)

Although not all preschool children develop this same moon theme, they commonly attribute human feelings and emotions to inanimate objects. Children believe they are ultimately protected from their fears by their all-powerful parents. Their overriding fear, then, is that they will somehow lose this parental protection. When a parent leaves home, this fear becomes realized. And if one parent can leave home, they conclude, what's to stop the other from going away as well? Youngsters' inaccurate sense of time and distance only aggravates that fear; they cannot discriminate between a parent's going off to work in the morning and moving to another state.

Learning how to master their fears is one way children realize they have control over their lives and are capable of handling uncertain situations. It is an important and necessary part of growing up. You can help your children through this stage by respecting their fears and never calling them "babies." Continually reassure them that they had nothing to do with their other parent's leaving home. Remind them that you will always be there to take care of them. When you must be away from them to go to work or out for an evening, be clear about who will take care of them, when you will return, and what they can expect while you are gone. If your children are at a day care center, make sure someone they know greets them in the mornings and helps get them settled. Avoid long separations. When possible, rehearse potentially fearful situations; at the least, talk about them or try role playing. For example, a few days before your child is to enter a new preschool, walk her through the school, show her to her room, and introduce her to her teacher. Have the teacher explain to her what her day will be like.

Ages Five Through Eight

By the time children are five years old, they have mastered some self-control over aggressive and emotional impulses and have begun to blossom into their own person. They are showing great curiosity at the natural world they live in and should be involved in a variety of activities, such as sports, artistic endeavors, and Scouts. The big task facing them now is to build on what they have gained so far to make a successful transition from home to school, establish a solid base for the many years of school to come, and learn to get along with friends and important adults in their lives.

Children of this age continue to have an active fantasy life, but it is generally different from that of younger children. They are preoccupied with heroes—from imagined ones like Batman to real ones like Dad—who can do what they themselves wish they could. Their fantasy life is like an escape valve: It allows them to channel their feelings and energy without harming themselves and (usually) others.

Not surprisingly, their parents' separation and divorce can throw them off track at this crucial time. With their growing but still limited intellectual skills, these children have a greater understanding of divorce and may feel more deeply the physical loss of the parent who has moved out of the family home. They have a great need for concrete answers to such questions as, Who will take care of me? What will happen to me? They long for their parents' reconciliation and may try to think up ways to bring it about. Loyalty to both parents is strong.

If the family's breakup appears to affect their school performance and ability to get along well with others, you should get help immediately. Ignoring the problem now will lead only to more serious problems later. Some warning signs are worsening grades, having difficulty making new friends, fighting with other children, excessive moodiness, isolation, unwillingness to leave the parent to stay overnight at a friend's house, and inability to follow rules at home or school.

Ages Nine Through Twelve

Children in this age range are making great strides in physical and mental abilities. They are gaining social skills as well, becoming more adept at starting, keeping, and ending friendships. For the most part, they are better equipped to handle the fallout from separation and divorce. However, they may be very angry about their parents' split and how it has changed their lives. They may bitterly resent a noncustodial parent who does not visit often. They understand that money is necessary to live and have certain things, and so they may condemn the parent who reneges on child support. Regardless, they greatly miss the parent with whom they do not live, particularly if the parent is of their gender. Also, children of this age are more likely to be used improperly as a confidant by a parent who continues to be enraged with the other parent.

Role models are particularly important for this age group. It is through watching their parents as well as other relatives, friends, and teachers whom they regard highly that they hone their skills at sharing, being a leader, developing friendships, and taking a positive, can-do attitude.

As they increase their repertoire of skills to deal with problems, their self-esteem and self-confidence flourish. If, however, they are unable to cope with demanding and stressful situations, their self-esteem suffers and a downward-spiraling course begins: the more they experience social and academic failure, the lower goes their self-esteem; the more their self-esteem suffers, the more they continue to fail. Thus, it is very important to help your children seek out social involvement through a variety of activities and to continue to monitor their progress at school. If they try to isolate themselves from children their age or refuse to join in any activities, you may need a consultation with your pediatrician or mental health professional.

As they reach adolescence (puberty), don't be hurt or surprised when they want to spend more time with their friends than with their family. This is a normal and necessary part of growing up. Part of the process of separating from the family is trying to become more like their friends through outward symbols: wearing the same style of clothes, getting similar haircuts or hairdos, talking a certain way, liking the same music, and so on. If your son suddenly wants to have an ear pierced or your daughter colors her hair an unusual color, it's probably because they are imitating their friends, not because their parents are divorced.

Their bodies, too, are beginning to undergo great changes that may concern or frighten them. You can probably still recall the anguish of your early adolescence when you thought that the tiniest pimple on your face was like a huge volcano threatening to erupt or that your nose was entirely too big for your face. When your son or daughter spends hours in front of the mirror on a search-and-destroy mission for blemishes or empties a can of hair spray while trying out new hairstyles, a dose of patience and loving respect, in addition to fighting the urge to tease, will go a long way in easing your emerging adolescent's insecurities and showing your understanding.

Children in this age group are developing an interest in sex. Boys, for example, may be looking at girlie magazines alone or with friends. But don't overreact; at this age, an interest in sex does not necessarily mean that they are sexually active. And keep in mind—particularly as you begin to date again—that they are beginning to become aware of your sexual dimension as well, a notion with which most youngsters are uncomfortable ("My mom would never do *it!*"). Be sure that you or their other parent prepares them for their bodies' sexual development, including menstruation in girls and nocturnal emissions (wet dreams) in boys. Discuss masturbation and assure them that exploration of their bodies is normal. Explain AIDS and other sexually transmitted diseases in language they can understand.

In broaching these topics with your children, it is not enough to leave relevant books and other materials around the house; you need to have an open and honest discussion with each child individually. You might want to talk to your pediatrician first for his or her advice and recommendations on appropriate books and videos. You might also want to think through your own values and views on dating and premarital sex so that you can frame your discussion of sexuality in a context that goes beyond mere facts and begin teaching your children what behavior is acceptable within your family.

A good technique for minimizing or avoiding embarrassing your youngster when you discuss sexual matters is to use a third-person approach. You might say to your eleven-year-old daughter, for example: "A lot of girls your age notice that they are beginning to grow hair in their private area. Do you know what that is?" This is preferable to "Do you have hair growing in your private area?" The first question is more apt to lead to a productive discussion in which she feels free to ask you questions and seek out more information.

If you think that a child is sexually active, acknowledge your suspicions. Although a generation ago the worst parents feared was an illegitimate pregnancy or an abortion, today the stakes are far higher—death. Once youngsters have become sexually active, there is no turning the clock back. The best recourse is to talk about the consequences of their behavior and encourage them to behave responsibly by always using condoms and some other reliable form of birth control.

Undoubtedly there will be a few rough patches ahead if your separation and divorce occur when you have a child on the verge of puberty. But remember, adjustment to the crisis will be made more easily if you can maintain a stable household and lay down rules that you consistently enforce. Don't waste time or emotional energy arguing about things that don't matter in the long run—like hairstyles and choice of T-shirt. They will outgrow their need to be different from others outside their age group in time. Realize that your child's growing independence is not a personal rejection of you.

When Will Things Get Better?

Your children's overt reactions to your marital breakup should recede after a time, usually six months to a year for a girl and up to one and a half to two years for a boy. But if they do not, or if they intensify, you need to seek professional help (see Chapter 12). It's important to realize, however, that some of these reactions are not based on time, and so there is no hard-and-fast rule about how long a child's adjustment should take. Children may still be having some problems and reworking some of these issues into college and adulthood. Karen, an attractive twenty-year-old, found herself attracted only to blond, blue-eyed men like her dad. She had never made the connection between the men with whom she became involved and her father until it was explored in therapy. Unfortunately, much like her parents' marriage, her relationships inevitably ended. One of her goals in therapy was to find out why so she could break this cycle.

What Your Children Need Most

Here are some important points to remember when trying to help your children deal with their feelings in the aftermath of the family's breakup:

- Make yourself available to your children by spending as much time with them as possible and inviting them to discuss their feelings. A useful technique is to say something like "You know, honey, Mommy's leaving has been hard on all of us, and I know we all have our own special feelings about it." Don't insist, however, that they share their feelings with you. Once they know you are willing to listen to them, most children eventually become more open.

- Acknowledge and empathize with their feelings—don't judge, deny, or make light of them.

- Don't criticize your children's other parent in front of them. Remember, they love both of you, and you should not only support but also encourage their continued attachment to their other parent.

- Try to keep the conflict between you and your ex-spouse to a minimum. At the least, do not fight in front of the children.

- Help your children deal with their feelings of loneliness. One important way is to help them become confident that they can handle almost any situation. Show them how to dial 911 and what to do in case there's a fire. Teach older children how to use the stove and how to prepare simple meals. When you are not home, be certain they know

(continued)

what they may *not* do. Of course, make sure they have not only your phone number handy, but also that of a neighbor or relative who is free at that time of the day to just talk to them or to help out in an emergency. (Some communities even have a phone number that children can call to talk to an adult when they get lonely.) Keep alcoholic beverages, pills, and poisons under lock and key.

- Don't punish or ridicule them for regressive behavior. They will abandon such behavior on their own if you provide them with consistent parenting, show interest in them and their feelings, and are patient with them.

- Do not rely on television or video games as time fillers or babysitters. Limit total time for such passive activities to a maximum of one hour on school nights and two hours a day on weekends—that is, assuming that schoolwork and chores are completed first. Help your children find more engaging ways to spend their time. Keep a variety of books, games, and art supplies on hand, or stationery to write to their other parent or friends. Help them develop a hobby they can pursue on their own and then share with you or their other parent. If you can afford it, buy a computer. Some of the educational software now available is so much fun they won't even realize they're learning something. And, as much as possible, encourage them to invite friends over. Although you may not like the extra noise or work, think of it as an investment for their teenage years: you are teaching your children that their friends are welcome in your home, and you'll know where your children are.

- Respect children's need for privacy and time away from others. If the children don't have rooms of their own, arrange their bedrooms so that each has a personal storage area and a section that doesn't have to be shared.

(continued)

- Keep tabs on your children, no matter how busy you are. You need to know where they are, and they need to know you know. "Do you know where your children are?" is not an outdated question to be asking yourself, regardless of the time of day. Likewise, keep your children informed of your whereabouts. They worry about you, too.

Chapter 6

IMPACT OF DIVORCE ON PARENTING

Within a few months of the separation from her husband, thirty-five-year-old Maureen realized that she had underestimated just how difficult life would be without him. The chores that were once divided between two people now fell to her. With sole custody of their two daughters, ages six and eight, Maureen was responsible for the family's welfare. They had no relatives in the area where the family lived; she and her husband had moved there right after college. When Maureen's ex-husband took a job in another state, the girls were devastated and she was deprived of a backup babysitter. Now whenever one of the children was sick, Maureen was caught between the no-win choices of begging time off from her full-time job as a nurse and sending a sick child to school. On top of it all, Maureen was trying hard to save extra money so she could buy a small townhouse in a neighborhood with better schools. Thus, she often worked extra shifts when the girls were away at their dad's.

More often than not, Maureen felt tired and overwhelmed, wishing there were more hours to take care of everything needing her attention. Ironically, the worst part of the day came when all her work was done. With the house quiet and the girls asleep, it was difficult to push memories of happier—and easier—times from her wandering mind, and she began to question what step she should take next in her life. Although she had to admit that her marriage couldn't be saved, she nonetheless missed the companionship and support it had once provided.

Maureen's situation is typical of many custodial parents within a year of their separation or divorce. Noncustodial parents don't have it much easier. Although the daily demands on their time and energy may be less, they find that missing their children and the routine of family life can be just as heavy a burden. Similarly, the amount of distress a person experiences is not entirely related to which spouse wanted or sought the divorce. Both spouses can expect some rough sailing in the days ahead.

People in Maureen's position are at a crucial point for both themselves and their children. How they approach restructuring their lives after the breakup of their marriage is another important factor in their children's adjustment to the new family situation.

The process of separation and divorce sets up an almost impossible situation for parents. At the same time, they need time out for themselves—to deal with the emotions and stress accompanying the loss of their marriage and to decide a new course of action—their children have the greatest need for reliability and for assurances of love. Absorbed in their own problems, parents may become less affectionate with their children or fail to discipline them consistently. The more parents pull back to regroup after a divorce, however, the more fiercely children show their need for attention. When both parents and children have lost their emotional equilibrium, they exacerbate each other's problems. The key to breaking this cycle is for parents to

➤ take control of their lives,
➤ create a nurturing, predictable environment for the children,
➤ learn to deal with the children authoritatively, and
➤ be aware of some of the problems that divorced parents commonly encounter, as described in this chapter.

Maureen was one of the lucky—or to be more precise, intuitive—parents. A few years ago she summed up her approach to this difficult time of her life to me: "Although it has been hard, I finally realized what my children needed most was a reasonably stable mother they knew they could count on." Although this may simplify what she in reality had provided for her children, her instincts were on the mark.

Common Problems of Divorced Parents

When a husband and wife first separate and divorce, they experience the gamut of emotions from sadness, anxiety, guilt, shame, and shock to elation over believing that all their problems are now solved. The spouse who didn't want the divorce may feel worthless and unlovable; the spouse who wanted the divorce may have second thoughts. There is no one order for these emotions; each may come and go again and again.

At the same time, there are new living arrangements to become accustomed to. The spouse with whom the children live may remain in the family home, reminding them of the loss of the parent who has moved out. If the family home must be sold and the proceeds split between the two spouses, both spouses will probably relocate to new neighborhoods. Perhaps the children must go to a new school and make new friends. The mother, in addition to leaving behind neighbors she chatted with regularly or could turn to in emergencies, may feel isolated and embarrassed if her socioeconomic status has dropped. If she has not done so already, she may be entering the work force full time. The noncustodial parent, more commonly the father, may be paying child support, but he may resent the fact that he too may have a lower standard of living and that he now plays a reduced role in his children's lives. Both parents may be wrestling each other in the courts over custody or visitation disagreements.

One of the most worrisome reactions is a parent's lacking the energy to go to work, keep up the daily chores, take proper care of the children—in short, losing interest in life itself. These are signs of a serious depression. If symptoms persist for a month or longer, a mental health professional must be consulted (see Chapter 12). If the person is thinking or talking about committing suicide, a psychiatrist should be consulted immediately.

As I pointed out in the last chapter, it is vitally important that parents overcome these reactions and, for the children's well-being, learn how to handle the stresses brought about by the divorce. The children's adjustment is directly linked to the parents' adjustment.

Adult Regression

Chapter 5 notes that children sometimes behave in ways typical of an earlier stage in their development in reaction to their parents' separation and divorce. In the same way, a keenly unwanted or brutal divorce has the potential for throwing an adult back into an earlier stage of development or leading to behavior that is unusual for that person. Some adults may go so far as to become helpless, depending on others—including their children—to take care of them.

Eve, for example, became extremely upset when her husband of ten years suddenly left her. Although she had run the household smoothly and taken good care of their son during the marriage, after her husband moved out she began to have difficulty making even routine decisions. When the roof leaked or the stove malfunctioned, she called her former husband to ask his help. After she had overdrawn her checking account a few months in a row, she asked him to take over paying the bills. Since he still felt guilty about his sudden departure, he went along with her requests. He soon found, however, that the more assistance he gave her, the more dependent she became on him. Within a few more months her helplessness and childish behavior made him fear for his son's safety and well-being. She came to see me for help when he began threatening to sue her for custody of their son.

Liz, too, was thrown into mental disarray after her divorce. To block out her pain, she tried to find solace in a procession of men. Up to that point, she had slept only with her husband and had prided herself on being a virgin on their wedding night. After a year of one- or two-night stands, she felt ashamed and embarrassed by her uncharacteristic behavior. Soon after entering psychotherapy, she decided to have herself tested for the herpes virus and the human immunodeficiency virus (HIV). So far, she has tested negative, but she will have to undergo more testing before she can be reasonably sure she is free of HIV infection.

Most people don't need to see a mental health professional to recover from regressive behavior. Usually such changes are temporary, remitting when the person is able to reestablish a sense of inner equilibrium and direction.

Parent as Child, Child as Parent

After a divorce, some parents experience a specific type of regression in which they become too dependent on one or more of their children. In essence, a role reversal takes place in which the children become the parents' caretakers, confidants, and counselors. These parents are most often troubled, depressed, and lonely; they are unwilling or unable to take responsibility for themselves. Sometimes they are alcoholics or are dependent on another drug. The result is a form of mental bondage and skewed development in the child and a faulty sense of reality in the adult. In its most destructive (but rare) variant, some adults go so far as to commit incest, using the child as a replacement for the lost marital partner. More commonly, they have the child sleep with them to alleviate their loneliness. (As I emphasize in Chapter 5, parents should not invite or permit their children to sleep with them.)

Most parents, however, are vulnerable to depending too much on their children in more subtle ways. Nancy, for example, was divorced after fifteen years of marriage. Because of her extreme shyness, she had never made many friends. When she was married, taking care of her family had filled her time, giving her a ready excuse to refrain from cultivating new friendships. Now for companionship all she had left was her ten-year-old daughter, Alexa. The two of them were inseparable. On weekends when Alexa wasn't with her father, mother and daughter spent much of their time at the mall, going to the latest movies, and taking short trips.

Within a year of the divorce, Nancy began to interfere with Alexa's visits with her father. When he would call to arrange a pickup time for Alexa, Nancy would tell him that Alexa was busy or that she didn't want to go with him that weekend because of special plans the two of them had already made. When the visits stopped altogether, the father consulted an attorney for enforcement of his visitation rights, and I saw Nancy and Alexa as an impartial examiner requested by the court.

The extent of Nancy's problem became clear as I interviewed the family members. Alexa noted that after her father had first moved out of their home, her mother's only apparent interest outside her job was the television set. Except for a few of Alexa's friends, no one ever came to visit them, and she and her mother, in turn, visited no one, not even relatives. A sensitive, insightful child, Alexa worried about her mother's spending too much time alone and took it on herself to liven up her mother's life. She eventually became afraid to leave her mother, for when Alexa wasn't around, Nancy would spend hours sleeping or watching TV.

Clearly, Alexa's life revolved around her mother. As she took greater and greater responsibility for her mother's welfare, she was increasingly being locked out of the normal growing-up experiences of a preadolescent. Her father was right to be concerned. I recommended that Nancy and Alexa enter family therapy to straighten out the roles of parent and child. Nancy also needed individual treatment to address other problems that became apparent in the evaluation. I also recommended that Alexa's visitation with her father be resumed immediately.

Some Warning Signs

Any one of these signs may indicate that parents are depending too much on their children:

- Relying on the oldest child to provide most of the care for younger siblings.
- Relying on the children to cook meals, take over the bulk of household chores, etc., to the point that these jobs interfere with the children's schoolwork and social activities.
- Describing financial troubles in detail.
- Asking for their children's permission to go on dates.
- Giving details of their dates.
- Sharing intimate details about their marriage and divorce.
- Talking about their sexual activity.
- Trying to alleviate their loneliness or depression by keeping children home from school.
- Trying to talk their children out of visiting with their other parent.
- Complaining to their children about "how hard life is."

The temptation to become too dependent on your children is always there if you don't have another adult to whom you can turn when you need advice or just someone to talk to. Although there is nothing wrong in soliciting your children's opinions in matters that concern them (in fact, doing so helps build their sense of responsibility and family commitment), avoid relying on them for advice that affects only you or that should be offered only by adults. For example, it's all right to ask your children to help pick out the family's new car, but you should not ask them whether you should go out on a date with someone you met recently at work.

Denial and Sublimation

Some people deny having any upset or angry feelings over their divorce. They claim they have adjusted just fine and have resumed living a full life in the single lane. Eileen, a former patient of mine, fell into this category. Her reason for seeking therapy, she said, was because of the difficulties she was having with her ten-year-old son. She couldn't understand why he was still having problems over the divorce three years afterward; she herself had absolutely none. This woman was extremely active in a number of causes in her community, chief among them water pollution and other environmental problems. She also held down a full-time professional job and did volunteer work at her son's school. In time it became clear that she had residual feelings about her divorce as well as other problems related to her rivalry with her sister and other family members. To protect herself from those unpleasant feelings, she funneled all her energy into keeping busy every minute of her waking hours. This is known as *sublimation*. In her case it took a long time to break down her defenses, but in the end she was able to rework her life so that she spent more time with her son and having fun.

People like Eileen, however, should not be confused with people who enjoy leading busy, full lives. All of us would do well to become involved in a variety of activities and causes. Devel-

oping interests outside the daily grind keeps our intellect growing and expands our range of friends and acquaintances. The
danger comes when we fill our schedules to the point where we
may be avoiding dealing with problems or may have little time
and energy left for our personal needs and those of the people
closest to us. This busyness may be an attempt to ward off depression. It will only postpone the inevitable.

Overburdening Children With Responsibility

For many harried, overworked single parents, it is sometimes all
too easy to fall into a routine in which they depend on an older
child to take care of the younger ones. Or they might assign
chores to the children that not only entail danger or an unrealistic degree of responsibility, but also take them away from
schoolwork and social activities normal for their age. An only
child may be put in an even more difficult bind: expected to
fend for herself, she has no sibling with whom to share her fear
of being alone and her distress about the absent parent.

Although it is not unreasonable for single parents to expect
their children to carry some of the weight of household duties,
such responsibilities should be assigned within certain limits:

1. The chores should be appropriate to the child's age. A nine-
   year-old child, for example, should not be expected to cook
   dinner and clean up afterward every night.
2. Generally, children under the age of ten should not be left
   unsupervised, and children under the age of twelve should
   not be put in charge of younger children. This is not to say,
   however, that once youngsters reach these magic ages, they
   are ready to be left alone or to babysit—a child's maturity
   and willingness are the determining factors.
3. Older children should not be given total responsibility for
   the care of younger brothers and sisters. They are siblings,
   not substitute parents. Not only does this practice overbur-
   den the older children, but it has serious consequences for
   the younger children as well: recent research indicates that

children cared for by older siblings may have a poor sense of self-esteem. This may be due to the younger children's not getting enough parental attention, to stresses on the family, or to older siblings' picking on younger children when the parent is absent.

4. Chores should not be heaped on a child to the extent that they interfere with schoolwork and sleep or preclude time with friends. Schoolwork is a child's most important job, and an active social life is a necessary ingredient of healthy development.

Instead of overburdening their children, some parents go too far toward the other end of the responsibility scale. To assuage their guilt over the divorce and its unpleasant repercussions, these parents exclude the children from household tasks and try to do everything themselves. Or they may use such faulty reasoning as "I had to do too many chores when I was a kid. I don't want to put my child through that." Such selfless intentions are unrealistic from the parent's point of view and do a disservice to the child. Being assigned and expected to carry out age-appropriate tasks creates a sense of accomplishment and self-discipline in children. It is a training ground for handling increasingly more difficult demands that will be placed on them by school, other institutions to which they belong, and eventually paying jobs.

Studies have noted that children with divorced parents reap unanticipated benefits from assuming a great deal of responsibility at a young age. Many of these children note that they have a greater sense of strength, independence, and capability as a result of their survival experiences in a postdivorce family. They are clearly proud of themselves and their ability to assist their parents at a time when the family's future was seriously jeopardized. Children whose parents are divorced—like all children—need to feel needed; thus, parents should not try to protect them from the vagaries of everyday life. The danger comes when the children are robbed of their childhoods, forced to grow up far before they are ready. They can never recapture those years.

Guide for Assigning
Chores and Responsibilities

Here is a rough hierarchy of chores and responsibilities for children according to age. It is not meant to be all-inclusive, but to give you an idea of children's general capabilities and how they can be built on as the children grow older.

1 to 2 Years

■ Begin to control themselves so that they do not deliberately make messes and break things.

2 to 3 Years

■ Pick up after themselves, such as returning toys to toy bin, with help and direction from parent.
■ Bring used silverware (forks and spoons) to sink.
■ Put trash in wastebaskets.

3 to 4 Years

■ Help set table.
■ Empty wastebaskets.
■ Put away toys with little direction from parent.
■ Put dirty clothes in hamper.
■ Help care for family pet.

4 to 5 Years

■ Make bed with help from parent.
■ Hang coat up on low hook.
■ Set table.
■ Brush teeth, comb hair, and dress with little or no help from parent.

(continued)

- Put dirty dishes on counter after a meal.
- Help with simple yard work: Pile up leaves in the fall, pick up sticks, help plant seeds, water outside plants.

5 to 6 Years

- Make bed (but not perfectly).
- Take bath and wash hair with little or no help from parent.
- Answer the phone properly (but not take messages).
- Write simple thank-you notes.
- Clean up bedroom.
- Assume more responsibility in caring for family pet.
- Water houseplants.
- Help fold and put away clean laundry.
- Put away silverware from dishwasher.
- Help wash family car.
- Begin to fold laundry and put it away.

6 to 8 Years

- Wake up to alarm clock.
- Pack simple school lunch (e.g., sandwich and cookies).
- Prepare simple snacks.
- Straighten up kitchen and bath after use.
- Take accurate phone messages.
- Rinse dirty dishes and put in dishwasher or place on counter.
- Sweep out garage, sweep sidewalks.

8 to 12 Years

- Put out garbage for pickup.
- Clean bathroom floor, sink, toilet.

(continued)

- Clean kitchen floor, counters.
- Wash and dry dishes.
- Wash family car.
- Vacuum and dust.
- Assume bulk of family pet care.
- Bag lawn clippings.
- Load, run, and empty dishwasher.
- Deliver newspapers.

12 Years

- Do minimal babysitting of siblings and nearby neighborhood children.
- Run washer and dryer.
- Iron clothes.
- Prepare simple meals.

Violence

A danger to watch for especially in the first few months after a divorce or separation is violence between the former spouses and child abuse. A father denied visitation because he's late on his child support payments may be tempted to strike the mother when she begins to belittle him in front of the children. A mother who comes home from work late one night to find that the children have spilled a quart of milk on the kitchen floor may slap the first child who approaches her with a question. Even the children may become violent with a parent. I once treated a twelve-year-old boy who, among other things, pushed his father down the porch stairs one evening when he tried to make him come in to dinner.

Although overwrought parents may be operating on short

fuses, there is never any excuse to become violent. If you feel yourself losing control of your temper to the point where you want to hit another person, you should leave the room or, if this is impossible, take a mental timeout to cool off. The old advice of counting to twenty or even higher is still sound. If you fear someone else is going to become violent, you should leave immediately and take the children with you. If you have guns in your house, get rid of them now. You should also insist that your former spouse do the same, or at the very least keep the guns off the premises when the children are present. Simply storing firearms and ammunition separately is not adequate protection.

Because family violence has received so much attention in the past decade, communities are doing a better job of offering an array of services and self-help groups to both victims and people who want to overcome their violent tendencies. Check with your local or state government for the phone numbers of appropriate agencies; information on self-help groups should be available from your local hospital or the phone book. Other good information sources are the local medical and bar societies.

Parents who harm their children physically are more likely to be found out today and reported to child protective agencies. More and more pediatricians, emergency room personnel, and other health care specialists are trained to spot injuries suggestive of child abuse. These professionals are required to report suspected child abuse to the local government authorities, who will investigate the case and, if warranted, take steps to protect the victim and other children in the home. This may range from mandated family counseling to removing the children or the parent from the home.

If you or your children are the object of your ex-spouse's violence, don't hesitate to get a restraining order to prevent him or her from getting near you or the children. Admittedly, such court orders have a limited value against someone determined to do serious harm, but they may deter some people and at least create a paper trail if you find later that you need to take further action. Several states have enacted antistalking laws designed to protect individuals from threat and harassment. Consult your lawyer about reasonable and effective steps to take.

Remember, your best bet in preventing a violent encounter is to remove yourself from the situation as quickly as possible. Next, be sure to tell someone about what happened—a relative or friend, for example—and get additional help if you fear the threat will continue. Tell your family doctor, who may be able to provide additional assistance and advice as well as medical care. Finally, don't blame yourself. You cannot cause someone to be violent; that person is solely responsible for his or her behavior.

Isolation Versus Hyperactivity

In the immediate aftermath of separation and divorce, many people tend to follow one of two patterns in their lives: they either isolate themselves from others or pursue a hyperactive social life.

People who follow a course of isolation may do so for many reasons. Some parents, for example, may be unable to afford a babysitter; others may feel guilty if they leave their children with a babysitter after being away from them all day. Although their motivations are different, both types of parents may come to resent their children. From these parents' point of view, the children are locking them out of opportunities to take a break from their demanding routines and spend some time with other adults.

Some parents, however, use their work and the children as a handy excuse for avoiding interaction with other people. They may still be sad and upset about the divorce—unable to put it behind them and take those first few shaky steps to reestablish their lives. They show no interest in dating again and may deny having any sexual feelings. Sometimes they harbor unrealistic expectations that their former spouse may someday return, and they thus choose to live in a "just in case" limbo.

Some people, overwhelmed by their grief and failure to set new goals, may lack the energy to do anything beyond the absolute minimum to survive each day. Making an effort to meet new people or to take on new challenges is simply out of the question. Such behavior often fosters overdependence on the children, since they become the parent's only focus in life. What will become of such a parent when the children break away and establish their own lives? In its worst form, isolation may lead to severe depression and other psychological problems. As I said earlier in this chapter, such people need professional help.

Jack's case is fairly typical of parents who isolate themselves after their divorce. As the custodial father of two girls and one boy—all under the age of ten—Jack found that his weekdays were an unchanging routine of hurried breakfasts, dirty laundry, and carpools. It seemed as though there was at least one family crisis each day demanding his attention—a sick child, forgotten homework—and weekends were often his only chance to get caught up on things around the house. On the few occasions when he had tried to bring in a babysitter, his youngest child would cry almost to the point of hysteria. Although Jack never regretted having custody of the children, he wished he had some time to spend away from home.

Jack's wish was not unreasonable. Spending time away from the kids to be with other adults can help people become better parents. It offers a chance to step back from the problems and tensions at home and put them in their proper perspective. After all, being a parent is only one of many possible roles in an adult's life.

At the other extreme of the social spectrum are those parents who are any place *but* home. With a full schedule of night classes, church activities, outings with friends, and so on, these parents leave the children with a round of babysitters, the children's other parent, and willing friends and relatives. Some may go so far as to replace the former spouse with a serious new love interest before they are emotionally ready, or they frenetically engage in indiscriminate dating and sexual relationships. Sometimes such parents are (subconsciously or not) trying to blot out the fact that they even have children, who are reminders of their failed marriage or a responsibility they wish they didn't have.

Obviously, the children suffer greatly by missing out on the consistent parenting and love they need, particularly in the first few months after their parents' divorce. Children's distress is compounded by the antics of an out-of-control parent and, not surprisingly, they often come to mirror that behavior back to the parent.

Moving On

In the first months to a year after separation and divorce, these and other effects of the emotional, financial, and lifestyle upheaval brought on by the dissolution of a family are very much on everyone's minds. When the dust finally begins to settle, however, there is the business of building a new life.

Your first task in this reconstruction is to put your failed marriage behind you and deal with any residual feelings of grief, anger, self-blame, or guilt. This is not a process that can be tackled overnight; working through your feelings takes time and a willingness to recognize your worth as an individual and your capacity to love and be loved again. In addition, you need to realize that your role as spouse is separate from your role as parent. Although your marriage ended in divorce, your parenting relationship goes on. Your children love you unconditionally; now it's up to you to show them that their love is well placed.

At some time in the future, the chances are good that you will remarry, but if you are in the first year or so after your divorce, you should take your time in establishing any new love interest. If it happens, that's all well and good, but it should not be a major focus of your life right now.

I am reminded of the divorced mother of a patient of mine who made this mistake. When the patient's mother was not at work, she spent every spare minute in relentless pursuit of a husband who would relieve her of her manless state and the necessity of being the sole provider for her and her daughter. Every Friday and Saturday night, she would douse herself in cologne, put on makeup and evening clothes, and join her other middle-aged friends at a local club frequented by her set. The mother's desperate behavior had sorry consequences for her child, who, left by herself when her mother was on the town, began to use drugs, shoplift, and fail at school. Of course, there were other problems between mother and daughter, but in the mother's single-minded pursuit of a husband for herself and a father for her daughter, she had little time and energy left to deal with her daughter's needs, much less carry on a normal mother-daughter relationship with her.

Next, you need to accept the permanence of your divorce. You and your former spouse will continue to have dealings with each other—and I hope, as I've emphasized again and again, that they will be free of conflict and characterized by compromise. Although your children's fantasies about the two of you reconciling may never entirely vanish, at some juncture they need to feel, as you do, at peace with the divorce. This is more likely to happen if they see that you have taken the lead in this direction.

That the children are able to come to terms with the divorce has important consequences, not just in the period following the divorce but in their adult years as well. Children with divorced parents are more likely to be divorced as adults themselves; they sometimes rush into relationships for which they are ill prepared in an effort to prove they are lovable and to fight against their fear of rejection. If they see that you can recover from such a devastating trauma, such reactions in their adult lives may be avoided.

Attaining an inner peace about the divorce partly depends on the quality of the relationship you and your ex-spouse are able to build as parents to the children you share. If seeing or thinking of your ex-spouse is emotionally charged for you, you may need to monitor your attitudes and behavior toward your ex-spouse in front of your children. Remember, although the two of you were unable to continue your marital relationship, this has nothing to do with the right or ability of each of you to be a good parent to your children.

Creating a Social Life

For many people, one of the most difficult aspects of single parenting is dealing with the social isolation that seems to be an inherent part of the job. More than one single parent has remarked to me, "I have no life outside my children. It's not that I don't want one; I simply don't have the time—or the money." Now is the time for you to realize that your ultimate well-being (and your mental health) depends on your ability to create a new identity for yourself in which being a parent is only one part, not the whole.

Ironically, having a life of your own will make you that much more effective as a parent, because it widens the perspective and outlook by which you can interpret and deal with your children's behavior and needs. This is true for parents who are married as well as those who are divorced. I've treated a number of women, now in late middle-age, who have devoted their entire lives to their families. These women never worked outside the home, or if they did, it was often to help put a child through college. Their volunteer work also centered on the children—perhaps the local PTA or Scout troop. Although their motivations were nothing less than laudable, and many can boast of well-adjusted, successful children, these mothers now appear helpless to refocus their energy in new directions. Particularly tragic are the parents who continue to inject themselves into the lives of their grown children and are then rejected.

Diving back into the social melee means more than searching for a new mate; it means redefining old relationships, as possible, with people who knew you as part of a couple and beginning friendships with people with whom you may now have more in common. It also entails finding interesting ways to spend your time that permit you to learn new skills or widen your social circle. Many newly divorced people take advantage of their single status to pursue school, career, hobbies, and other pastimes for which they didn't have the time when they were married.

Perhaps the easiest, and safest, way to enlarge your social circle and pastimes is to "exploit" your natural interests as well as family and friends. You are more apt to meet people like yourself when you meet them in connection with activities that interest you or people you already know.

I knew one woman, for example, who had a lifelong interest in art but never felt she was good enough to pursue it. Deciding she had nothing to lose after her divorce, she signed up for an art course at a community college. One of her classmates was a local hospital volunteer who invited her to come to the hospital once a week and share her talent with the children on the pediatric ward. Her self-esteem got a double boost—not only did she feel good about her art, but she also felt appreciated and needed by the children.

Another woman took up the fiddle and clog dancing. She met her second husband during a week-long fiddle camp in Georgia.

If you belong to a church or synagogue, or would like to, you can take advantage of dozens of opportunities for becoming involved in interesting activities and meeting new people. Many churches and synagogues now have special groups for single people, although you certainly don't have to limit your involvement to belonging only to them. Activities sponsored by religious organizations also offer the advantage of being sensitive to the demands of parenting. I know one choir director who welcomes members' children at rehearsals, setting aside a play area for them in the rehearsal hall. During the church service, the children can participate in a Bible study or child care group in the church basement.

Most communities now have a chapter of Parents Without Partners (see Chapter 15). As its name implies, this group offers members a chance to meet and provide support to other single parents. Similar groups have sprung up in most communities as well. In my area, for example, one of them is the Ski Club. It is true that some people avoid such groups for fear that they will be branded as being on the hunt for a new spouse, or stigmatized in other ways. But most people who attend seem to enjoy the emotional support they provide and to appreciate the fact that children are often included in the social activities. Furthermore, the nature of these groups makes it easy to participate or drop out as your needs shift or as the groups become less useful to you.

Dating

Many divorced people have said to me in one way or another, "I have no interest in dating or ever getting married again. I've learned my lesson. I don't ever want to risk getting hurt again." Although this reaction is not uncommon in the early stages after a divorce, when memories are fresh and wounds still raw, it rarely holds up in the long run. At some point, most divorced people do date again and eventually remarry.

Your beginning to date again marks still another transition for your children. Although you have a right to your social life, you also have a responsibility to handle it so that your children make a healthy adjustment to seeing you with someone who is a potential love interest. This collides head-on with their lingering fantasy that you and their other parent could someday reunite.

Sometimes children try to dissuade their parents from dating. Earlier I discussed parents who become overdependent on their children; the reverse is not unusual either. When a parent begins to date again, an overdependent child may feel less needed and become despondent over assuming a less important role in the parent's life. Once the parent may have shared confidences with the child; the parent now has someone else in his or her life for that purpose. As a result, the child may try to interfere with new relationships or may cleverly set ambushes to prevent the parent from leaving home. Such a situation is one proof that parents need to build a life for themselves and help their children do the same so that neither becomes too dependent on the other.

Understandably, venturing into the world of dating is intimidating and confusing. The conflicting emotions you experienced when you were dating during adolescence and young adulthood were probably easier to handle than those associated with dating as a divorced adult. At that time you were learning as much about yourself and the concept of relationships as you were about sex and the person you were dating. And because of your age, dating was only one facet of your life. You had school to think about, a career to launch. The stakes are now different. Many social mores and values have changed since then, and your children figure into the new equation.

Here are some points to keep in mind about dating:

➤ *Don't think of dating as a search mission for a new spouse.* It can be simply another way to spend time with a friend you particularly like or have something in common with.

➤ *Act your age and be yourself.* Some newly single people think they can make themselves more attractive by sporting trendy haircuts and wearing clothes designed for teenagers and young adults. They may buy a sports car and begin hanging out in nightclubs frequented by the college-age crowd. Some may even enjoy what they think is harmless flirting with a child's girlfriend or boyfriend. Rather than appearing sexier or more with-it, such people are little more than caricatures of their younger selves, more to be pitied than admired. Their children often grow to resent them for not looking or behaving like the adults they expect—and need—them to be. In particular, preadolescents and adolescents may feel that they are in competition with mothers and fathers who are so obviously trying to increase their sex appeal and recapture their youth.

Of course, a laudable goal at this time may be to improve your appearance by losing some weight, increasing your physical fitness, or getting a new hairstyle, but be clear about your motives: you should do such things to please yourself, not as a lure for a new partner.

➤ *If you are in the process of divorcing and your soon-to-be exspouse begins to date, try not to share your anger or hurt with your children.*   Remember that although you are still legally married, the line between separation and a legal divorce is thin.

➤ *Don't try to hide your dating from your children—you won't succeed.*   Youngsters will pick up on the cues and may react more strongly to your duplicity than to the dating itself. "I always know when my mom is going on a date," complained ten-year-old Evan, half-amused, half-insulted. "She always says she's going to Aunt Rhonda's house."

➤ *Introduce dates to your children in a direct, reassuring manner but without providing more information than they need to know.*   A mother might say, for example: "Marty, this is Mr. Smith. We are going out to dinner tonight at the new restaurant beside the movie theater. I've given the phone number to the babysitter, and she can call me if something comes up. I'll be home around eleven P.M. I know you'll be fast asleep by then, but I'll check on you and kiss you good night again."

This kind of statement shows that you respect their concern about your whereabouts and safety and lessens any feelings of abandonment that might be resurrected by your temporary absence.

➤ *Let common sense be your guide in sexual matters.*   For example, do not engage in sexual activity in front of the children or bring home various dates to spend the night with you. The time for intimacy is when the children are away from home—for example, visiting their other parent. Also, do not fall prey to one-night stands; they are not uncommon among newly divorced people, who may be trying to make up for the deprivation they suffered in their marriage or to prove their sexual desirability.

You may think that because you are an adult, the rules should be different from those you will set for your children when they reach adolescence, but in actuality, they probably shouldn't be that far apart. After all, you will be one of the most formative influences on your children's sexual behavior. "Do as I say and not as I do" doesn't make much of an impact on an adolescent whose hormones are in overdrive. Furthermore, it is nothing short of stupid to ignore the possibility of becoming infected with HIV and other sexually transmitted conditions.

If you are involved in a stable, long-term relationship, it is probably not harmful if that person stays overnight at your house. But under most circumstances, I would caution against sharing the same bedroom. One exception is if the person moves in with you for what is intended to be the long term.

➤ *Don't engage in a succession of short-term, intense relationships.*   You want to keep your home life as stable as possible, and that means refraining from introducing to your children a variety of people who will subsequently drop out of their lives. Each time it happens it represents another loss and abandonment to the child. This may seem like another tough hurdle to dating. But remember, you can take advantage of times when your children are with their other parent.

➤ *Be careful about dating and engaging in sex before your divorce is final.*   If your spouse is suing you for custody of the children, such activity can be used as negotiating leverage against your position.

➤ *Do not think of your dates as stand-in parents.*   You alone are responsible for the care and discipline of your children. However, it's all right to ask a person well established in your life to act as a friend to your children. A mother could ask her boyfriend to advise her six-year-old son on how to handle school yard bullies, or a father might ask his girlfriend to help his twelve-year-old daughter pick out a special dress for her first school dance.

➤ *Do not use your dating activities as a means for hurting your former spouse or proving to him or her that you are sexually attractive.*

➤ *Never encourage your children to report on your private life when they are with their other parent.*   (You can reasonably expect that they will make reports of their own, coached or not, but such tales should be free of your influence.) Likewise, you should respect your former spouse's right to a private life and not pump your children for information about him or her.

➢ *If your former spouse is dating someone steadily, don't turn your children against that person when they all appear to be getting along well together.* The children will feel confused and disloyal to you if you are sending messages that conflict with their perceptions. Be thankful that there is one more person in your children's lives who cares about them. There is no need to feel insecure about your place in your children's affections. No one can ever replace a parent in a child's heart.

There are few events in a person's life that equate with the trauma of divorce, and you need as many friends and relatives to rally around you as possible. Although rebuilding your life may take time and patience, it is possible to do so in a way that will benefit you and your children.

How to Get Involved

Here are some proven ways to meet other people who may share your interests. If you can't afford a babysitter, exchange babysitting services with other parents.

■ Volunteer in community organizations, such as your local hospital, library, and political parties. Becoming active in your children's parent-teacher association is also a good idea. Not only can you meet other parents—married or not—who may be able to help you in school-related emergencies, but you will also get to know the school administrators and teachers. Your involvement will show them that you take your children's education very seriously.

(continued)

- Join the local chapter of organizations for divorced people, such as Parents Without Partners. (See Chapter 15 for more information on this organization.)
- Join the local chapter of your professional association.
- Take adult education courses sponsored by your community college or local school system (the school system courses are often quite a bargain). Don't limit yourself to academic or enrichment topics—many schools offer a broad range, from gardening to fixing cars. Also, by taking courses on parent effectiveness and classes for divorced parents, you can meet other parents with similar concerns while sharpening your parenting skills.
- If you've ever thought about finishing your college degree or switching careers to improve your earning capacity, this may be an opportune time to do it. Although it may make life more difficult in the short term, you and your family will benefit from your working in a field that makes you happier and offers greater income. Also, check with your employer to see whether tuition assistance or reimbursement is available.
- Get involved in activities sponsored by your church or synagogue. Some of the activities are entirely social in nature, such as groups for single people, or involve a special interest, such as music or visiting sick people.
- Take stock of your special abilities or areas you have been interested in but have never taken the time or opportunity to pursue, such as gourmet cooking, playing bridge, or mastering a musical instrument. There are probably groups already formed that you might be able to join. For example, say you have a special interest in local history. You might contact your local historical society or organizations that support or run historical sites in your area. If

(continued)

you have difficulty finding a relevant group and have an institution of higher learning in your area, a phone call to the appropriate academic department may provide the answer.

■ Do any of your friends or relatives have an interest or hobby that fascinates you? Let them know of your interest, and they may be able to get you started or introduce you to other people who could be helpful.

■ Don't reinvent the wheel. You almost certainly have a relative, friend, or acquaintance who has been divorced for at least a few years. Ask what was helpful to him or her—and what wasn't—in making the transition from married person to single parent. Try to query as many people as you can. What worked for one person may not be right for you.

VISITATION AND RELATED ISSUES

Studies show that one of the worst aspects of divorce for children is the loss of contact with a parent. Children need and want regular, frequent interaction with the parent they no longer live with, and most of these parents are highly motivated to keep their relationship with their children as strong as possible.

It is through visitation that noncustodial parents and their children maintain important face-to-face contact. Unfortunately, visitation has many limitations. Perhaps the biggest is that it has little to do with genuine needs and wants. That parent and child miss each other and simply want to be together is often less a consideration than what day of the week it is or whose turn it is to have the kids this weekend. Even the term *visitation* underscores its defects. It stigmatizes noncustodial parents as little more than hosts to visitors who require entertainment. Many experts prefer the term *coparenting time* because it more accurately sums up what should take place between noncustodial parents and their children when they are together.

Understandably, some parents cannot bear the pain of being constantly reseparated after each visit and tend not to see their children regularly. Some go so far as to fade out of the children's lives or abandon them completely because of their frustration over the abnormality of the visiting relationship. Other parents erroneously believe that because they may not have been good parents before the divorce, it's too late to try, or that because they were poor spouses, they're also poor parents. Although dropping out of the picture may be easier, these parents don't realize the sometimes irreparable harm they do to their children. The mother of one ten-year-old boy whose father had disappeared for two years summed up the situation when she said, "Abandonment is much more traumatic than divorce to children. They are always left wondering what's wrong with them or why they drove their parent away. Nothing can fill the void left by a parent."

Visitation is one of the most emotionally loaded issues divorced parents must deal with. Picking up and dropping off the children provide opportunities for former spouses to keep their marital conflict alive if they have not made the effort to put it to rest and get on with their lives. When the noncustodial parent is late picking up the children, for example, the custodial parent charges, "He doesn't care enough to pick you up on time." When the noncustodial parent sees that his son's shirt is too small, he says, "I give your mother enough money to dress you right. What does she do with the money?" Such remarks show that the parent's thoughts are not centered on the children's welfare but on unresolved feelings about the ex-spouse.

From the children's point of view, visitation also can be more of a quandary than a happily anticipated event. Many divorced parents do not live in the same neighborhood or even in the same city, and so visitation requires that the children leave their home community to travel to their other parent's. This makes it difficult for youngsters to participate in activities typical for their age—sports teams, Boy Scouts or Girl Scouts, art or dance classes. Furthermore, visitation forces children to leave one parent to be with the other. They may miss and long for the parent they have left behind. The children's needs are once again pushed to the background because of the divorce.

Even when visitation goes smoothly initially, there may be some problems when the children reach the age—around eleven to thirteen—when they begin to have their own friends and schedule of activities. When these children say they would rather be with their friends, their choice usually has little to do with the parent vying for their time. In other words, the children are not choosing to forsake that parent; instead, they are doing what is natural for a preteen—hanging out with their friends.

Making Visitation Work

Although visitation makes great demands on all family members, most parents observe that it helps their children make a better adjustment to the postdivorce family. With a little work and cooperation between the parents, visitation can become a rewarding part of the family routine.

The primary relationship in visitation is that of the noncustodial parent and the children, but the success of visitation hinges on the commitment of *both* parents. If the custodial parent fails to support and encourage visitation, it is headed for failure. Also, the former spouses must be determined to keep their disagreements to themselves and not let them spill over into the visiting relationship. This means that visits should never be used as

➤ Rewards for paying child support: if the checks stop coming, so do the children. (This may be backward thinking anyway; 1990 census data confirm that noncustodial parents who have a lot of contact with their children are more likely to pay child support voluntarily.)

> ➢ Weapons for forcing the noncustodial parent to behave in the desired manner.
> ➢ A powerful tool for controlling the noncustodial parent by making him or her beg for the visitation privileges already agreed on or granted by the court.
> ➢ Spy sessions, after which the children are interrogated on their return home about the other parent's love life, economic status, and other matters.
> ➢ A means by which messages can be passed between the former spouses.
> ➢ A test of the children's loyalty. Some custodial parents schedule fun activities for weekends the children are going to be with their other parent in a backhanded effort to lure them into saying they don't want to go. Other custodial parents make their children feel guilty for looking forward to spending time with their other parent.

When a custodial parent is having difficulty communicating with the other parent or obtaining child support payments, the two of them need to work out their differences directly. They should choose a time when the children are not present or within earshot.

Exchange Times

Much of the conflict between divorced parents over visitation revolves around the exchange of the children—that is, at pickup and dropoff times. This conflict compromises the children's anticipation of spending time with their other parent. Ultimately, the children may reach a point where they don't want to go at all just to avoid the open hostility between their parents or the depressed look of the parent they are leaving behind. One mother used to tearfully kiss her kids goodbye and retreat to her bedroom about ten minutes before her ex-husband was scheduled to pick the kids up. Her eight-year-old son, Ross, told me he would try to get her to come out, but she refused, saying, "Don't worry about me. I'll be OK. You just go and have fun with your dad." As soon as Ross would get to his dad's house, he'd phone his mother right away and throughout the weekend to make sure she was all right. Needless to say, Ross directed more energy to his mother than to his father during visits and felt worried and guilty the entire time.

To make the exchange less stressful for parents and children alike, the parents need to agree in advance on the logistical details surrounding the visits, such as who will pick up (or drop off) the children, when, where, and how. The children should then be informed of these details. To prevent the children's disappointment and further feelings of loss and abandonment, the parents should make every effort to stick to the agreement.

If parents cannot put aside their interpersonal problems long enough for the exchange to take place, they should consider choosing neutral territory instead—perhaps the house of a supportive friend or relative or even a favorite babysitter. Alternatively, the friend or relative can do the picking up and dropping off.

Parents should remember to inform the appropriate officials exactly who has permission to pick up the children from their day-care center, school, after-school program, or other activities in which they are enrolled. Children should be clear about who is going to pick them up from day to day. One little boy complained that his divorced parents took turns getting him from school and sometimes traded off afternoons if one was held up while the other was free. Although this sounded like an ideal coparenting situation, the boy told me, "I never know who's going to come. One day no one came, and I wasn't sure who to call. I felt like I didn't have any parents at all."

In addition, noncustodial parents should be aware of their right or limits to have access to or pick up the children. In some locales, noncustodial parents are not permitted to take a child if they are not on the child's official list of people permitted to do so, whereas in other places, they cannot be stopped from taking the child even if their name does not appear on such a list. If the visitation agreement does not permit the noncustodial parent to have access to the child at school, school officials may ask for a copy of the legal documentation.

Checklists

Another source of conflict is what the children are permitted to take with them to their other parent's house and what they are permitted to take back home again. Before each visit, parent and child can draw up a checklist of things to pack. This list also can be used in repacking to go home. The noncustodial parent can add to this checklist the items that he or she gave the children and that can go home with them. (Still, the noncustodial parent should be somewhat prepared by keeping some basic items on hand, such as toothbrushes, pajamas, and extra clothes, in case anything is lost or forgotten.) It's also a good idea to pack a favorite doll or toy to serve as a transitional object between the two homes.

Although creating lists may seem time consuming and petty, it is often the little things that lead to misunderstandings and hurt feelings. "Just because I forgot to pack Ian's good pants, you used that as an excuse not to take him to church on Sunday again," one parent charges, while another complains, "You didn't pack Lisabeth's sneakers on purpose so I'd have to buy her new ones." Checklists also serve a practical purpose, however. A child on medication, for example, needs to continue taking it during a visit and remember to bring it home again. A child who sleeps with a special blanket or stuffed animal may be inconsolable if it's forgotten at either parent's house.

Schedules

Once a visitation schedule is established, the children benefit immensely if both parents stick to it and keep changes and cancellations to a minimum. The children's lives will take on a regular rhythm in which they know they will be seeing their other parent in a predictable routine. Disappointment over cancellations and changes only reawakens their feelings of rejection and insecurity and undermines their trust in adults.

Although adhering to this basic schedule is important, extra or spontaneous visitation should also be permitted, as long as both parents can agree on the details and the children's school schedules are not disrupted. Such visitation lets the children and the noncustodial parent be together when they need or want to, not just when the schedule says they must. (One word of caution, however—noncustodial parents shouldn't surprise young children by visiting them in the school yard. Legal issues aside, this may only upset and confuse them. It also can be dangerous if they are tempted to follow the parent when he or she leaves.) Furthermore, both custodial and noncustodial parents should be open to trading off time so that events important in the child's or family's life won't be missed, such as a school play or a grandmother's birthday.

Children can be given a calendar on which they or the parent can mark the dates and times they will be going to visit their other parent. This helps reduce confusion and prevent scheduling conflicts, reassures the children of future visits, helps young children better understand when they will next see their other parent, and permits older children to organize their time better.

Sandra, the custodial mother of ten-year-old Rachel, worked out a system with her ex-husband that has been fairly successful. At the start of every year, she notes all holidays, birthdays, vacation trips, and other important events that she would like to have her daughter home for. Then she and her ex-husband negotiate for the days that conflict with his visitation rights. For the days they can't agree on, they stick to the letter of the visitation agreement. One time Sandra had to interrupt a ten-day ski vacation when the schedule called for Rachel to be with her dad six days into the trip. "Rachel's missed some family events because of our visitation schedule," says Sandra, "but the most important opportunity in her life right now is to be with her dad."

Location

When parents live relatively close to each other, the usual arrangement is for the children to visit with their other parent in his or her home. When the parents live more than a few hours' drive from each other, however, it is best if visitation occurs in the children's location to minimize the disruption to their lives. Families may want to try meeting on middle ground to preserve as much time as possible for visits and make it possible to visit more often.

For example, one family occasionally holds visits in a motel located halfway between the parents' homes. Although this is not a natural setting, it permits the father to spend less time on the road and more time with the children. And the motel offers certain amenities they all enjoy, such as the pool. The mother either returns home or stays in another nearby motel for her own minivacation. Small local motels and budget chains make this option affordable for the family.

If the parents live very far apart, more planning is necessary. When young children are involved, it is far better for the distant parent to try to visit the children in their own location as many times a year as possible than to host the children in an unfamiliar locale requiring solo air travel.

Dan, for example, was a wealthy businessman who moved to California after his divorce. His former wife, Jeanne, remained in Michigan with their three-year-old daughter. Dan offered to pay for the child's airfare for weekend visitation twice a month, but Jeanne rightly refused until their daughter was older.

Since most parents can't afford to accompany their children when they fly or to have someone else do it for them, there are real safety issues to consider. Many children are terrified at the prospect of traveling on their own, even when they are with siblings, and their fears should be respected. Airlines are notorious for flight delays, misplaced baggage, and other problems that make one wonder how well they can keep track of bewildered and frightened children.

Some commonsense steps, however, will reduce parental worry and the likelihood that children may become scared or lost:

➤ When you are making the flight reservations, ask the airline about its guidelines and restrictions on children flying without an adult.

➤ If the children have never used a pay phone before, have them rehearse placing pay and collect calls.

➤ On the day of the flight, such information as the children's names, parents' names, home address, relevant phone numbers, flight information (especially if they have to make connecting flights), and destination address should be written down and stowed in a safe place, such as an inside pocket of their carry-on bag.

➤ Pack carry-on items that will give the children some measure of comfort during the flight, such as a favorite snack, stuffed animal, or book, and items that will keep them occupied, such as a coloring or puzzle book. (Don't pack toys that might be disruptive to other travelers, however.)

➤ Introduce the children to the attendants on their flight, and, if permitted, take them to their seats to get them settled in.

➤ If possible, call the person who is meeting the children at the destination airport to confirm the children's flight and expected arrival time. Every effort should be made to minimize the amount of time the children are without someone they know.

Stick to Your Word

Parents should not make promises to children that they do not intend to keep or that there is a high likelihood they cannot keep. Often parents who continually break promises don't mean to hurt the children, but their efforts at trying to save them some pain in the short run only result in more pain later and show up the parent as unreliable and untrustworthy.

Lanore, for example, had a poor track record at sticking to the visitation schedule she and her ex-husband, Frederick, had set up for their five-year-old son. Frederick couldn't stand to see the little boy cry whenever his mother failed to show up, so he fell into the bad habit of trying to reassure him that Lanore would definitely show up "next time." The next day Lanore would call full of apologies and promises that nothing would interfere with their next visit. And so the cycle went.

Although Frederick deserved praise for not making malicious remarks about Lanore to his son, he had to learn a new response to the situation for his son's sake—simply to comfort his son and stop making promises on Lanore's behalf. He also had to tell Lanore in private that she was harming the boy emotionally.

Including Significant Others

Generally, noncustodial parents should not include their girlfriends or boyfriends in visitation activities. As I emphasized earlier, the purpose of visitation is to strengthen the relationship between the noncustodial parent and his or her children. When a lover is included in visitation plans, the parent usually pays more attention to that person than to the children. Furthermore, the children often resent including a person who is outside the family and who may be perceived as responsible for their parents' breakup.

Another danger of including significant others is that children often form attachments to them and run the risk of being hurt and further disheartened if the relationship breaks up. If this becomes a pattern, children stop forming attachments to avoid potential pain. However, parents shouldn't go so far as to hide a relationship until marriage plans are made. At the point where a long-term relationship or remarriage looks like a solid possibility, the person should be introduced to the children and included in activities on a limited basis. Children of significant others should be introduced later in the relationship to avoid jealousy and fears of abandonment.

When visitation is longer than a week or two, the parent can hire a babysitter or ask a relative to stay with the children if he or she wants an afternoon or evening out.

Discipline

It's helpful to everyone in the family if parents can agree on an approach to discipline and house rules (see Chapter 10) and cooperate with each other in this area. Not only will this make discipline more effective, but it also permits the parents to present a united front to the children, making it less likely that they will try to play one parent off the other. The kids will soon lose their incentive to make such remarks as, "But Mom lets me ride my bike in the street!" or "Dad lets me stay up till eleven every night!" And if one parent has assigned a punishment (such as loss of TV privileges for a week) for some misbehavior, it can be continued when the child is with the other parent.

Sometimes, however, continuing a punishment will not work. The parent to whom the job falls may resent having to be the "bad guy" by enforcing the other parent's rules. In this case, the punishment can be resumed when the child returns. In addition, some parents misuse punishment of a child as a way to punish their ex-spouse. One mother routinely heaped unreasonable punishment on her son just hours before he was going to spend a weekend with his dad (one time it was the loss of two weeks of television for failing to put out the garbage the day before). The mother would rant about how lax her ex-husband was when he failed to enforce her penalties. The father understandably complained, "She's ruining his time with me."

If parents cannot agree on a similar approach to discipline, all is not lost. Children are remarkably flexible and will not be confused by having to follow two sets of rules, as long as each set is enforced consistently and fairly.

Special Days and Holidays

No matter what arrangements are made with regard to who gets the kids and when for holidays and birthdays, the probability that someone will feel cheated or disappointed is high. Some common courtesies between the parents, however, will go a long way in smoothing over such feelings and assuaging the children's guilt when they know it's impossible to make both parents happy.

➤ On each child's birthday, the parent whom the child is with should have the child call the other parent or make arrangements for the other parent to call at a specific time. The same can be done on special holidays, such as Christmas and New Year's. This will help the parent who is not with the child feel less lonely and closed out of times the family used to celebrate together.

➤ When the children will not be with a parent on that parent's birthday, the other parent can remind the children of the upcoming birthday and make plans to mark it accordingly. For example, the children can be encouraged to call the birthday parent as well as be helped to make or buy a gift to be mailed or presented later. One bonus of this thoughtfulness is that it permits the children to express their feelings of love toward both parents without fear of ridicule or rejection. As the children grow up, they will come to respect their parents even more for the maturity and consideration they showed toward each other, even under difficult circumstances.

➤ More and more divorced parents are deciding to spend certain family events and holidays together with their children and other family members, from grandparents to stepchildren. Since everyone is usually on his or her best behavior, the children benefit from seeing their family interact happily together. It is a reminder to them—one they need—that their family came about through love and has now evolved into a different but no less caring family. In addition, the children feel less stressed because they don't have to take sides or "abandon" one parent to be with another. Before you take such a step, however, weigh both the risks and the benefits. It may reawaken reconciliation fantasies in the children as well as spark rivalries between old and new spouses. If you and your family are able to share special times together, congratulate yourselves, for you are truly exceptional!

Normal Reactions to Visitation

In the period before children go on a visit and after they return home, it is normal for them to feel anxious and upset. (In fact, if a child isn't upset to some extent at this time, there's often something wrong with the child's attachment to the noncustodial parent.) If the noncustodial parent has been unreliable in the past, the child may be worried about whether the parent will show up. Younger children sometimes fear that the custodial parent will be gone when they get home.

Each time the parent and children meet, there is a period of adjustment until they feel at ease with each other again. When the visit is over and the children are back home, they experience a letdown and feelings of sadness. They may cry or be angry and take out their frustration on the parent with whom they live.

When children behave in these ways, many custodial parents automatically assume that the noncustodial parent did something bad or hurtful to the children. They then throw out questions around one theme: "Just what did your father [or mother] do to you?"

The answer in most cases is an honest "Nothing." The stress of anticipating the visit, having to reexperience some of the trauma of the divorce (after all, had there been no divorce, there would be no visitation), and leaving the parent over and over again can sometimes be too much for youngsters to handle. Put yourself in your child's shoes and think how you'd feel having to say goodbye to one parent to spend time with the other.

When children appear to be struggling under emotional overload (assuming no abuse is involved), the most helpful action a parent can take is to let them have some time to themselves and share what's on their mind when they are willing and ready. Parents should not ask leading questions out of their own curiosity or plant suggestions in the children's minds that their other parent somehow caused their distress. More productive is to show empathy by saying something like "I know this must be pretty hard on you, Adrienne" or "It must be difficult for you to leave Mommy after you've had such a good time with her." When the child is ready to talk, she'll be more apt to approach a parent who has made an effort to acknowledge her feelings, not judge or deny them.

Making Visits as Natural as Possible

Certainly it is difficult for noncustodial parents to maintain the kind of involvement and close connection with their children that were possible when the family was intact. What often results, then, is not surprising: noncustodial parents sometimes pursue their children's love and attention in inappropriate ways. Frequent gifts, trips, no set bedtimes, and lenient or no discipline are not uncommon and lead to a whole new set of problems. "My time with my children is so short," one father told me, "that I want to spoil them a bit. I want them to think being at my house is fun."

The best way to approach visits, then, is by trying to make them as much like normal family life as possible. The time should be passed largely in routine ways, not constant "superspecial" events. Although outings to the movies, zoo, ice cream store, sports events, circus, roller-skating rink, and so on can be enjoyed occasionally, they should not make up the bulk of visitation time. Such outings don't encourage or permit close communication or chatter about commonplace things, the stuff of everyday lives. A child can't share a problem with a parent when they are zooming down the newest thriller roller coaster at the amusement park.

Beyond that, the children need to achieve a sense of normality with both parents—to be part of their everyday lives and vice versa—for it is in living out real-life situations that a strong, rewarding two-way relationship can be fused. If, for example, Mom has to tend to the lawn while the children are visiting, she

Suggestions on How to Spend Visitation Time

- When you and your children are together, leave the television set off and avoid the urge to pack each visit with one special outing after another. Visits should be planned to allow ample time for you and the children to really talk to each other and keep the connection between you alive.

- Establish a schedule for visitation days. Although it should not be too rigid, it should permit a routine to settle in. Assign chores to the children to help them feel they are a part of your home and learn more about the importance of responsibility.

- Include visits to nearby relatives. Be generous enough to occasionally visit your former spouse's relatives who live nearby. Your children will benefit from being able to continue *all* these important relationships.

- Encourage your children to meet and play with other children in the neighborhood. The more people they know in your neighborhood, the more at home and connected they will feel there.

- Keep the children's ages and level of development in mind: older children may enjoy participating in entertainment and sports activities with you; younger children may be more in need of nurturing activities, such as playing or drawing with you, going on walks, and story telling.

- Have the children bring their homework, and help them with it as necessary. (Don't do it for them, however.)

- Take advantage of such community amenities as the public library, the swimming pool, and so on. While they are having fun with you (maybe learning new skills), your children also will make new friends and come to appreciate your community more.

(continued)

- Give each school-age child a book to read while he or she is away from you. Then discuss what the child has read when you are together again.
- Take turns planning occasional special outings. A parent can stand only so many video games at the arcade, and the children can put up with only so many visits to museums.
- Take each child to work with you occasionally, one to one. This helps give a child an idea of how you spend your time when you two are apart and creates in his mind a more solid composite of the person you are.
- Take advantage of your children's interests and skills by planning relevant activities, such as ice skating, or consider an area in which you and your children could both develop an ability by taking a class.
- Keep up the evening rituals you had before the divorce, and launch some new ones. Try to spend some time with each child individually and share some special activity at bedtime, like telling a story or reading a book.
- Permit the children to call their other parent as they wish. Have them call at least once during brief visits, more during longer visits.
- Consider a long-term project in which all of you can participate—such as building a miniature village, doing complicated puzzles, constructing a tree house, or collecting rocks and insects. This gives the kids something special to share with you and look forward to between visits.
- Don't let your gender or that of your children limit the kinds of activities you share. Dad can go shopping for a school wardrobe as well as wash the car with his daughter, and Mom can play basketball as well as make brownies with her son.

can make them feel needed and teach them some gardening skills by including them in the work. Instead of taking the kids out to dinner, Dad can plan a meal in which the cooking is part of the fun and everyone pitches in. Perhaps it's possible to arrange for the children to participate in local Scouts or take music lessons in accordance with the parent's visitation schedule.

During visitation, parents should approach establishing a routine in much the same way as before the breakup. Consistent discipline, set bedtimes, maintaining such family rituals as eating dinner and attending religious services together, doing chores, shopping, and creating new rituals are important. If possible, each child should be given a place—whether it's an entire room or just a drawer or two—where the child can store some of his or her things permanently. This will help children feel that they "live" in the parent's home and that a part of them remains there at all times. Another way to promote this feeling is by having a pet. During a visit's first few awkward hours, when parent and child are warming up to each other again, a pet can be a real ice breaker—it permits the child to lavish affection on it as the child gradually reattaches to the parent. Dorothy bought her nine-year-old daughter, Edie, a cat. "I'm going to see my cat this weekend," she once told me happily. That was easier for her to say than "I'm going to see my mother this weekend."

During visits, parents should not abandon the children to relatives or babysitters or permit children to idle away the time in front of the television set or completely on their own. Although leaving the children with others occasionally is not harmful when the children are visiting for longer periods, to reduce this limited time with them on a regular basis further defeats visitation's purpose.

Between Visits

Noncustodial parents should make it a high priority to maintain contact with their children between visits. This not only keeps parents plugged into their children's lives, but also makes visitation less strained in its initial moments. Wise and committed custodial parents permit and assist the children to communicate in various ways with the other parent between visits. Granted, frequent contact may seem intrusive to custodial parents—especially those who want little or no contact with an ex-spouse—but think of it from the children's perspective: they are happy and comforted to hear from Mom or Dad. One of the best gifts you can give your children is permission to love their other parent.

Here are some suggestions on how parents can stay in touch with their children between visits:

➢ *Phone calls:* The telephone is an obvious way for noncustodial parents to connect with their children between visits. Both parent and child should feel free to initiate calls. Custodial parents can dial the phone for youngsters who have not yet mastered this skill.

If long-distance calling becomes too expensive, the noncustodial parent might want to get an 800 phone number so children can call at any time at no expense to the custodial parent. Using an 800 number through some long-distance telephone companies may be less expensive than calling collect if the volume of calls placed in a month is large enough.

If calls *constantly* come at a bad time—like dinnertime or right before bed—the noncustodial parent can be given specific time blocks to place calls so that they won't interfere with family routines. Also, these calls are meant to take place between the child and the absent parent. They should not be used as an extra opportunity for former spouses to fight—for example, about late child support checks or other problems between the two of them.

➢ *Letters and cards:* Who doesn't like to receive mail? Both parents and youngsters will enjoy receiving and sending letters, silly notes, interesting or unusual postcards, photos, and other surprises on a regular basis. To facilitate mail communication, noncustodial parents can supply each child with stationery and preaddressed, stamped envelopes.

➤ *Audiocassettes and videotapes:* Many parents record themselves reading bedtime stories, singing favorite songs, or just sending greetings on audiocassette or videotape to their children. Messages can be personalized for each child and played over and over again. Some parents find it easier (and more fun) to prepare tapes than write letters, and children appreciate the sense of immediacy they offer.

➤ *Photographs:* Children should be permitted to keep a photo of each parent at the other parent's house as part of their personal belongings. Noncustodial parents can also display the children's photos in their homes to show the children that they are indeed part of the household.

➤ *Computers:* With home computers increasingly more affordable and an integral part of school curricula, more parents are purchasing systems for home use. If both parents' homes have a computer, communication is possible via modem or disks hand-delivered or sent through the mail. Some families have found that sending e-mail through on-line computer services is less expensive than long-distance calls and faster than regular mail. It can be read immediately or when the recipient has time.

➤ *School conferences:* The noncustodial parent should make it a point to attend report card conferences and school open houses. If the custodial parent is not cooperative in sharing information on dates and times, the noncustodial parent can contact the school directly. Furthermore, at the start of the school year, the noncustodial parent should meet with each of the children's teachers and ask to be kept informed of the children's progress and any problems they might be having.

If you do not have sole or joint legal custody of the children and the school refuses to give you information about the children, ask your ex-spouse to contact the school and give written permission (or whatever the school requires) for your involvement. If your ex-spouse refuses, check with your lawyer to see what your rights are. Don't give up.

➤ *School, religious, and community events:* Noncustodial parents should attend as many events as possible in which their children are participating, such as religious ceremonies, school plays, and sporting events. If the custodial parent is not forthcoming with the relevant information, the children may be the next best source of information for events of this type. Another way to keep tuned in is to become a volunteer in the parent-teacher association and organized activities in which your children participate.

When Children Don't Want to Visit

The custodial parent has a legal—and I believe a moral—responsibility to see that the children spend time with their other parent. When children say that they don't want to visit their other parent, the custodial parent should firmly tell them that they must do so, not provide a willing ear to their litany of complaints. Young children and preteens are usually happy once they are with their other parent.

This is not to say that the children's complaints are not valid, for indeed they sometimes are. Visits may reawaken the trauma children felt before and during the divorce. If the other parent has a new lover, they may feel uncomfortable around him or her. Perhaps the parent spends little time with the children, instead letting them overdose on television or making them play with the neighbor kids. One young girl I know in the custody of her father complained, "My mother doesn't understand the real *me.*" Although the daughter loved outside activities and sports, her mother, a teacher, planned their weekends around visiting museums and other cultural activities.

These kinds of complaints take on special significance when custodial parents reframe them in terms of assuming

"I'm the better parent." All parents—whether married or not—approach their role differently; no two parents are alike. One parent's judging the other in that role as either good or bad (so long as abuse is not involved) misses the point of visitation, which is meant to keep the connection alive between children and the noncustodial parent. Someday the children themselves will be the judges—the only judges who in the end really count.

Some parents I've dealt with have encountered difficulties in this area by following their lawyers' advice. One lawyer instructed a mother to videotape her child screaming into the camera that she did not want to visit her father anymore. The mother did not consider the harm this would do to her child, only that it might help get her ex-husband's visitation rights suspended.

Dealing With Angry, Alienated Children

In divorces characterized by particular acrimony, it is not uncommon for one parent to turn the children against the other parent, either consciously or subconsciously. When accomplished to the degree that the children refuse any contact with the parent who has now been cast in the role of villain, this is called *parental alienation syndrome.*

Christine, age thirty-two and the mother of a boy, seven, and a girl, three, was devastated when her marriage broke up. Her husband left her when she found out she was pregnant with their third child. About two months later, she miscarried and blamed it on the stress she was under. Although Christine never admitted to herself what she was doing, she subsequently began a dogged campaign to prove to her children their father's unworthiness. Over time, her plan worked. Within a year of the divorce, the children flatly refused to spend any time with their father. When he came to pick them up, the older child became angry and screamed hateful things at his father; the younger one became hysterical and clung to her mother. "See? They don't love you anymore," Christine said triumphantly after one attempted visit.

These are the kinds of cases that end up in court—the spurned parent brings action against the custodial parent to enforce the visitation agreement. But time is on the custodial parent's side; his or her attorney knows all the delaying tactics that prevent these cases from being heard for months, even years. By the time the parties are before a judge, the children's feelings are so entrenched that they are nearly impossible to undo. Under such circumstances, judges are reluctant to rule that the children must spend time with the noncustodial parent. Other judges, however, enforce visitation (sometimes supervised by a professional on neutral territory) in the hope that it may result in the relationship's eventual repair.

Still, it is worth the effort for noncustodial parents to go through these painful and often expensive motions, for a number of reasons. If the visitation agreement is enforced, sometimes it is only a matter of time before the children thaw and respond affectionately to the outcast parent. They may have gone along with the custodial parent's emotional blackmail because they were fearful of losing his or her love or wanted to support a needy parent. Once out of the domineering parent's presence, their true feelings surface. Furthermore, at some point the children will come to understand how they were misled and badly used by the custodial parent. If the noncustodial parent gives up too soon, the children may feel resentful, making it difficult to resume the relationship later.

In addition to taking legal action, noncustodial parents whose children refuse to visit or even talk with them can continue to demonstrate—through frequent letters, birthday cards, gifts, and so on—that no matter what, they still love them, want to have contact with them, and look forward to the day when they can be together again. If there is a good chance that mail may be intercepted, a mutual friend or cooperative relative can be asked to make deliveries directly to the children. These parents should also keep in contact with the children's teachers and attend school conferences and other events in which the children are involved.

In Christine's case, her ex-husband gave up the fight when the children first refused to spend time with him. About two and a half years later, Christine remarried. By then, all her animosity toward her ex-spouse had dissipated, but her attempts at encouraging the children to spend time with their father fell on deaf ears.

Another woman handled her situation in a different way. Gail's former husband, who has custody of their two children, began to turn the children against her shortly after the divorce. Although his crusade against Gail had little influence over their daughter, it was quite successful with their son—within six months he refused to spend any time with his mother. But Gail hung in there. She continued to invite him to her house each time she picked up her daughter for visits and mailed him letters and cards. She volunteered to be a monitor on school field trips and help out with other class activities. When her ex-husband saw how determined she was to remain in her son's life despite the rejection, he pulled back. Undoing the damage, however, has been a slow process. Although the mother-son relationship is still strained, her son is now willing to spend some time with her.

"Once he said to me, 'If you take me to the movies, I'll come visit you this weekend,'" Gail told me. "Sure, it was manipulative of him, but I wasn't going to pass up any opportunities to be with him and show him I love him."

Some parents have told me that trying to maintain a one-sided relationship was simply too hard on them, so they stopped seeing and trying to communicate with their children altogether. But parents should not make such a monumental decision on their own. It is best that they discuss the situation with a mental health professional. This person may be able to suggest some avenues yet left to explore or provide badly needed support at a time when the odds seem impossible. Such intervention also often helps prevent more serious psychiatric problems, like depression, from developing later.

Safety Issues

Although some custodial parents try to interfere with visitation by citing their concerns about their ex-spouses' inability to care for the children adequately, such fears are usually unfounded. Still, it's a good idea to reach agreement on some basic safety issues for the good of all. (For more serious problems, such as suspected child abuse, see Chapters 8 and 12.)

➤ Children under forty pounds or the age of four should ride in a car seat at all times. If the noncustodial parent does not have a car seat, the custodial parent should send the seat along with the child. Older children should be made to use their seat belts.

➤ Parents should refrain from drinking alcohol around the children. Although an occasional beer or glass of wine with dinner may not be harmful, imbibing any more than that compromises the children's safety and the parent's judgment and ability to drive or respond in emergencies. (Children should not be permitted to stay with any adult who drinks to excess or takes illicit drugs.)

➤ Children should be permitted to go or be taken only to appropriate places. For example, they do not belong in bars or nightclubs, nor should they be left unattended at the local mall. They should ride their bikes and play only where it's safe.

➤ House rules should be explained to the children in terms of what they are and are *not* permitted to do and where they are and are *not* permitted to go.

➤ Children should know whom they are allowed to go with and *not* go with, even if the person is a parental friend or "seems friendly."

What Children
Think About Visitation

Here are some of the most frequent comments children have made to me about visitation:

Negative Points

- No matter which parent I'm with, I always miss the other one and wish we could all be together.
- I miss my friends when I'm at my dad's, and I wish I didn't have to miss out on all the fun stuff they do while I'm gone.
- I miss my pet.
- I get tired of all the packing and unpacking.
- My mom always looks real sad when I have to go back home again.
- My parents can't even make the arrangements for my visits without fighting over every detail.
- I get tired of being used as a messenger between the two of them. I wish they'd just talk to each other and leave me out of it.
- My mom plans every last minute of our time together. We never have time to just sit around and talk.
- I never know when I'm going to see my dad. The last two times we were supposed to get together, he canceled at the last minute because of a business trip.
- I wish I could see my dad more, but every time I bring up the subject, my mother says she's too lonely when I'm not around.

Positive Points

- I have a lot of fun.
- I get to see my dad, and this gives me something to look forward to when I miss him.

(continued)

- I get to visit my grandparents and other relatives, too.
- I have a lot more friends than I used to, since I have friends at my mom's house and at my dad's house.
- I like to help my mom around the house when I go to visit her. It makes me feel good to know she counts on me.
- My dad pays more attention to me now than he did before the divorce.
- I've got two sets of toys—one at my mom's house and one at my dad's.
- I get to travel a lot more and see new places.
- I have *two* families, and they both love me.

➤ Since the point of visitation is for noncustodial parents and their children to spend time together, children should not be left with babysitters during brief visits. When visits are longer, such as over the summer, babysitters may be used occasionally if they have been carefully screened for qualifications and references.

➤ Children should know basic safety survival skills: how to state their name, address, phone number, and parents' names; how to answer the telephone and dial 0 and 911; how to use a pay phone; what to do and where to go in case of fire; what to do if they get a cut; and so on.

➤ Young children should not be left at home without adult supervision. Generally, children should be at least ten (and that age in maturity level) before they are permitted to stay home alone, and approximately twelve before they are charged with the care of younger children.

➤ If the noncustodial parent is not responsible for the children's health insurance coverage, he or she should obtain policy and coverage information. This information may be needed if visiting children need medical care for sickness or injury.

Chapter 8

SPECIAL
PARENTING ISSUES

After her parents divorced, five-year-old Sandy lived with her mother, Deborah, and spent time on a regular basis with her father, Mike. Father and daughter were very close — she was the veritable apple of his eye — and being apart from him between visits confused and upset her. Within six months of the divorce, their lives took a turn for the worse when Mike became very sick and had to be hospitalized. Extensive testing showed Mike had Hodgkin's disease, but with treatment, the doctors felt that his long-term prognosis was promising. Mike's hopeful outlook soured, however, when he saw how the drugs ravaged his body and clouded his mood. Balding and losing weight, Mike decided that he didn't want Sandy to see him like this. He was afraid it would scare her and destroy her image of her strong, competent father. Deborah concurred.

Told that she could not see her father, Sandy initially peppered her mother with such questions as When could she see her dad again? Was he dead? If he still loved her, why didn't he come anyway? Would he ever get better? Deborah's answers did not seem to make Sandy feel any better, and she began spending more time alone in her room. Sporadic phone calls from Mike did little to cheer her up. When Sandy began to suck her thumb again and refused to play with her friends at school, Deborah came to see me.

Among other things, I advised Deborah that short visits with Mike would help Sandy as well as Mike. Before Sandy saw her dad for the first time in months, Deborah and I sat down with her to prepare her for the visit. We discussed Mike's illness, the treatment he was undergoing, and how it had affected him. I encouraged Sandy to make drawings of her and her dad, and we used these as a springboard for discussing her feelings. After a few visits with Mike, the two of them were soon able to joke about his lack of hair and made up stories about his magic medicine. Although Sandy was still clearly worried about her father, the combination of seeing Mike regularly again and unlocking her feelings helped allay the worst of her fears.

The relationship between a child and a parent is never problem free. Just as in traditional two-parent families, it is full of good times and bad, happy times and sad. Trying to protect children from less-than-perfect parents—whether custodial or noncustodial—robs them of important opportunities for growth and for learning that life is made up of a variety of experiences and different kinds of people.

In most cases, unless there is a serious question about their safety or well-being, children should not be shielded or cut off from a parent. There may be a need, however, for working around a particular difficulty or obtaining assistance from a mental health professional to keep the relationship going.

Here are some other kinds of parenting problems I've often encountered in working with families of divorce and how to deal with the situations they present.

The Uninvolved or Absent Noncustodial Parent

There are many reasons that noncustodial parents reduce the amount of contact they have with their children or stop seeing them altogether. Perhaps they cannot deal with the pain of the constant separations from their children, or they are embarrassed at their reduced financial circumstances and poor accommodations for the children when they visit. Still others move far away after the divorce, lack the self-confidence they need to continue parenting their children, become mentally or physically ill, or replace their "old" family with a new one. And sadly, some, although a small minority, are just not willing to work hard enough to keep up a relationship with the children.

Sometimes uninvolved fathers are created by otherwise well-meaning professionals who believe that overnight visitation with children under the age of two or three should not be permitted. I don't agree; it is a rare father who is incapable of taking care of an infant or toddler or can't be taught to do so. It's nonsensical that parents are quite willing to leave small children in day-care centers while they are at work and yet are unwilling to leave those same children with their other parent.

Whatever the reason, custodial parents often assume that their ex-spouses become uninvolved because they are no longer interested in the children. This is almost always untrue. For the children's sake, therefore, the responsibility falls to the custodial parent to make every effort—and encourage the children to do likewise—to get these drifting parents back into the children's lives. The children should continue to send letters and cards, extend invitations to special events in the children's lives, send copies of report cards and school papers, keep in touch with relatives from that side of the family, and so on. If the door is kept open, there is a good chance that reinvolvement will occur.

One father once told me, "I didn't know what to do with a youngster who was still in diapers and couldn't talk much yet, and so I was uncomfortable being alone with him. My ex-wife, however, kept sending me pictures of Ronnie and tapes of him gurgling and trying to make words. Well, I finally couldn't stay away anymore—I felt I was missing too much. My ex-wife had been right—I did learn to have fun with my child and take care of him despite his young age. I have to hand it to her for sticking in there, especially since our divorce was not one of the most friendly."

There is no denying that it takes an exceptional custodial parent to behave like Ronnie's mom, but the reward is knowing that the children will benefit immensely and come to appreciate the custodial parent's wisdom and generosity.

As noted in Chapter 2, boys need a strong male presence in their lives. When fathers drop out of a child's life, custodial mothers might want to enlist someone close to the family—a favorite uncle or family friend—to provide some of the male guidance growing boys require. Another option is participating in a Big Brother program or one of the other programs for boys sponsored by local police departments and other community groups. Conversely, if a noncustodial mother becomes uninvolved, the father can make a similar effort to involve an aunt, grandmother, or family friend in the children's lives.

The Overinvolved Parent

At the other end of the involvement continuum is the overinvolved parent. This is the parent who calls the children several times a day, contacts teachers for weekly progress reports, is always concerned about the children's health, wants to know everything about the children's friends, and so on. Although any one of these activities by itself might be legitimate, taken together they indicate a person with neurotic fears and anxieties. In short, this parent (who can be the custodial or the noncustodial parent) doesn't know how to let go of the children.

Overinvolved parents aggravate everyone, especially the

children, who feel they are being smothered and have no freedom. Ultimately the children are robbed of learning how to become responsible and self-reliant, and they suffer from the
conflict between the two former spouses about their differing
parenting approaches.

Not long ago I got a call from a parent who was concerned
about his ex-wife's particular pattern of overinvolvement.
"Dawn's always been a hypochondriac, and now it seems like
her health worries extend to the kids," Frank told me. "She's
taking the kids to the doctor all the time, and they're complaining about all the tests they've been getting. My oldest son told
me Dawn kept him out of school for three days last week because she thought he had the flu. He said he felt fine, but Dawn
wouldn't listen. I'm really worried that she's going to turn the
kids into hypochondriacs, but on the other hand, I don't want to
take any chances that they might really be sick and need to see
the doctor."

I told Frank that he should obtain his ex-wife's permission to
call the children's pediatrician and discuss his concerns. The
doctor could either assure Frank that Dawn's concerns were
valid or talk to Dawn about her overconcern about the children's health. Frank was wise not to confront his wife directly,
because she probably would have taken the offensive by accus-
ing Frank of not caring enough.

One effective way of dealing with overinvolved parents is to
set limits for them. If, for example, a noncustodial parent has a
habit of always calling at dinner time, the custodial parent can
set aside a block of time each night during which calls can be
taken—maybe 7:00 P.M. to 9:00 P.M. This works, too, with custodial
parents who constantly call the children while they are visiting
their other parent.

The Mentally Ill Parent

Being mentally ill does not mean that a person is unfit to parent;
it depends on the nature and extent of the illness and whether

the person is receiving treatment. Even if the mental illness affects a person's functioning, visitation is sometimes possible if it is supervised.

The past twenty years has seen great strides in the understanding and treatment of a wide variety of mental illnesses. As a result, mental health professionals are able to help many more people lead happy and fulfilling lives once again. Many of the psychiatric medications now in use are much safer and have fewer side effects than the medications commonly used years ago, and the growing body of data on psychotherapy (also known as talk therapy) confirms its effectiveness for a variety of disorders. There are few instances, then, in which children should not be permitted to visit with a mentally ill parent. Among them:

➢ People who are seriously mentally ill and refuse to get help. These people may reach the point where they are no longer able to care for the children or where repeated exposure to the parent's illness may hurt the children in some way, psychologically or physically. For example, some people become so depressed that they stop taking care of themselves or stay in bed all day. The children may start taking care of the parent instead of the other way around.

➢ People who drop out of treatment prematurely or who are not taking prescribed psychiatric medication to control their illness. For example, I was brought in as an impartial examiner in a visitation dispute where the father had manic-depressive disorder but refused to take his medication. When he was in the manic phase of his illness, he behaved dangerously, and the mother was afraid that the children would not be safe with him. After conducting my evaluation, I recommended against the father's being permitted to have unsupervised visitation with the children. (He is now complying with treatment, and visitation has been resumed.)

➢ People who have a psychotic disorder and lose touch with reality. Being with a parent who is totally withdrawn or saying things that don't make sense frightens young children. Not old enough to understand what psychosis or hallucinations are, they take the parent at face value and believe that the behavior is directed at them.

One of my patients is a divorced father with a psychotic illness. What has worked for his family is short, structured visits with the children supervised by grandparents who have been trained to act in a variety of roles—as protectors, interveners, and reality interpreters. When the father is very sick, the visits are suspended.

If your ex-spouse falls into any of these categories, your first responsibility is to protect your children. You should see your lawyer about having the visitation or custodial arrangements suspended until your ex-spouse enters treatment and is capable of caring safely for the children once again. But don't use the illness as an excuse to cut off his or her contact with the children indefinitely; an evaluation should be conducted to determine whether supervised visitation is possible in the interim.

The Alcoholic/Drug-Abusing Parent

Much like the mentally ill parent, the parent who abuses alcohol or other drugs poses a variety of safety risks to the children. Because of the unpredictability of his or her behavior, there also is a legitimate concern about the potential for physical and emotional abuse. This parent should never be permitted to take the children, or be with them, while under the influence of alcohol or other drugs. Supervised visitation may be possible once the parent admits he or she has a problem and has entered treatment.

If your ex-spouse abuses alcohol or drugs, it's best to take steps now to enlist the aid of a lawyer to end the visitation or custody until your ex-spouse stops the substance abuse and enters a treatment program. Not only is the children's well-being at stake, but also you run the risk of putting yourself in danger by refusing to hand the children over to your ex-spouse when he or she is drunk or high.

The Physically and/or Emotionally Abusive Parent

At the time of their divorce, most people know whether their spouse abused the children in some way, and this should have been addressed when the custody and visitation arrangements were being made. In some cases, however, parents become abusive later.

Comments like these from a parent (or other adult) may indicate a child is being mistreated: "I can't take you anywhere that you don't cause trouble." "You're so stupid [dumb,clumsy, ugly, careless, etc.]." "You don't have any brains." "You're the most selfish child I've ever seen." "You're not deserving of any love." "You're just like your mother." Children may reflect back what they are hearing by saying something like, "Dad says I'm the biggest klutz he's ever seen." "Mom says all I do is embarrass her in front of her friends."

Any of these statements on its own may not be evidence of abuse, but once a pattern becomes obvious, the emotional well-being and self-esteem of children to whom these statements are directed are sure to suffer. With their simple faith and unquestioning love, children believe what their parents tell them.

Not uncommonly, emotional abuse is coupled with physical abuse: when parents fail to capture their fury with words, some move on to pushing, hitting, beating, and other acts incomprehensible to loving parents. Obvious signs of physical abuse are cuts, burns, bruises, bumps, broken bones, and black eyes that the child is reticent or fearful about explaining, that are in unusual places (like the genital area), or for which there appear to be a pattern. Another sign of abuse is a failure to grow and develop consistent with the child's age, caused perhaps by poor nutrition or isolation from other people.

Many parents who resort to name-calling or cursing at their children are not necessarily bad parents; often they are over-whelmed by stress and lack effective parenting skills. Perhaps tired and frustrated, short on time and money, they have learned that yelling or hitting makes a misbehaving child straighten up or disappear fast. Unfortunately, what they have not learned is that these "methods" are not only inhumane but also ineffective in the long run (see Chapter 10).

If your ex-spouse fits this description, you may want to see a mental health professional for family counseling. Often the family approach is less threatening for the abusive parent and helps the children deal with their feelings about the abuse. Additionally, participation in parent effectiveness programs now offered in many communities may be helpful as well for learning specific child discipline techniques.

If, however, the abuse is more serious—possibly sexual or physical—have the children examined by a doctor immediately. The doctor must file a report with the relevant authorities in your area, who will conduct their own investigation. You should also see your lawyer to discuss the possibility of suspending the current visitation or custodial arrangements; the court may approve supervised visitation in the interim before the case is heard. For more information, refer to the section in Chapter 12 on sexual and physical abuse of children.

The Parent Who Is Incarcerated

In dealing with families in which one of the parents is in jail or prison, I've noticed that parents' reactions fall at two extremes. Some try to keep it a secret from their children, whereas others take the attitude that "it's no big deal." Both of these extreme reactions can cause problems. Instead, children should be told that their parent is in jail or prison and why. The amount and type of details supplied to them depend on their ages. Obviously, the younger the child, the simpler the explanation should be. The seriousness of the situation should be imparted to them, but they should be reassured that there's nothing wrong or bad about them and that their parent's behavior will not rub off on them. They should also be coached on how to deal with the inevitable gossip.

In most cases, the children should visit the parent if the penal institution permits.

The Parent Who Dies

A child's attachment to a parent has little to do with whether the family has been divided by divorce. Thus, when a parent dies, the children have the same need to acknowledge the death and go through the grieving process as they would have if the divorce had never occurred.

Most divorced parents don't prevent the children from attending the other parent's funeral and saying a final farewell, but many fail to help them work through their grief. Being empathic may be difficult for many parents, because they don't share the children's positive feelings toward a person from whom they may have been divorced for many years.

If your children's other parent dies, encourage them to talk about their memories of that parent and the happy times they spent together; share your happy memories as well. Expect them to be sad and tearful, and at such times, follow their lead: listen if they want to talk, or let them have some time to themselves. Invite them to keep pictures of the parent displayed in their room, and help them keep in touch with relatives on that side of the family. In addition, expect their behavior to be less than perfect for a while; they may be angry that the parent died, and some children express their sadness as anger. In addition, the children may have a greater need to cling to or depend on you. Young children in particular may fear that you, too, will die and leave them completely on their own. Above all, don't feel threatened by the depth of their feelings for the deceased parent—be secure in the knowledge that they still love and need you.

If the parent died by suicide, you should explain to the children what happened in language they can understand. Don't overload them with information or lurid details they don't need to know or may not be able to handle. You should not guess or make up reasons about what led the parent to commit suicide, but be specific that the children were not the cause.

Without being prompted, some children won't take the initiative to ask questions or talk about a parent's suicide. Ken, nine, came home from school one day and found his father dead on the living room floor from a drug overdose. Despite the horror of the sight and the shock he must have felt at the time, he never asked a single question about what had happened until he was in therapy two years later. Unfortunately, the adults around Ken had assumed that his silence indicated acceptance of his dad's death.

If the children's needs and questions go beyond what you can handle, you may want the family to see a mental health professional.

The Parent With a Different Value System

Jim was an avid hunter. Raised in a rural area of a farming state, he learned at a young age from his father and uncles how to hunt deer, geese, ducks, squirrels, and rabbits. He enjoyed his memories of weekends at a mountain cabin with the men in his family. Now as an adult, he hoped to teach his son the rudiments of hunting and dressing animals and infuse in him the same kind of appreciation and respect for nature that Jim's father had passed on to him.

Jim's wife, Ellie, had never approved of his hunting but understood that it was something important between him and his family. Now that they were divorced, however, Ellie did not want Jim taking their son, Tad, eight, on hunting trips. She feared for

Tad's safety and no longer wanted to hide her feelings that hunting was a cruel and needless sport.

When Ellie refused to let Jim take Tad for weekends during hunting season, Jim went to court to have his visitation rights enforced. The judge ordered the visits to continue, saying that Ellie's personal feelings toward hunting did not constitute valid grounds for denying visitation.

This case raises a question commonly faced by many families of divorce: What happens when divorced parents have clashing value systems and each parent wants the children raised according to his or her own values? To Jim and Ellie, the issue was hunting; in other families, it may be religion, sexuality, philosophy toward life, schooling, approach to discipline, and definitions of right and wrong.

Although two adults can learn to accommodate each other's differences, it's quite another matter when children are involved—flexibility and tolerance may lose their importance in the zest to raise offspring as perfectly as possible. When divorce occurs, the situation becomes more complicated as each parent hopes to put his or her own imprint on the children. Not surprisingly, the result is conflict between the two parents that places the children in a no-win situation. Regardless of their opinions on the matter, the children fear that if they take Mom's side, Dad will feel that he doesn't count; if they take his side, Mom will feel they don't love her.

Raising children is not a matter of perfection. They are a little bit of all the major figures in their lives and the sum of all their experiences, with a good dose of genetic influence thrown in. Exposing them to different value systems will not undermine their development; in fact, it will probably enhance it as they begin to think for themselves, make their own choices, and understand the consequences of their choices. One of a parent's most important jobs is to help a child build the foundation for making these kinds of decisions competently and confidently. If they have done their job well, parents have little to fear.

One mother, Lara, once said to me, "How can I let a man

that I no longer respect or even like take care of the most precious thing I have—my son?" Her ex-husband liked to spend his weekends watching sports on television, drinking beer, and trading gossip with his friends. He and his friends shared depressingly parochial views; they spoke disparagingly of almost everyone not like themselves, from people outside their race and women to college graduates.

Lara did not think it proper that her son be placed in this stifling environment, yet she knew that it was important for him to spend time with his dad. So instead of trying to prevent visitation, she talked with her ex-husband about establishing certain ground rules, among them no drinking by him or his friends during visits, limiting television, and serving nutritious meals. He agreed.

By the time their son was eleven, she noticed that he was not excited at the prospect of visiting his dad anymore. "There's nothing to do there," he complained. "Dad never wants to do anything with just me—he always has his friends around and I'm supposed to just fit in. Besides that, I don't like the way he treats Grandma when she comes over to visit. He never says anything nice to her." Lara, to her credit, did not use any of this as an excuse to end visitation; she still encouraged him to go, but she discussed things he could do at his dad's other than just hang out with the guys.

"He's finding out on his own that he and his dad don't have very much in common," Lara told me recently. "If I had tried to prevent him from seeing his dad, he probably would have held it against me and made his dad out to be the greatest person on earth."

Chapter 9

PARENTING TECHNIQUES TO BUILD YOUR CHILD'S SELF-ESTEEM

The self-esteem of nearly all children whose parents divorce is injured to some degree. If Dad or Mom really loved them, they wonder, how could he or she just leave? On top of that, many children blame themselves for the divorce or believe they contributed to it. Awash in confusion and guilt, they don't understand why they are having so much trouble negotiating their limited world.

During and after the immediate trauma of the separation and divorce, there is a lot parents can do to help their children attain or regain an image of themselves as competent, happy, and self-assured. An important starting point is recognizing that the divorce and how it is handled, now and in the future, have a significant bearing on children's feelings about themselves.

In this chapter I discuss techniques for building children's self-esteem and creating a supportive home climate. The next chapter deals with discipline.

What Is Self-Esteem?

Self-esteem is the sum of a person's feelings and thoughts about himself or herself in terms of competence, value to self and others, and the ability to be self-reliant, confront challenges, and respect others. Individuals who develop healthy self-esteem as children become adults able to manage and take charge of their lives. They know who they are, feel connected to others, show a positive attitude, and have a purpose to their lives.

Children, of course, can't say in so many words that their self-esteem is suffering. Instead, they send out signals that something is wrong through declining school performance, a battery of physical complaints (headaches, stomachaches, and so on), accidents, problems with peers, difficulty in concentrating, helplessness, and increased aggression. One method I use to get an idea of children's feelings about themselves is to ask them such questions as "If you had three wishes, what would they be?" "What do you want to be when you grow up?" Having no aspirations or wishes, or bizarre ones, may be a sign that a child needs special attention or even professional help. Lucy, for example, told me that she wanted to be a threshing machine. Lucy was tall for her age and very obese; she had great trouble getting along with kids her own age and recognized that she was different from other children. With no vision for her future as a professional, friend, mother, or wife, she saw herself as a machine known for its destructive ability.

Parents can enhance children's self-esteem by making them feel that they are the family's highest priority and that they are loved and appreciated unconditionally, for nothing more than being themselves. How parents do this goes beyond just telling them in so many words. These sentiments need to be conveyed every day in the ways children are taken care of, talked to, touched, and disciplined. Underlying it all must be sincerity and honesty.

Doreen found this out the hard way. As her daughter, Jackie, was growing up, Doreen kept telling her that she was the most beautiful child in the world. By the time Jackie was eleven and overweight, she knew it was not the truth, but her mother never faltered in delivering this compliment. Trying to live up to her mother's praise, she constantly dieted and eventually became bulimic. She is now in treatment. "I learned that what Mom said was not the same thing as what she thought," Jackie told me. "How can I ever believe anything she says?"

Special Issues for Children With Divorced Parents

Techniques for building or reinforcing children's self-esteem are the same regardless of their parents' marital status. However, divorced parents and their children must confront a number of additional issues that can have a great impact on the children's emotional development.

Obviously children whose parents are divorced are living in a situation where arguably the two most important people in their lives—the foundation of their existence—have gone their separate ways, and the children can live with only one of them at a time. It is nearly impossible for adults to imagine the depth of despair children feel about this predicament. What they desperately need, then, is permission to love and spend time with both their parents. When they have it, the gains are big: supportive parent-child relationships buffer youngsters from much of the stress related to divorce and ease long-term adjustment.

If, however, children constantly get the message, overtly or not, that loving one parent means they don't love the other, they begin to question their perceptions and ability to trust their own judgment. They also fear they'll be rejected by one parent for loving the other, and this in turn makes them even more insecure and needy. They've already lost one parent, they think; they will do anything to avoid losing their other one.

Divorced parents would do well to look at each other through their children's eyes. In most cases children see something wonderful in both parents, and nothing will be gained by leading children to believe they are wrong. Parents who are successful at turning the children against their other parent will eventually find that it's a short-term gain. These parents not only jeopardize their children's emotional well-being, but when the children grow older and figure out how they were misused, the parents also run the risk of losing the love they wanted so badly.

An extension of this principle involves parents' love relationships, which may include a new spouse (see Chapter 13). If the children are able to form attachments to the new partners in their parents' lives (and vice versa), they will benefit from having a wider support system and a genial atmosphere in which to live or visit. Sometimes as children begin to like, even love, a parent's new partner, the other parent, out of jealousy or insecurity, begins to send out signals that this new person is "bad" or "stands in the way of Mom and Dad getting back together." The children become confused. Their positive assessment of the new partner contradicts the other parent's negative message. Out of loyalty and the need to resolve their conflicting feelings, they start to believe, "Gee, Dad's new wife seems nice, but if Mom doesn't like her, then I shouldn't either."

Another important area is the quality of the relationship between the two parents during and after the divorce. Parents can teach their children valuable lessons about handling disagreements maturely by working them out through discussion, negotiation, and compromise. If conflict persists, however, parents *must* protect the children from it; if they don't, the children can be expected to be more aggressive, anxious, and frustrated.

As I've stressed previously, many children—especially the younger ones—feel guilty about their parents' breakup. If they continue to think that it was all their fault, they may come to believe that they can't do anything right and that they are somehow bad. Getting children to stop thinking in this egocentric fashion is very difficult—in fact, it's impossible if they are five or under. Thus, parents must remind the children over and over and over again that the breakup was because of a problem between the two parents and not because of anything the children did or didn't do. Similarly, if one parent fails to live up to his or her responsibilities to the children after the divorce, the other parent can step in to reassure them that it is not their fault.

If parents want their children to have a healthy self-image, they must possess one themselves. The aftermath of a divorce is indeed a difficult time for all family members. Parents who make the effort to handle stress, take some time out for themselves, and think positively are more likely to have the energy and patience to create an atmosphere in which their children can thrive. The better parents feel about themselves and their accomplishments—that is, the higher their self-esteem—the better prepared they are to influence their children through positive role modeling.

As you deal with these many issues, remember that one of your most powerful tools is showing your children you love them through physical expression. Be generous with hugs, kisses, pats on the back and shoulders. Look at your children and make eye contact when you talk to them. Cuddle up daily with the younger ones. Touching is another way of making children feel wanted and secure.

Active Listening

As children, many of us were raised to believe that "children should be seen and not heard"—the parent talks, the child listens and heeds. The problem with this approach is that it assumes the child is something of an empty slate, a robot; it overlooks the fact that children have thoughts, needs, and feelings that deserve our attention and respect. When children are raised with an iron fist, they often rebel at the first possible chance, never learn to think for themselves, or fail as adults to develop a give-and-take relationship with others.

A far more constructive approach is to create a home environment in which the children's feelings and needs can be safely expressed and acknowledged. This does not spoil them or make them more demanding, as many parents mistakenly believe. When children's needs are met most of the time, they gain a sense of security and learn that they can count on the adults around them. This approach actually makes them less demanding and more trusting.

Keep in mind that the way you handle your emotions will make a great impression on your children. Children model their behavior after their parents'; if they see you retreating to your bedroom when you are sad, or losing your temper when you are mad, they are likely to behave the same way. They will become confused when they try to copy your behavior and you tell them that it's wrong. So try to practice what you preach—it may sound trite, but it still works.

Here are the basic components of active listening:

1. Listen attentively as your child speaks. Don't interrupt or assume you know what your child wants or is talking about.
2. Acknowledge what you are hearing with words or comments that encourage the child to continue talking. Do not denigrate, criticize, or make fun of the child or deny the child's feelings. Your goal is to match your words and facial expressions with the child's emotions; they should be in sync with each other.
3. When the child is finished, reflect back what you think you have heard. Give a label to the child's feelings if possible.
4. Empathize with the child. An easy way to do this is to imagine yourself in your child's shoes. How would *you* feel in this situation?
5. As appropriate, comfort the child. All that may be needed is a hug or a few kind words.

Here's an example of active listening. Nine-year-old Mark approaches his mother with a concerned look on his face. Mom decides to say nothing at first to see whether Mark will begin the conversation on his own.

MARK. Mom, Dad just called.

MOM. *[She stops what she's doing and looks at him.]* Mm-hmm.

MARK. He says I can't come to his house for the weekend. *[Mark pauses, looks as though he might cry.]*

MOM. That's too bad, Mark. *[She waits for him to say more.]*

MARK. I can't believe he's done it to me again! This is the third weekend in a row that he says he's got to work.

MOM. Yes, I know, honey. That must be very disappointing.

MARK. Well, I'm more mad than disappointed. Gosh, sometimes I feel like he doesn't love me very much if he never wants to spend time with me.

MOM *[continues eye contact with Mark, then speaks]*. Your dad loves you very much, and I'm sure he'd rather be with you than at work. *[Mark begins to cry, and Mom fights back the urge to keep up the stream of conversation or vilify his father. She hugs Mark instead.]* I know I'd be sad if someone I loved very much disappointed me.

MARK. Well, he did say he'd call me tomorrow and that we'll try to plan for another time.

MOM. That's good. Maybe we can find something else fun to do this weekend. *[She gives Mark another hug. He stops crying and goes back to playing.]*

Contrast the above conversation with the following:

MARK. Mom, Dad just called.

MOM. What did *he* want? *[Her tone conveys suspicion.]*

MARK. He says I can't come to his house for the weekend.

MOM. He's always letting you down. Isn't this the third weekend in a row that he's canceled plans with you? *[She attacks the father. She completely misses the distress in Mark's voice.]*

MARK.   Well, yes, but I'm sure he has a good reason. [*Mark reacts defensively to Mom's attack on Dad.*]

MOM.   He never has a good reason. He just doesn't plan his time well enough, and then you have to suffer for it. [*She denies his feelings, keeping up the attack on Dad.*]

MARK.   Gosh, Mom, that isn't true! I saw him a lot over the last few months. [*Mark looks as though he might cry.*]

MOM.   Well, I don't know why you're so upset. It's no big deal—you can see him another time. We'll find something else to do this weekend. [*She again denies his feelings and fails to empathize with his disappointment.*]

Another feeling that children have a lot of difficulty handling is anger, especially if they've been exposed to a lot of fighting and abuse between their parents. As a parent, your goal is to help your children learn to recognize when they feel angry and then express it assertively. They should neither swallow it nor become aggressive by hitting, hurting someone's feelings, or being destructive.

Here are basic principles you can use to help your children learn how to handle their anger:

1. Anger is a feeling. Feelings are not bad. It's how you express your feelings that matters.
2. When you feel angry, you have a right to acknowledge it, but in ways that won't hurt anyone or anything.
3. Take the time to figure out why you are angry. What is it that you want or need?
4. Just acting angry isn't going to help you get what you want or need. You are more likely to reach your goal in other ways—for example, by talking about it, asking for it, or figuring out a solution to a problem. What do you think you can do to reach your goal?
5. If your goal can't be realized, what can you do to make yourself feel better?

Here's one way to talk about anger, using these principles. You'll need to repeat the process a number of times before the youngsters catch on, but perseverance will pay off.

Aaron, eight, is playing with his sister, Becky, six, one Saturday morning. They are building a tent by placing a sheet between the couch and the coffee table when Becky knocks the tent over. Dad is watching from the kitchen. "Now look what you did!" Aaron yells at Becky. When he has difficulty putting the sheet back in place, he loses his temper. "You've ruined my tent. You're just a stupid baby. You're always messing up everything I try to do. Go away!" Aaron pushes Becky so that her head knocks into the coffee table, and Becky starts to cry. Dad comes into the living room and makes sure Becky is all right.

(1. Anger is a feeling. Feelings are not bad. It's how you express your feelings that matters.)

DAD.   You seem to be very angry with Becky.
AARON.   She's ruined my tent. I worked real hard on it.
DAD *[using active listening]*.   I would be angry, too, if someone ruined my tent.
AARON.   Yeah, I'm really mad at her. I hate when she does stuff like that.

(2. When you feel angry, you have a right to acknowledge it, but in ways that won't hurt anyone or anything.)

DAD.   Having feelings and being able to recognize them is good, Aaron. But there are right ways and wrong ways to express your anger. You cannot hit or push or otherwise hurt Becky or call her names when you're mad at her. Do you understand?
AARON *[reluctantly]*.   I suppose so.

(3. Take the time to figure out why you are angry. What is it that you want or need?)

DAD.   Aaron, stop for a moment and think about why you're so mad at Becky.

AARON.   Because she's just a goofy girl, and she's always getting in the way and messing up my stuff. I'm just tired of her!

DAD.   Gosh, that's a lot to be mad at! But hold on. You just mentioned a moment ago that you were angry because she knocked your tent down.

AARON.   Well, yeah, we were having fun until then. I wish she hadn't done that.

DAD.   So if you're mad that she knocked the tent over, what do you think would make you feel better?

AARON.   I want the tent up again so I can go inside and read my new comic book.

(4. Just acting angry isn't going to help you get what you want or need. You are more likely to reach your goal in other ways—for example, by talking about it, asking for it, or figuring out a solution to a problem. What do you think you can do to reach your goal?)

DAD.   Pushing Becky isn't going to get your tent built up again, is it? What do you suppose will?

AARON *[after thinking for a few moments]*. I guess I just have to start all over again.

DAD.   You're right, Aaron. Here, let me help you and show Becky what to do.

(5. If your goal can't be realized, what can you do to make yourself feel better?)

If for some reason (such as that Becky refuses to cooperate) rebuilding the tent doesn't work out, Dad can redirect Aaron's attention.

DAD.   Maybe we can build the tent later. Is there somewhere else you can read your comic book?

AARON.   Yeah. I think I'll go to my room for a while.

In this example, the father focused on Aaron because his behavior was the more dangerous at the moment. But the father also could have used these principles to help Becky deal with why she knocked the tent over. Moreover, if Aaron hadn't been able to calm down and discuss his feelings with his father, the father could have ended tent play for a set time—say the rest of the day—and tried talking later. This type of cause-and-effect action is called applying *logical consequences* to misbehavior, which is discussed in the next chapter.

Anger is a very strong and sometimes scary emotion for most children to contain easily, and it will take time before they are able to think first before striking out or losing their temper. So in addition to encouraging them to talk out their feelings, you can direct them to physical outlets or ask them to suggest some ideas. Some examples: punching a pillow, ripping paper, kicking a ball or running outside, taking a shower or bath, lifting small weights, or shooting baskets.

Drawing is another good outlet. It is safe, it can be done virtually anywhere, and the drawings can be used to spur further discussion between parent and child. Drawing is particularly useful with younger children, who are not skilled at identifying their feelings and lack the language to describe them. Notice, too, that drawing and the principles for helping children deal with their anger can be used to handle a variety of feelings—sadness, loneliness, frustration, failure.

It doesn't take that much time and practice to master these principles and active listening skills. But sometimes, in the heat of a crisis, parents forget the fine points. If that happens to you, think of these three words: empathize, empathize, empathize. Just taking the time to try to connect with your children's feelings can defuse almost any difficult situation.

Encouraging Cooperation

In many families, parents and children seem to be on opposing teams. While parents try to get the children to do what they want them to, the children expend their energy doing anything but. This leads to tension in the family. Getting the children to do chores, homework, and so on does not have to constitute a clash of wills, however; teamwork is possible when parents treat their children with respect and come to expect the best from them. The result is that the children feel they are capable and important to the smooth running of the household.

Here are some ways to encourage children's cooperation:

➢ Teach the children how to do the jobs you expect them to do. For example, demonstrate how to make a bed, take out the garbage, fill and empty the dishwasher, take a phone message. Go through all the steps, watch while they do it, and give constructive advice. Once they are familiar with a job, allow them some latitude in doing it. There's more than one way to carry out most chores.

➢ Adjust your level of expectations to the child's age and level of development. For example, a five-year-old can't lift a huge bag of garbage but can empty the trash cans throughout the house.

➢ Be clear about general responsibilities. For example, no fair yelling when you come home from work that all the lights are burning in the house if you have not instructed the kids to turn out the lights when they leave a room. Other examples: All toys must be put away before the children go to bed at night; dirty plates should be rinsed and placed in the dishwasher; food can't be left out on the kitchen counter. (More on house rules is covered in Chapter 9.)

➢ Assign responsibilities equitably. Set up a schedule as necessary, and post it in a prominent place.

➢ Don't criticize or go on the attack when a job hasn't been done. Instead, state what needs to be done, using as few words as possible, and give the child credit that he or she knows what to do. Example: "Shanice, the toys are still on the floor" or even "Shanice, the toys." (Shanice knows that you are telling her to pick up the toys and put them away where they belong.) Not: "Shanice, how many times do I have to tell you that you must put your toys away before you go to bed? You know they belong in the closet. Can't you ever remember without my reminding you?"

➤ Be sensitive about the way you talk to the children. Although you probably know that you should try not to yell at them (sometimes a Herculean task, I know!), many parents don't realize that they sometimes use a tone of voice that sounds like yelling to the children.

One day Roberto overheard his mother engaged in what he thought was a fight with her best friend. He approached the two women, who were sitting at the kitchen table, and said fiercely, "I hate when you fight!" The two women were surprised by this outburst. "We were only having a discussion about politics," the perplexed mother told me later. "We weren't fighting at all." Roberto, who had been exposed to roughly two years of parental quarreling before his parents divorced, could not distinguish between friendly intellectual sparring and hateful argument. It all sounded the same to him and elicited the same kind of emotional upset.

➤ Give choices when possible. Children are more likely to cooperate when they are given some say in the process. Example: Asking "Would you like to wear your green outfit or red pants and shirt today?" is more likely to get a child moving than shouting "You'd better get dressed right away or you'll be late!"

➤ Let the children know how you feel when they don't cooperate—but, again, without lectures or personal attacks. Example: "Mickey, it frustrates me when you forget to empty the dishwasher after you come home from school, because it delays my starting dinner." Not: "You never remember to empty the dishwasher. All you do is make more work for me!"

➤ Avoid giving in to the temptation to do or finish jobs assigned to the children. Although many parents say doing the job themselves saves them time and keeps the peace, it hurts the children's self-esteem as they come to realize that the parent doesn't really count on them or trust them to behave responsibly.

➢ On occasion, let the children "overhear" you telling other adults about their accomplishments, big and small. They will pay more attention to the tone of pride in your voice than what you are actually reporting. Use specific terms delivered in proportion to the accomplishment: "Dylan got an excellent grade on his spelling test the other day. He studied very hard for it." Not: "Dylan is so smart—he always gets the best spelling grade in his class."

Helping Your Child Shine

Every child can do something well. Parents who have trouble identifying a child's strong points can benefit from adopting a more creative approach to appreciating their children.

Many parents think that a child who shines is one who shows talent in such areas as music, sports, academics, dance, and so on. These are the children who perform perfectly at recitals, get straight A's, and lead the team on to victory. But how children perform on an everyday basis in all sorts of things is far more important and deserving of a parent's attention and praise. It also presents far more opportunities for parents to single out the children's successes and build on them.

Here are some examples of everyday behavior worthy of notice:

➢ Coming home from a friend's house on time
➢ Going to bed without a fuss
➢ Doing chores well
➢ Washing hands before dinner
➢ Helping or sharing with a sibling
➢ Showing improvement in a school subject
➢ Cleaning up after making a mess

➤ Showing compassion by saying "I hope you feel better" to a sick parent or "Can I help you?" to a busy parent
➤ Taking care of the family pet
➤ Putting dirty clothes in the hamper without being reminded
➤ Taking a complete phone message

If the job is not done perfectly, the parent can comment on the part that is done reasonably well instead of focusing on the part done poorly or incompletely.

Other areas to single out for recognition are those in which a desired behavior is being taught or reinforced. Almost anything is fair game. For example, when a three-year-old boy flushes the toilet after he uses it, the parent can comment, "I liked how you remembered to flush the toilet!" or simply "Good job!"

You'll notice that commenting on these kinds of accomplishments represents an important shift in attitude in the home. Instead of dwelling on the negative—what the child failed to do or did wrong—you are building on the positive. In this way, children eventually get the sense that most of the time they are capable, competent, and thoughtful, not stupid, lazy, and forgetful.

Of course, parents should encourage their children to, for example, participate in sports activities, take lessons in areas in which they show an interest or aptitude, or get involved in school and community theater. This will give them additional opportunities to build their confidence. If individual lessons are out of financial reach, another option is group instruction offered through local schools or community programs.

Here are some other ways to help children feel capable and competent:

➤ Set aside a spot—the refrigerator, a door, a bulletin board—to display drawings, poems and stories, school papers, and so on. If the children don't offer you their work, ask for it—even commission it. ("Sylvia, could you draw us a Thanksgiving turkey to put on the refrigerator?")

➢ Assign responsibilities to each child, taking into consideration each child's abilities, personal style, and interests. For example, the early riser can be assigned the job of bringing in the newspaper each morning, while the outdoor lover can be put in charge of watering the family garden.

➢ Set aside a special time (ideally daily) when the children know you are available for them on a one-to-one basis without interruption. This will make them feel special and encourage them to share their thoughts with you regularly.

➢ Look for ways your children can create their own opportunities to stand out. A child who likes to draw can enter art contests; one who likes to play teacher can sign up to tutor younger children. Building toy models and participating in plays, clubs, and sports sponsored through the school or community are additional outlets for their talents and interests.

➢ Encourage your children to keep a diary or journal. Writing in one helps reduce anxiety and is another avenue for getting out thoughts and feelings.

➢ Show an interest in the children's day. They'll tell you more if you use the active listening techniques described earlier rather than quizzing them with a barrage of typical parent questions.

➢ Set a series of realistic goals with your children in areas where improvement is needed or desired. Recognize their efforts as they attain each goal.

➢ Teach your children to rely on themselves first in certain situations instead of depending on you. For example, when they ask you to spell a word for them, direct them to the dictionary. Instead of opening a bottle of soda for them, show them where the bottle opener is stored and how to use it. If they ask you a question like "How do caterpillars turn into butterflies?" ask them what they think first and help them look the answer up.

➢ Teach your children how to interact with adults—for example, how to address adults, approach people (such as teachers and policemen) when they need help, and look at people as they speak to them. Having these skills makes it more likely that adults will respond positively to your children, which in turn feeds their self-confidence and enlarges their support system.

➤ Encourage your children to play, and allow them to act their age. In the rushed way most families live their lives these days, opportunities for playing and just being a kid are in short supply.

Giving Praise

Praise is one of the strongest tools an adult can use to reinforce desired behavior and enhance self-esteem. It is much more effective in the long run than material rewards. Children given those learn to do what's expected of them only if they "get something" for it. In contrast, children who earn praise have an opportunity to learn something about themselves and bask in their capabilities. But how praise is delivered determines whether it is perceived as insincere and hackneyed or useful and valued.

An effective statement of praise doesn't center on the child but on the child's behavior. It is also realistic, intended to give the child honest feedback, and not out of proportion to the behavior. And it should not set up expectations of perfection in the child.

Sometimes words aren't even necessary. Kyle, the little boy in Chapter 5 who was scared of the moon, liked shaking hands with his mother whenever he did something praiseworthy.

Compare the following:

1. "Sally, you washed the dog's dishes, put away his toys, and cleaned out his pen, and it wasn't even your turn. That's what I call being thorough and thoughtful!"
2. "Sally, I'm glad you tried to clean up the dog's things, but I

see you forgot to put away the dog food again. But thank you anyway."
3. "Sally, you are wonderful! You are the best daughter a father could have."

The first scenario demonstrates the most effective way to praise a child. The father comments on what the child has done, praises her for her work, and gives her two words—thorough and thoughtful—that she can now use to describe herself. In the second scenario, imagine how Sally must feel after she has worked so hard. Obviously, this is a father who can never be pleased, no matter what the effort, so why try? In the third scenario, the scale of her father's reaction does not match that of the job she has done and imparts no usable information. Worse yet, Sally's now saddled with having to live up to the impossible standard of being the best daughter a father could have.

Giving Criticism

Criticism, too, can be delivered in such a way as to teach, not tear down, a child. In fact, much of the advice for giving praise holds true for criticism. It should describe the event and not the child and be delivered in an attitude of love and support. If done properly, the child should learn something of value that will help him or her handle or avoid similar mistakes in the future. Also, when criticism is balanced out by praise, it is more likely to be accepted.

Consider two more scenarios:

1. "Luis, how could you be so stupid as to lose your winter coat! Do you know how much it cost? What are we going to do? Maybe I'll ask your father for more money this month so I can buy you a new coat. Wait until he hears how careless you are."
2. "Luis, you lost your winter coat, but I know you didn't do it on purpose. However, that coat was to last you for the rest

of the winter, and replacing it is going to be expensive. You'll have to earn the money yourself. I am very disappointed, but I know you can be more careful in the future."

In the first scenario, the mother labels Luis stupid. If Luis hears that message often enough, he'll eventually come to believe it. Also, the mother drags Dad into this. Now Luis not only has lost his coat but also may be the cause of a fight between his parents. The mother's reaction in the second scenario is the appropriate one. She lets Luis know how she feels but lets him save face by giving him a way to right the situation. She also reaffirms her faith in him—that he can be more careful. Luis knows he has a chance to live up to her expectations of him.

Solving Problems

In the above example, Luis's mother could also have used his mistake as an opportunity to build his self-esteem in another way: by helping him consider the problem himself and come up with ways he could handle it on his own. In this way, Luis learns not only that he is (at least partly) in control of the outcome but also that mistakes can be fixed.

MOM [states the problem and shares her feelings].   Luis, you've lost your winter coat. I know that sometimes it's hard for you to remember everything when you're in a hurry and thinking about something else. But I get upset when you're careless with your things. We don't have the money to replace expensive items. But that's not really the point. It's important to be responsible and take care of the things we own. So what are we going to do about this problem?

LUIS.   Well, I'm not sure if I really lost it or not. I had it at lunchtime today, but I took it off in the school yard when I got warm playing ball. I think I forgot to bring it in with me when we went back to the classroom.

MOM.   —Mmm. So it could still be somewhere at school?

LUIS.   Yes.

MOM.   What do you think you should do?

LUIS.   Well, I could look in the lost-and-found box at school tomorrow.

MOM.   That sounds like a good idea.

LUIS.   And I could look around the school yard in case it's still there.

MOM.   That sounds good, too. What if you don't find it? What should we do? There are still two more months of winter left.

LUIS.   I could earn the money for a new coat if you'd let me.

MOM.   How could you earn it?

LUIS.   I could do extra chores around the house. And maybe Dad would let me do some around his house, too.

MOM.   Yes, I think we could do that. But money is tight this month. We'll have to look for a coat on sale, and we can't be choosy.

LUIS.   OK.

MOM *[reminds Luis she still has faith in him]*.   I'm sure you can do better in the future. Do you have any ideas on how we can prevent this kind of problem?

LUIS.   Well, I probably shouldn't take off my coat in the school yard. I'll make sure that I keep it on or that I don't take it out of the classroom in the first place.

MOM.   I think that's a good plan. I know you can be responsible if you put your mind to it.

The mother in this scenario uses an effective problem-solving approach. Instead of attacking her child, she acknowledges both Luis's and her feelings. Then she encourages him to think of ways he could solve the problem while she remains nonjudgmental about his ideas. She also could have made suggestions for them to mull over together and vetoed any that were unworkable. This same kind of approach can be used in family meetings to solve problems that affect the entire household or disrupt family harmony. Examples of such problems are the children's fighting over the bathroom when they all want to use it at the same time in the morning, lack of cooperation when the parent asks the children to do something, and misbehavior in the car.

Allowing children to handle their own problems carries with it the assumption that the children are intelligent and capable enough to do so. Herein lies this technique's success at building children's self-esteem. Even though the parent retains control of the process and the final course of action, the children act in partnership with the parent. They have a stake in the outcome because they helped determine it.

This approach can be used for small as well as big problems. Sometimes parents, in their zeal to protect their children, are too quick to step in and take control for them. But when left to their own devices, most children are quite capable of handling many of life's everyday problems.

For example, one day four-year-old Winnie was playing in the yard with a neighbor boy while her mother worked in the garden. Suddenly, Winnie came running at her, tears streaming from her eyes. "Frankie hit me!" she sobbed. Patricia later told me that she decided to let Winnie handle the problem herself to see what would happen. She was concerned that Winnie wasn't learning to stand up for herself very well.

"I bet that makes you very mad," Patricia told Winnie, using her best active listening skills.

"Yes, it does. He shouldn't have done that." She cried a little while longer while Patricia patiently listened.

"Mommy, come tell him to stop it!"

"Winnie, I think you can handle this yourself. What do you think you should do?"

The girl stopped crying and looked intently from her mother to Frankie. "Well," she said after a few moments of reflection, "I guess I could tell him not to hit me anymore."

"OK. Anything else?" asked her mother.

"Yes—that I don't like when he hits me!"

"Good, Winnie. Why don't you give it a try?"

Winnie ran back to Frankie. From the sidelines Patricia wasn't sure what Winnie said to him, but she was pleased when the two children resumed their play.

Teaching Survival Skills

Children who know how to take care of themselves and are prepared to handle common crises face every day more confidently and less fearfully. They depend less on the adults in their lives and more on their own ingenuity. These are some of the skills children should be taught and rehearsed on, according to their age and level of maturity:

➤ *Self-identification:* How and when to state name, address, phone number, and parents' names.
➤ *Using a phone:* How to answer the phone, take messages, dial, and use a phone book. Emergency numbers, parents' work numbers, and other important numbers should be posted by the phone. Children too young to dial a seven-digit phone number should be taught how and when to dial 911 or at least 0. Children should be rehearsed on how to give their name, phone number, and address.
➤ *Handling emergencies:* What to do in case of injury; fire; bad weather conditions, such as thunderstorms, tornadoes, or snowstorms; and other situations that are potentially dangerous or scary, such as a parent's failing to come after school.
➤ *Safety skills:* How to answer the door, cross the street, ride a bike and play safely, and deal with strangers. Children can be given a code word known only by the parent and other selected people so that they will not talk to or go with anybody who doesn't quote it to them first. Children also should be taught how to say "no" and protect themselves if someone tries to touch them in their private areas or in ways they do not like.
➤ *Living skills:* How to prepare simple meals and snacks, use eating utensils correctly, pour drinks, use household appli-

ances safely, fold and put away clothes, wash dishes, sew on a button, make a bed, clean up after themselves, show good manners, and practice good personal hygiene habits.

➤ *Handling money:* How to carry money without having it get lost or stolen; how to pay at a store and count change; how to comparison shop; how to manage an allowance and make decisions regarding saving and spending their own money.

Just as important, children should be clear about what they are *not* allowed to do and where they are *not* allowed to go. Both custodial and noncustodial parents may want to cover these points with the children.

Having a Pet

Having a pet and being responsible for its care can go a long way in building up a child's self-esteem and reducing the feelings of loneliness and sadness associated with divorce. Many divorced parents blanch at the idea of having one more living creature around the house to care for, but the extra work may be worth it. A pet is a window to children's emotions. How they interact with it is often an indication of how they feel or what's on their minds. It also is another way of identifying with the nurturing aspect of a parent—children often imitate the ministrations of a loving parent as they "parent" their pet. Almost every little girl, for example, has taken the family cat for a ride in a baby buggy. In contrast, some children take care of a pet in the way they wish they were parented.

The first choice of most children, of course, is a dog. From a parent's point of view, it's not a bad one. A dog provides unconditional love and gives great comfort to latchkey children or children who tend to keep all their feelings to themselves. A cat can be a good choice, too, but its independent spirit makes it less accessible emotionally, and some breeds do not do well with children. Still, a cat eats less and doesn't require midnight walks outside—facts that may help persuade an undecided parent to take the pet plunge.

If something on the order of a cat or dog is out of the question, however, children's natural fascination with animals leads them to form attachments with other kinds of pets as well: hamsters, birds, turtles, fish.

If you decide to get a pet, first read some books on selecting the right one. The children should read the books, too; if they can't read, you can review the information with them. A local veterinarian or humane society also may be helpful resources. If possible, allow the children to earn some of the money to purchase the pet and its supplies. This heightens their feeling of ownership of the pet.

Once you bring the pet home, make it clear from the start that your children (depending on their ages) are in charge of it. Show them how to care for the pet and then let them do it, keeping a watchful eye to make sure that the pet is not neglected or abused. Then look for opportunities to praise your children for a job well done.

Chapter 10

DISCIPLINE: PARENT AS GUIDE AND TEACHER

F ollowing divorce, parents often abandon their role as effective disciplinarians. So much energy is being devoted to survival issues that disciplining the children in any systematic way gets eclipsed by more pressing matters.

In many families, this process may have begun long before the divorce papers were signed. As parents get caught up in their marital problems, the proper raising of children may no longer be one of their most pressing priorities. Sensing the state of anarchy, the children take advantage of the power vacuum. Thus, by the time the divorce occurs and the family begins to function in its reconstituted form, there is a great need for firm and consistent authority.

Many divorced parents, however, are uncomfortable disciplining their children. Some parents, especially custodial parents

179

who were not accustomed to being the family disciplinarian before the separation, fear that their children will reject them or want to live with their other parent if they take too hard a line. Other parents abandon disciplining their children in an attempt to make up for the unhappy period surrounding the divorce or to alleviate their own guilt over the breakup, when they think the breakup is the cause of their youngsters' misbehavior.

Still other divorced parents, already struggling with the numerous day-to-day demands on them, exert control only when their children have committed some transgression that can't be ignored. Perhaps it is a teacher who notifies them that their child is failing or fighting with kids in the school yard. Otherwise, these parents assume that little intervention is called for, considering the circumstances. They may rationalize their position by saying they are too tired or too busy. In contrast, some parents exert too much control and try to dominate their children's every move.

Whatever their reasons, parents who abdicate their responsibility to discipline their children effectively and to set limits for them run the risk of their children's getting into trouble with other authority figures, performing less well in school, and getting along poorly with peers. Ultimately, the children lose respect for their parents and flout their authority. "I like Daddy better than you!" one child may say when told to do something she doesn't want to do. "You can't make me. I'll go live with Mom," threatens another. By the time this stage is reached, it is nearly impossible to get everyone back on track again without professional help.

Children want and need discipline; they depend on their parents to set limits when they themselves are not able to. Testing these limits may be the only way children can be sure their parents will stand fast and thereby protect them. When parents don't take control, the children will, by default.

This chapter will help you devise a disciplinary plan for your family that puts you in charge while at the same time respecting each child's autonomy and unique needs. Good disciplining skills don't come naturally to most parents—it takes hard work and careful thought. By having a plan, you will know how you want to raise your children and how you will respond when they misbehave.

As you go about implementing your plan, think positively. Have confidence that you can raise your children as a single parent. Don't get caught up in thinking, as so many people do, that you can expect a big dose of trouble from your children now that they live in a "broken home." Discipline under these circumstances may be more of a challenge, but keep in mind that the more you and your ex-spouse help your children deal with the many emotions they experience in reaction to the divorce and as they grow up, the more successful you will be in teaching them how to control their behavior.

What Is Discipline?

In the first year after divorce, children can be expected to show a variety of behavioral problems, including aggression, impulsiveness, destructiveness, whining, anxiety, and withdrawal. As I point out in Chapter 5, these symptoms usually abate over time, but the ways in which parents deal with them make the difference for a child between becoming a well-adjusted individual, tempered by overcoming adversity, and losing his own precious sense of self. (More serious problems, such as suicidal behavior and depression, generally require professional help. They are discussed in Chapter 12.)

As an experienced parent, you've probably read a variety of magazine articles and books on how to discipline children. Most of them make the point that discipline and punishment are not the same thing; in fact, they may even be at odds with one another. Punishment may teach children what *not* to do, but it won't teach them what they *should* do. It focuses their attention on the action taken against them, eliciting revenge fantasies against parents. And, like prisoners, children often think that paying for their crime brings the matter to an end.

The verb *discipline* means *instruct* or *teach*. Discipline, then, is systematic teaching or training intended to produce desired behavior and encourage moral development. Desired behavior, however, is more than just a parent's idea of "being good." The goal is for children to be able to put limits on their own behavior—that is, acquire self-discipline; develop a conscience and sense of right and wrong; learn how to interact successfully with others; express such negative feelings as anger through words, not internalizing or acting them out; and capably manage their frustrations and conflicting emotions.

Disciplining children is indeed tricky business, for how parents choose to discipline children is just as important as what they want to teach them. It needs to be accomplished in such a way that parents help their children feel good about themselves and confident about their budding abilities. This means that parents should be sensitive to their children's needs and limitations. Demanding more than they are capable of handling or attacking them personally for their misbehavior only erodes their sense of self and kills their unique spirit.

Consider some of the worst reactions to misbehavior I've come across in parents: biting kids after they bite someone else, putting them in a garbage can, making them sit in a corner while wearing a dunce hat, locking them in a closet or bedroom, making them wear clothes they've soiled with urine or a bowel movement, putting a sign around their neck saying "Dummy." Is it any wonder that children shamed and humiliated in these ways lose self-esteem or self-confidence? Would you feel any different?

In the last twenty years or so, many parents have chosen to act more like their children's friends than parents. They purposely avoid disciplining their children, fearing that it might blunt their creativity or self-expression. They seek a democracy in which each family member gets a vote. This approach to parenting developed in reaction to the traditional, authoritarian view that parents should govern their children with an iron fist and make sure they obey all their numerous commands and rules.

Time has proved that these approaches to parenting are

largely unsuccessful. Instead, parents should be like guardrails on a highway—they should set limits within which the children are free to travel, and if the children stray too far from the intended path, should gently guide them back. Parents should neither be absent from the highway altogether nor behave like tow trucks, with their children tethered tightly behind them.

A Reasoned Approach to Discipline

Whether it's called playing or learning, or some combination of both, what children are really doing most of the time is exploring their environment and trying to figure out where they fit within it. When children "misbehave" or make mistakes, they are usually not looking for ways to irritate a parent or manipulate him or her to do their bidding, as many parents erroneously suspect. The two-year-old taking a bath and splashing water all over the walls and floor is not trying to make more work for her mother; she is fascinated by the sound of the water, the bubbles' luminous patterns as they drip down the wall, the way a toy floats in the tub after it's dropped. The eight-year-old who rides his bike too far by himself is not trying to upset or worry his father; he is probably just curious about what's around the next corner or trying out the independence furnished by his wheels. Yes, children can be expected to test their parents' limits and push them as far as they can on occasion, but children need to be reminded, for their own good, that these limits are firm.

Unfortunately, many parents—following the example set by their own parents—typically react with anger when their children misbehave. Parents' fuses are even shorter when they are under a great deal of stress, as many divorced parents are. (Indeed, parental stress and child abuse are directly linked.) Losing control in this way, however, scares and intimidates children and doesn't work in the long run—they will indeed learn something, but it will be the wrong lessons: to avoid getting caught and thereby escape parental wrath and to lash out at others when angry or upset.

Much of effective discipline is a matter of the proper attitude.

Reacting in the right frame of mind to children's behavior is more likely when parents take the time to see things from their children's perspective. It also increases appreciation of children's learning process and the role of play. Keep in mind, however, that understanding the behavior is not the same as accepting it.

Parents can take advantage of the fact that children learn by example. If they treat their children with the same respect they show close friends and others they love, their children will treat others that way, too. Children want to please their parents, and they bloom under their approving smiles.

This is not to say that on occasion parents should not let their children know when they are angry with them. The key is to convey their feelings in a controlled, temperate manner. This is discussed further under the section "How to Correct Children."

Behavior Carries a Message

Sometimes children do elicit parental attention by misbehaving. When children do this consistently, parents need to ask themselves why. After a divorce, children's emotions are in turmoil, and they are in particular need of reassurance and attention; when their emotions are out of control, so, too, will be their behavior.

Understandably, single parents' time is often stretched to the limit by having to run the entire household virtually all by themselves. Their attention is drawn to whatever appears to be the most demanding at any given moment, whether it's overflowing laundry, an empty refrigerator, an overdue report for work, or a broken-down car. Children who have their basic needs taken care of often become a less compelling priority, and parents may become lax in keeping tabs on them. Although expedient for the moment, this can lead to more problems later. When parents attempt to reestablish control or assert their authority, the children, accustomed to their relative freedom, balk at the tightened reins. Such a pattern is not uncommon between divorced mothers and their sons.

Children who feel neglected often discover on their own that one sure way to get a parent's attention is to do something "bad" or something that can't be ignored—and, in their minds, even though they elicit irritation or anger, it is better than nothing at all. You can prevent this from occurring by investing some time in your children on a regular basis. Make it a part of your daily schedule to spend a minimum of fifteen to thirty minutes with each of your children alone. If this is out of the question, try doing it on a rotating basis with each child. You'll find that such a plan offers a bonus: Children often hurry to finish their homework and chores in the evening to be sure they have time with you before they go to bed.

This special time should be spent interacting with each other—not watching television or engaging in some other passive activity. Some ideas: board games (not video games), a walk around the block, a trip to the local playground, reading books aloud, doing arts and crafts, playing sports in the yard, even doing chores together. I know one family who spent weeks painting ceramic figures for a Christmas crèche, and another built a miniature railroad. A mother and her two daughters got into the habit of taking a stroll through their small development each night and eventually graduated to jogging together and entering community runs.

As you consider activities, don't impose your choice on the children; encourage them to make suggestions. Don't be like the father who insisted that all he would do with his son was play sports, and if his son wasn't interested, that was too bad. And above all, don't deny them this special time with you when they've misbehaved.

Be Prepared: Have a Plan

One of the most important elements of successful discipline is determining in advance what you want to teach your children, why, and how. Your plan should be rooted in positive goals, not simply in terms of punishments for misbehavior. Be prepared to enforce your plan firmly and consistently.

Having a plan helps you as well as your children: all family members know what's expected of them and what happens when they don't follow through. This greatly reduces the likelihood that you'll either overreact to minor misbehavior or underreact to more serious misbehavior. It also reduces the amount of conflict in your home by taking the spotlight off you as the "mean parent" and putting it on the house rules. Instead of your old reaction—"I told you that you had to do your chores before you could go out and play"—you now can say, "You know the rule. Chores come before playtime." With less time spent bickering and negotiating, you'll have more time to use productively.

Your Family's Values

Here are some points to consider in devising a plan:

1. Your family's values: Ask yourself what values are important to you in raising your family. Joseph Novello, M.D., author of *Bringing Up Kids Family Style*, recommends that you ask yourself the question, "What kind of person do I want each of my children to grow up to be?" The rest of your plan springs from your answer.

   First, identify broad categories of values, such as self, love, health, religion, honesty, responsibility, work, friends, and personal philosophies. Use these to get started, but don't feel bound by them; identify your own and work from there.

   In each of these broad categories, determine what specific values are important to you, and state them in terms of family goals. For example, under "self," you might state that your child's development of a strong self-identity and the ability to be self-sufficient are primary goals. Under "religion," it might be educating your children about the family's particular religion and participating in your church or synagogue community. Under "love," you might decide that your children must show respect and courtesy to other people.

2. Next, you need to *operationalize* these values by listing ways your children can come to internalize them. For example, if self-sufficiency is a value you selected for your children, you could list something like "Teach Jenny how to do things for herself—make her bed, prepare her lunch for school, put her clothes away, etc.—with the goal that I won't have to remind her very often." If you've decided that your children should learn the tenets of their religion, you could write, "We will go to services each week."

   If your ex-spouse questions the values you've selected (and this is not uncommon), don't worry: your plan is not doomed to failure. First, you should review these values with your ex-spouse. You might be surprised to find that you agree more often than you don't. He or she may appreciate the groundwork you've done and find it easier to go along with you than to disagree. In the areas where you cannot come to agreement, see whether a compromise is possible. If it is not, then tell your children that your plan holds in your house and that they are expected to abide by it. There is no negotiating on this point.

3. With values in place and a road map for teaching them, you are ready to set down the rules of the house. Here's an example:

➤ *Value:* Education.
➤ *Goal:* Children must graduate from high school and enter a skilled profession or go on to college.
➤ *How you will teach this value:* Periodic discussions on the importance of education and outlining realistic expectations for each child. Daily school attendance (except when sick) and homework are the children's top priorities.
➤ *House rules:*
   1. All homework must be done before doing anything else on school nights, such as watching TV, playing video games, and playing outside.

2. Each child is responsible for knowing homework assignments every night.
3. No going out on school nights. Exceptions are participating in such organized activities as Scouts, school rehearsals, and sports.
4. If more than one grade drops to a C or below, outside activities will be eliminated until the grades are brought up.
5. Bedtimes are in force during the school week.

Rules need to be realistic in allowing for the children's ages, level of understanding, and physical capabilities. Although children need to be challenged to be and do their best, they should not be set up for failure and constant conflict with you. Parents who make too many demands without recognizing children's limits and needs are emotionally abusive; those who make too few demands are often neglectful and uninvolved in their children's lives.

There should not be so many rules in a household that they collapse under their own weight or create a military atmosphere. In addition, the children should be able to participate in setting some house rules and have a say in their enforcement. Although the parent is in charge of the household, the children need to feel that they have input, too. This will help them build a sense of responsibility and increase their understanding of the reasoning behind the rules.

4. Spell out in advance, as much as possible, the consequences when major house rules are broken. You may have already noticed, however, that just by stating the house rules, you are already ahead in this part of the exercise. In the above example, a child already knows, without Mom even having to remind him, that if his grades should drop to a C or below, he forfeits outside activities until his grades improve.

Some Disciplinary Techniques

Here's an outline of some of the techniques you can incorporate into your plan for preventing or dealing with misbehavior and teaching desired behavior.

Set a good example for your children.   Parents should model the behavior they would like their children to learn and avoid behaving in ways they don't want their children to behave. Children who see their parents approach everyday living with upbeat confidence and competence will learn to do the same. The corollary, of course, is that children whose parents are unhappy, depressed, angry, anxious, and so on are likely to mirror these back as well.

Some key areas to pay particular attention to are the ways in which you handle stress, anger, and frustration; accept responsibility; show self-reliance and dependability; solve problems; approach unwelcome tasks; get along with others; and seek out the help of others when necessary.

Look for opportunities to reward your children's good behavior.   Positive reinforcement works much better than negative reinforcement (punishment). But beware—this statement applies to both "good" and "bad" behavior. That is, although you want to be sure to reward desired behavior, you want to avoid accidentally rewarding undesired behavior. For example, a father and his four-year-old child go to the grocery store to pick up a few items. As they wait in the checkout line, the child demands that Dad buy her a candy bar. You know this scene—you've either lived it or watched it! If Dad gives in, which is the most expedient thing to do, the child will learn that whining and crying get her what she wants. Her undesired behavior has been amply rewarded, and it's certain that she'll try this technique again. Instead, Dad should firmly tell her "no candy" and keep on repeating this message. If the child is really acting up (screaming, arching her back, throwing things, etc.),

Dad should take his daughter and leave the store. That may be hard to do, especially if time is limited and the groceries are badly needed, but it's laying the groundwork for her future self-control and cooperation.

A most effective reward to children is praise. The praise should be focused on the event, not the child (see Chapter 9). For example, a parent who sees her six-year-old making her bed without being reminded should comment on the child's initiative, not gush about how wonderful she is.

Also, care must be taken not to punish a child accidentally for being good. The mother in this example would have taken away any future incentive for the child's doing chores on her own by remarking, "Well, it's about time you made your bed without being told! And look! You didn't even make it right. Here, I'll do it."

To help children master specific behaviors, a reward system is often effective. Once the behavior is accomplished, the reward can be faded out. For example, to help a five-year-old stop his constant battling with his younger brother, the parent can draw up a chart that has blocks for each day of the week, broken into several periods: breakfast to lunch, lunch to dinner, and dinner to bed. For each period the child plays nicely with his brother, he is awarded a star or a check in the appropriate block. Stars or checks are assigned a value so that at the end of each week the child can "cash" them in. Although material rewards such as toys can be earned, much better are rewards that encourage family interaction: an extra story at bedtime; extra time alone with you; a trip to the movies, ice cream store, zoo, museum, library, or the like; and other special privileges—maybe even coming to work with you for a day if that's possible.

These kinds of rewards also can be used occasionally to encourage children's cooperation—for example, a trip to the ice cream store when the dishes are all done or an extra story at bedtime if they get their baths finished fifteen minutes early. But don't overdo this; children should learn to complete jobs—and do them well—because it gives them a sense of accomplishment and pride.

Are you sure there's a problem?   Some things are just not worth flexing parental muscle over. Ask yourself, "Does it really matter in the long run?" Perhaps some flexibility on your part will help avoid needless bickering and demonstrate to your children that you trust their judgment and input. When they see your willingness to negotiate on some matters, they may more readily accept your firm stance on those that are tied to your values for the family.

For example, one mother looked the other way when her eight-year-old son chose to play in oversized T-shirts and fluorescent-colored shoelaces in his high tops. She held the line, however, on what was permissible attire for church.

Avoid putting children in situations they will have difficulty handling.   For example, a parent who must take the kids along while grocery shopping should try to go at a time when they are not tired or hungry. When visiting relatives or friends, the parent can take games and coloring books along so the children have something to do other than explore the closets and jump on the furniture.

Ignore the behavior when appropriate.   Just because a three-year-old whines for a new picture book, the parent doesn't have to get dragged into a discussion on why he can't or doesn't want to buy it. The parent should simply say no and walk away; the child will soon follow right behind. If irritating behavior occurs while at home, the parent can retreat to another room. As I pointed out above, giving in to a wheedling, whining child only teaches the child to persevere the next time.

Parents should remember that even with older children, they don't have to allow themselves to get caught up in arguments or endless negotiating. When a ten-year-old pleads to go with friends to see a movie that the parent doesn't approve of, the parent should stand fast in his refusal. There is no need to answer the expected litany of arguments; doing so suggests that the parent's mind may be open to persuasion. "Dad, Jack and Matt are allowed to go. . . . They'll think I'm a baby if I don't go. . . . The movie isn't what you think—it's really not that bad. . . . " Instead, the parent should empathize with the child's desire to go to the movie and, if possible, give him another option: "Jeff, I know you're disappointed that you can't go to that movie. It has an R rating and contains too much violence. If you'd like to see the new Disney movie, I'd be happy to drive you and your friends."

Less is often more.   When a parent disapproves of a child's behavior, sometimes getting the child to stop requires only a stern look, a raised eyebrow, a hand on the child's shoulder, or a terse "Stop that!" or "I don't like what you are doing." Very young children are motivated by wanting to please Mom and Dad. Older children, who generally know right from wrong, respond well to (and even appreciate) gentle reminders when they find it hard to rein in their own behavior.

Let children deal with their own mistakes.   The seven-year-old who spills Kool-Aid all over the kitchen floor shouldn't be yelled at or called clumsy. This won't clean up the mess, and, in fact, may lead to making him feel bad about himself and perhaps result in more accidents. Nor should the mess be cleaned up for him. Instead, the parent should empower the child to right his wrongs by himself, a lesson that will serve him well throughout his life. It might also teach him to be more careful next time. "Here's a bucket of hot water with a little soap in it. Here's how you wring out the cloth and sponge up the sticky juice."

Let children's actions lead to their own inevitable conclusions, with the parent staying out of the situation altogether.   This is known as *natural consequences*. The child who doesn't put his dirty clothes in the hamper will have to go without clean clothes. The child who forgets to bring her homework to school must explain her forgetfulness to the teacher.

Connect children's misbehavior to a logical outcome, known as *logical consequences*.   Unlike natural consequences, logical consequences are imposed by the parent. The child who can't get ready for school in time to catch the bus can be plopped on the bus, with shoes and socks and whatever else in hand, to finish dressing there. After the first time this happens, she'll probably be too embarrassed to let it happen again! If a child steals something, the parent makes her return it to the store manager and apologize. The child who fails to put his tricycle away loses riding privileges for the next day.

Here's another logical solution to a problem common to many busy families. When children leave their things lying around the house and don't put them away, the parent can stash them in a closet or some other storage area with a lock. The door is opened only once a week—no exceptions, no matter what gets scooped up. I know one father who went a step further than that: he put his son's clothes and various other belongings on the front lawn one night—no yelling, no lectures. The son retrieved them the next morning while amused neighbors watched. I don't recommend this practice, but I offer it to share with you one parent's ingenuity. By the way, it worked.

Using natural and logical consequences teaches children that their choices have particular outcomes and that they have the power to influence those outcomes to their advantage. By letting children exercise that power—for good or for bad (and in time it will be more good than bad)— parents are helping them grow in self-esteem and become more independent and self-reliant. Parents need to let go of the well-meaning but misguided notion that they need to "save" their children from themselves. This only makes children more helpless and dependent, the exact opposite of what you want to achieve.

Punish the child directly for the misbehavior.   These punishments should be used sparingly. Here's a hierarchy of choices:

1. Time-out: When a child appears out of control—such as when he throws a tantrum, argues, or hits—the parent sends the child to a neutral, isolated spot. It may be sufficient to put young children on the stairs or in a chair out of sight of the rest of the family. Older children can be sent to their rooms if they're not crammed with all kinds of electronic gadgetry. If a child won't stay put but instead sidles off the stairs or out into the hallway, it's all right so long as the child remains isolated. The time, too, varies according to the age of the child: five minutes may be sufficient for a five-year-old, fifteen minutes for a ten-year-old. The child can be given a stopwatch or an egg timer to keep track of the time, which should be passed reflecting on his or her behavior.

   When a toy or another object is involved in the child's misbehavior, it can be put in time-out instead of the child.

2. Negotiation: Negotiate with the child on a punishment, and occasionally let the child choose the punishment. I've often found that when given a choice, children are harder on themselves than their parents are. When this is the case, parents can modify the suggested punishment to make it more appropriate.

3. Financial penalties: Imposing monetary fines can be effective for limited, specific behaviors, such as swearing.

4. Grounding: This technique is useful mostly for older children—those who have begun to have their own social life. Grounding means that the child is confined to home for a set period. When using grounding, be specific about the term and don't overdo it. Grounding a child for a month, for example, overshadows the significance of the original offense and serves only to keep parent and child battling for that same period.

5. Restricting privileges: This involves taking away something the child enjoys for a defined period, such as watching television or playing with a favorite toy. Notice where this comes on the hierarchy of consequences—last. Yet many parents

try this first, with no rhyme or reason behind the restriction. Because taking away a privilege is usually not related directly to the misbehavior, its teaching value is minimal.

Choosing a punishment is a heavy responsibility. If done incorrectly, the punishment and cruel words can convey a sense of shame that will haunt children for a long time to come or cause emotional scarring. After four-year-old Sam had accidentally soiled his pants while at the store, his father placed him in a cardboard box, saying, "I'm not going to let you dirty my car." What a difference some kindness and understanding would have made to Sam at such an embarrassing moment.

In selecting any punishment, the key is to match its scale to that of the crime. Say an eight-year-old breaks her six-year-old brother's favorite toy the day before her mother had promised her a special outing to the movies for just the two of them. The mother's first reaction might be to take away the private date; the problem is, this punishment is too severe and lacks the element of teaching necessary for effective discipline. In this case it would be especially hurtful because it would deprive her of something she needs—time alone with her parent. Much more effective would be having her pay for a new toy out of her allowance.

Many parents automatically mete out their favorite punishment or the one that first pops into their minds regardless of the seriousness of the misdeed. Sometimes parents are guided by their moods: the worse their mood, the more severe the punishment. The result of this lack of thinking things through is sometimes as nonsensical as Johnny's being grounded for a week for hitting his sister the first time but being sent to his room for fifteen minutes the next.

Spanking and other forms of corporal punishment are not on this list. That's because they don't work and in the long run create a whole new set of problems more difficult to deal with than the original misbehavior. Children who are spanked are more likely to be aggressive themselves. They are also more likely to avoid a parent who causes them physical and psychological pain. Although corporal punishment may terrorize children into compliance for the moment, it teaches them inappropriate ways to deal with anger. By the time they are teenagers—too big to be spanked—they may be out of control and beyond the point, without professional help, of responding to any attempt at parental discipline. Additionally, with today's growing knowledge and laws pertaining to child abuse, parents who injure a child—with their hands, belt, or any other object—could rightly be charged with child abuse.

How to Correct Children

When correcting children, parents should focus on the behavior and not the child. They should keep their remarks short and to the point, making eye contact as they talk. They also can comment on how they feel about the behavior. The child should never be called names, which in excess is another form of child abuse; the parent gains power only by undermining the child's self-esteem and creating an atmosphere of fear.

Here's an example of how to correct a child who has told a lie: "It is wrong to lie. You know that one of our most important family values is to be honest at all times. Trust is built on honesty. While I'm disappointed that you lied, I expect that you can do better next time." The lecture ends with a hug or similar expression of affection and perhaps the use of one of the disciplinary techniques described earlier. The parent should not rattle on, "You are nothing but a liar! I am *very* disappointed in you. This is the third time this week I've caught you lying! Do you lie at school? I'm going to talk to your teacher tomorrow. You had better never lie again." No child can live up to "never."

Furthermore, parents should not use their love as a reward or withhold it as a punishment. Children need to know, no matter what, that parental love is unconditional, given to them simply because they are their children. This is a particularly important point for children with divorced parents, since many of these children already live with the fear of abandonment and rejection. Parents should not make such remarks as, "When you hit your sister, I don't love you. Maybe I'll love you later if you don't hit her again" or "I'll give you a hug if you pick up your toys."

Ideally, disciplinary action should be administered as quickly as possible after an infraction occurs. Young children in particular have no sense of time—tomorrow could just as easily be next year. However, first issue a clear warning to the child to stop the behavior, and state what will happen if the child persists. For example, three-year-old Kerry bangs his new toy car on the coffee table. Mom says, "Kerry, please don't bang your car on the furniture. That'll scratch it." When he does it again, Mom now says, "Kerry, if you continue to bang your car like that, it will have to be put away for fifteen minutes." If he does it again, Mom should stand firm and follow through on her stated intention— she shouldn't negotiate with him or give him another chance.

Consequences should be administered consistently. If, after Mom returns the toy to Kerry, he again starts banging it, Mom should take the same action to reinforce her message. If she doesn't, he'll learn that it's worth taking the chance to see if he can get away with doing what he wants to do.

A common mistake that many parents make is to react with the same ferocity to all misbehavior, whether it's scribbling on a wall or running out in traffic. To be effective, parents need to match the intensity of their reaction to the seriousness of the offense. Otherwise, the children will soon tune out.

When a parent is particularly angry with a child, or too tired or hurried to deal properly with a misbehaving child, the situation can be addressed fully later. It is far better that the parent take a few moments, even overnight, to collect her thoughts than to make an unfair or ill-conceived response. But the misbehavior shouldn't go unnoticed: "Janie, I am very angry at you right now for breaking one of our house rules by not calling me and telling me where you were going after school today. For your safety and my peace of mind, I need to know at all times where you are. However, it's been a long day, and I'm trying to get supper on the table right now. You and I will talk about this later. Please set the table."

In this example, the mother noted the house rule that was broken, stated her feelings, reminded her daughter why the house rule is important, and made it clear that the problem would be dealt with later. It would have been unfair to say nothing to the child and then jump all over her at bedtime or another day.

Special Issues for Divorced Parents

Sound approaches to discipline are the same for every family, whether they are led by two parents or one. But divorced parents—both custodial and noncustodial—have a few additional issues they should keep in mind.

➤ Create a stable home for your children in which there are regular meals and bedtimes and consistent rules that the children know and understand.

➤ Although your house doesn't have to look like something out of a magazine, try to create a home that is comfortable and inviting—a place that family members enjoy. You can buy used household items to teach your children about value and make a game out of searching for "recycled" items.

➤ Continue to *parent* your children. Although you may sometimes feel that "we're all in this together," you are not your children's peer and should not behave as though you were. You are still their parent, and they need you in that role. In all likelihood you were a good mom or dad before the divorce, so don't stop now. Yes, it might take more time and energy, but your children need you now more than ever.

➤ When you are tired or under stress, admit it to yourself and your kids. But try as much as possible to keep up your discipline plan no matter what. Being consistent is important to the plan's ultimate success. Be aware of the times when you feel particularly stressed so that you can react calmly and reasonably if your children misbehave.

➤ You can't fill the role of the absent parent, so don't try. If you were the disciplinarian before the divorce, and your spouse the negotiator, you can't try to absorb both roles now. In time you will find your own new style of parenting.

➤ Set a good example by treating your ex-spouse with respect and demonstrating that disagreements between people can be solved with words in a rational manner. Children whose divorced parents continue to keep their conflict alive show more behavioral problems; the bulk of the adults' attention is going to keeping the marital war alive, not to the consistent parenting of the children. Many youngsters respond with negative behavior to force their parents to pay attention to them.

➤ Collaborate with your ex-spouse on discipline. It makes the children's adjustment from one parent's home to the other's go more smoothly. Try to agree on a disciplinary plan, at least for major family values, and consider continuing punishments begun at one parent's house at the other's. For example, if a child is grounded for a week, the punishment can be continued until the week is up, no matter where the child is. (If this is not possible, the punishment can be interrupted when the child is with the other parent and resumed again until the entire seven days are up.) If you and your ex-spouse can't agree on discipline, however, don't give up. If you are fair, firm, and consistent, your children will respond to your efforts. And tell them that you expect them to cooperate with the rules in both houses.

➤ Never punish children by taking away a visit with their other parent or other close relatives such as grandparents. It is always an unfair and inappropriate punishment. It also has the effect of punishing the other parent and affected relatives and may violate the visitation agreement. Parents who do this are probably looking for excuses to prevent the children's other parent from spending time with them and are avoiding coming to terms with their own feelings over the divorce.

➤ Never say to your children, "You are just like your mom [or dad]" or some variation on this theme when they misbehave. The implication is that there is something wrong with their other parent. As discussed earlier in this book, you need to support the children's relationship with their other parent, not undermine it.

➤ Don't undercut or criticize the efforts of your ex-spouse at disciplining the children. If the children's other parent is effective at disciplining, you will benefit as well.

➤ Don't delegate your responsibility as disciplinarian to anyone else, be it your oldest or most capable child or a lover. That role is yours solely as parent.

Chapter 11

MAKING USE OF OTHERS' SUPPORT

Long before Anne's father walked out on her mother, Anne was emotionally distant from her family. Her father, an abusive alcoholic, taught family members early on to stay out of his way if they didn't want to be the target of a punch or verbal dressing down. It didn't take much to set him off; he was particularly mean after losing money at the racetrack or having a bad day at work. Anne's mother did little to protect herself or Anne from him, believing that it would invite only more trouble.

When Anne entered kindergarten, a whole new world opened up to her. School turned out to be a safe haven from her stormy home. The adults there—from the principal to cafeteria workers—were warm, helpful people who always had a kind word for the naturally cheerful little girl. Blossoming under the attention, Anne easily befriended many of these adults and continued to do so as she moved from grade to grade. When Anne was in second grade, her teacher gave her special books to take home to read. The next year the school's music teacher invited her to join the glee club and worked with her privately at no cost when she discovered that Anne had a lovely voice.

The more attached Anne became to people at school, the more detached she became at home. When school was closed for holidays and summer vacations, she felt as though her life were on hold.

Anne's father left the family shortly after her ninth birthday. Although things were much quieter and a little more predictable at home, it was still unpleasant. As bad as the marriage was, Anne's mother had been very dependent on her husband and could not cope well on her own. For the most part, Anne was expected to take care of herself, which she really had been doing for years anyway. Her father stopped coming around after a few months.

That Anne was able to turn to other adults when those in her own life failed her so miserably was a protective factor in her development. Most children, regardless of the quality of their home situation, can similarly benefit from interaction with other reliable people in their lives.

I had the pleasure to watch a real pro in action on a long flight home recently. I call her a "real pro" out of admiration and awe at her skill in engaging people and having them react positively to her. Marissa, who was eight, had not an ounce of guile or manipulation in her. Within minutes of the plane's taking off, she turned to the woman on her left and quietly asked, "What's your name?" As the conversation unfolded, Marissa learned not only the woman's name but also her occupation, the reason she had visited the city she was now leaving, and her impressions of the city, which was Marissa's hometown. In turn, the woman learned Marissa's name, age, favorite subjects in school, and where she was headed. Marissa explained that her parents were divorced, and she was going east to visit her father's relatives.

Her mother had remarried, and Marissa had a half-sister who was now four.

When lunch was served, the woman automatically cut Marissa's meat and helped butter her roll when she had difficulty using the airline's odd-shaped knife. After lunch, Marissa pulled out her art supplies and drew pictures for the woman. A bond was clearly developing between the two.

Marissa's father was also on the flight, but had to sit behind her because of late seating on the plane. Had they sat together, Marissa's behavior probably would not have been any different. My hunch was confirmed when on the second leg of the flight, after a brief layover that left some seats vacant, Marissa chose to stay seated beside the woman.

Marissa's skill at entering two-way conversations with adults, combined with her innocent openness, makes it likely that she will continue to get the attention and care she needs from adults. Although not all children are inherently as engaging as Anne and Marissa, parents can make it possible for their children to develop rewarding relationships with important adults in their lives. Having such relationships helps children learn to place their trust in adults again, provides additional opportunities for role-modeling opportunities, and takes some of the burden off custodial parents to try to be "everything and everybody" to their children.

Who are these adults? Almost anyone with whom children have significant ties—the children's grandparents, aunts, uncles, and cousins on both sides of the family, close family friends and neighbors, clergy, coaches, teachers, doctors, babysitters, and so on. Already your children may have adult friends you might not even be aware of; their choices are often unpredictable and surprising. I knew one ten-year-old boy who became quite attached to his school bus driver. Because the boy was the first stop in the morning and the last stop in the afternoon on a long rural route, he and the driver had plenty of time to chat and joke together. After the boy's parents divorced and his dad moved away, the school bus driver became a kind of father figure to him. Even though the two spent only an hour together on school days, the regularity of a familiar face was comforting.

General Considerations

A couple's relatives and friends have their own idiosyncratic reactions to a divorce. Some people rally around the spouse with whom they have the primary friendship or family tie; others take the side of the spouse to whom they are not connected (even parents sometimes do this). Many people simply avoid both spouses because they don't want to take sides, or they claim that they don't know what to say. In the back of their minds they may fear that the divorce will rub off on them.

Second-guessing people's reactions can be a waste of time. Thus, it's best to confront these kinds of situations by taking control yourself. As I've emphasized in earlier chapters, you should tell the significant people in your children's lives about the divorce as soon as possible after the decision to separate has been made. Depending on your relationship with each person, this diminishes the awkwardness of dealing with people who otherwise would have found out via the grapevine or the children, demonstrates that you are reasonably accepting and calm about the decision and want to get on with your life, and sets the tone for future interaction. It also opens the door to discussing ways in which others may be of help to you and the children at this difficult time.

Communicating openly in this way with your ex-spouse's relatives is particularly important so that your children may enjoy continued contact with them. One of the most serious mistakes that divorcing parents can make is to cut their ex-spouse's relatives out of their children's lives. Not only is this unfair, but it also robs them of some continuity in their lives and shuts off a possible source of emotional support.

Most divorced parents find that many of their relatives and friends are happy to pitch in if they are told in specific ways how they can be helpful. Perhaps they could invite the kids over for a meal once a week; babysit on weekends; go on special outings, such as to the movies, the zoo, or a Saturday lunch at a favorite fast-food restaurant; or attend sports events at the local school. The exact nature of outings matters less than that they occur on a regular basis.

Parents should not feel guilty about making use of friends' and relatives' availability. This is not "dumping the kids on someone else for free babysitting," as one parent once described the practice to me, but an important opportunity for children to forge or strengthen their relationships with other trustworthy, reliable adults. It also gives them a chance to talk about things that for many reasons may be difficult to discuss with a parent, perhaps because they fear they'll alienate a parent or further upset a parent who is already quite stressed.

For example, ten-year-old Tina was having a difficult time dealing with her parents' divorce. She was torn between feeling that she had driven her father away, because of his disappointment over her being learning disabled, and anger that her mother didn't stop her father from leaving. But Tina hesitated in confronting her mother, who was still upset about the divorce. Without going into details, an aunt Tina was very close to was able to give her a chance to air her feelings and explain that her parents divorced because they didn't love each other anymore.

To ensure that friends and relatives are more help than hindrance, they need to be aware of some important guidelines:

➤ They should never disparage the children's other parent in front of them. Even remarks made casually or intended to comfort a child can be wounding, such as "You'll be much better off now that your dad is gone" or "I never liked your mom much anyway."

➤ They should refrain from discussing the divorce or either parent in such a way that suggests they are taking sides. Instead, they should make every effort to support the children's need to remain loyal to both parents.

➤ They should not ask the children questions about either parent's personal life. There is nothing wrong with asking such general questions as "How's your mom doing these days?" or "I hear your dad got a new job. Does he like it?" These kinds of questions give the kids a chance to talk about the other parent in a positive way. The danger is in going beyond normal social pleasantries to ferret out personal information, dig for "dirt," or look for signs of an inability to cope. Some examples of inappropriate questions: "I hear your mom's having a rough time these days." "Is your dad dating anyone now?"

➤ They should permit the children to talk about their feelings if they so desire but shouldn't press them if they don't. When the children do want to talk, the best approach is empathic: "Something seems to be troubling you, Nikki. You seem kind of down today." "Yes, I'm sure you miss your dad very much. It must make you very sad when you want to be with him and can't."

➤ They should continue to treat the children much as they did in the past and not expect problems with them just because of the divorce. The children are still the unique individuals they were before the divorce and should continue to be enjoyed as such.

➤ They should respect the children's confidentiality. Fearing that other adults will report back to the parent anything they say defeats one of the purposes of spending time with adults other than parents. In particular, it reinforces the belief characteristic of many children with divorced parents that adults are not to be trusted. If a problem is so serious that the other adult feels it must be shared with the parent (say a health problem), the adult should explain why the parent needs to know and should encourage the child to tell. If this fails and the adult informs the parent, the parent should try to get the child to talk about the problem without revealing the source of the information.

Relatives

Grandparents

Grandparents on both sides of the family can be a real boon to divorced parents and their children. These relationships will be easier to tap if they and the children were close before the divorce, but even if they were not, creating a strong bond now is worth the effort for everyone's sake. Permitting these relationships to flourish expands and strengthens the children's family circle and sense of family history, takes some of the burden off parents, and creates many warm memories to draw on in later years. Boys in particular appear to benefit from a close relationship with their grandfathers. Unfortunately, research shows that parents tend to turn to grandparents only in a crisis.

Grandparents often are less hurried and have more time to lavish on the children than do custodial parents. Many also have greater financial resources, making it possible to provide certain opportunities to children—such as dance lessons or a special trip—that parents may not be able to afford. Conversely, children can grow emotionally and learn the value of family interdependence by helping aging grandparents with errands and chores around the house.

In many states today, grandparents have an independent right to visitation with their grandchildren, and in other states, they can sue for that right. However, long before the situation deteriorates to the point where grandparents have to fight to see their grandchildren after a divorce, wise parents should work with them to set up some kind of schedule that permits visits as regularly as possible. If the parent with physical custody of the children refuses to take this step, the other parent should try to include the grandparents during visits as much as distance permits.

When a family is split by divorce, some grandparents may back their own child, and others may side with their son- or daughter-in-law. Either way, choosing sides is only human, and expecting complete neutrality is unrealistic. Nonetheless, when it comes to dealing with the grandchildren, parents must insist that grandparents keep their feelings about the divorce to themselves and follow the guidelines above. If they try to turn the children against a parent or behave in a way that creates that effect, visits may have to be supervised or stopped altogether. Before such drastic steps are taken, however, parents should sound a warning and explain that ultimately, grandparents' words and deeds harm the children, not the parent against whom grandparents are embittered.

In some cases, grandparents refrain from seeing the children after a divorce. Perhaps they want to avoid seeing the parent with whom the children are living, or they may believe that the divorce has weakened family ties. Whatever the reasons, parents should let them know that the door is always open and that they are always welcome should they change their minds. In the meantime, the children should be encouraged to send them birthday cards and holiday greetings and extend invitations to them for family events.

Other Relatives

Parents' aunts, uncles, brothers, sisters, and other relatives also can play important roles in the children's lives. With their regular involvement, children learn that they have a supportive network of loved ones whom they can rely on or turn to as necessary. This is especially important for buttressing their feelings of security at a time when they are still suffering the aftershocks of their nuclear family's dissolution.

The adults in an extended family can serve as additional role models for children. For young children, same-gender role modeling is particularly beneficial to development. If these adults have families of their own, it may be possible to include the children in their family activities.

Children's cousins may make particularly good playmates because of the family bond and history they share. There is usually little awkwardness between them, because they have probably known each other since birth.

Friends

Many couples, particularly if they live a long distance from relatives, develop close friendships with other individuals and families who together make up an extended surrogate family. When one of the families is disrupted by divorce, the children may still be able to visit back and forth and be included in outings in which the extended family participates. Regardless of their own feelings of embarrassment or avoidance, parents should do all they can to keep such rewarding relationships alive. In addition, close friends of the parents may be able to act much like aunts or uncles to a child.

Another important source of comfort and continuity is the children's own friends. As children grow older, their friends play a larger role in their lives, and typically they prefer turning to a trusted friend before approaching a parent or another adult with a problem or, for that matter, good news. You can be sure that the divorce and their reactions to it will be one on a long list of topics they'll talk about with friends.

Parents can take advantage of children's need for peer support by making sure that the children have time for friends and for involvement in organized activities and groups. Children's lives should not be consumed by an unrealistic schedule of chores and other responsibilities they are too young to handle. The relationships they develop as children will teach them important social skills they'll need throughout their lives.

Another outlet for peer interaction is discussion groups for children with divorced parents, offered through schools and led by a trained teacher or another professional. Parents can check with their local school to see whether one is available there. One eight-year-old boy who had participated in such a program told me, "It made me feel good to talk to other kids who have divorced parents. I thought I was the only one who still cries at night because I miss my dad so much."

Teachers

During the school or work week, many children spend more waking hours at school or in day care than they do at home. How they are treated in these environments can have a powerful impact on their development, particularly in terms of their self-esteem, readiness to learn, and ability to get along well with others. Because school is a structured and predictable place, it has the potential to impart a sense of security that may still be lacking at home, as it did for Anne, the little girl described at the beginning of this chapter.

When a couple separate and divorce, their children's teachers should be informed as soon as possible. Many experienced teachers know that something is wrong before they learn exactly why. (If the family has relocated to a new school district as a result of the divorce, new teachers should likewise be informed.) Ideally, both parents should talk to each teacher together. This vividly demonstrates that both parents are committed to their children's education. If going together is impossible, the parents should arrange to go individually—the important point is that teachers meet *both* parents.

Here are few major points to cover with teachers:

➤ Give teachers a general idea of the family's situation—whom the child is living with, any difficulties the child may be having, related to the divorce or not, and so on.
➤ Point out each child's strong academic areas so that teachers can try to build on them. By emphasizing strengths, you are creating an upbeat picture of your child in the teacher's mind.
➤ Ask teachers to report any academic difficulties or behavior changes they pick up in the children. The earlier parents and

teachers take remedial steps, the more likely it is that the children will adjust.

➤ To bolster self-esteem, ask teachers to try to assign special responsibilities to the children. Also point out any special interests and abilities your children have that the teacher may be able to call on and thereby give the child an opportunity to shine. For example, nine-year-old Kee had artistic ability; her teacher asked her to help him design and set up some of the bulletin boards in the classroom. In another example, after his parents divorced, seven-year-old J.J. had trouble sitting still for long periods. His teacher made him the class messenger to the school office so that he could take a break now and then. J.J. felt special for having been singled out for this task.

➤ Encourage teachers to give the children a little extra time or empathy if they seem upset or distracted.

➤ Attend teacher conferences with your ex-spouse. If he or she refuses to do so, tell teachers now so they can be prepared to hold separate conferences. Schools in some jurisdictions, however, may not be willing to hold separate conferences for the parent who does not have sole or joint legal custody. If that's the case in your school district, and you are the noncustodial parent, ask your ex-spouse to contact the school on your behalf. You can also contact a lawyer or judge. The point is to try—don't give up. In some custody decisions, the noncustodial parent is given certain rights.

➤ Check with teachers or the school administration about programs or special services for children whose parents are divorced.

➤ If you haven't done so already, get information on athletic, musical, theatrical, art, and other programs the school offers appropriate for your children's ages. Involvement in such extracurricular activities gives children additional opportunities to attain new skills, interact with others, and feel good about their abilities. This helps reduce the likelihood that they'll develop behavioral problems.

➤ Noncustodial parents who live a great distance from the school should make the effort to meet their children's teachers. They should also ask teachers if they are available for progress reports by phone.

Although parents may find it hard to talk frankly with their children's teachers in this way, it may help to remember that most teachers are experienced at dealing with children whose parents are divorced and often go out of their way to show them extra kindness. Moreover, because of their training, teachers are often more perceptive and objective in analyzing a child's behavior and making sound recommendations to parents. If a teacher suggests that a child needs a psychiatric or psychological evaluation, parents should not be offended; most likely, it is good advice.

Still, parents need to be attuned to the (I hope) rare teacher who appears to have a stigmatizing attitude toward children with divorced parents, lumping them all together as "problem children." Such teachers may expect less from these children academically, and, when problems develop, may dismiss them with "Well, what else can you expect from children who live in a broken home?" Parents who believe that their child has such a teacher should talk to the school administrator about the problem. It may become necessary to place the child with a different teacher.

If a school is not providing what a child needs, parents should take the initiative and speak up. I know one mother of a severely physically handicapped child who worked with the school to provide the special services and attention that her child needed. The child was able to form special bonds with some of his teachers and aides that gave his self-esteem a much-needed boost, and his grades greatly improved. When the school wanted to discontinue the services, the determined mother enlisted a legal aid lawyer to show that the services had been successful and were still needed. What this mother lacked in money and education, she made up for by educating herself about her child's rights and by not being afraid to use the system to his benefit.

For their part, parents need to be sure to meet teachers halfway. Teachers are not surrogate parents and can't fill the gaps created by inadequate parenting. Children should be sent to school well rested, clean, fed, properly dressed, and prepared for the day ahead. This requires that parents devise routines in which the children put schoolwork first, go to bed at a reasonable hour, and have enough time in the morning to dress and eat a good breakfast. Many teachers I know complain about the increasing number of children who are sent to school tired, hungry, or poorly dressed. They are in no shape for a day of challenging academic tasks.

How to Support Children's Need for Others

Here are some examples of how relatives and friends can support your children's feelings of love and attachment to their other parent. (You might want to make photocopies for them.)

Should Do:

1. Ask them general questions about their parents.
   "How's your dad's new job?"
   "Is your mom excited about moving?"

Shouldn't Do:

1. Don't disparage the children's other parent in front of them.
   "Your mom never has anything nice to say about anyone."
   "Did your dad come to even one of your baseball games?"

2. Encourage them to talk about their feelings.

> "Something seems to be troubling you. . . ."
> "You seem a little pre-occupied today. . . ."

2. If children don't want to talk or share their feelings, don't force it.

> "Cat got your tongue?"
> "I know you're not telling me everything."

3. Empathize with their feelings.

> "I would be angry, too, if my mom didn't seem to pay attention to me. . . ."
> "I can understand why you feel very lonely sometimes. . . ."

3. Don't tell children how they should feel.

> "I don't know why you are unhappy about sharing a room with your brother. The two of you will be able to have a lot of fun together."

4. Encourage them to talk about their own lives with open-ended questions or comments.

> "Your mom told me you did a terrific job on your science project. How'd you get that idea?"
> "I hear your Girl Scout troop is going on a camping trip. What activities does your leader have planned for you?"

4. Don't spend your time with the children by doing all the talking or constantly directing the conversation.

5.   Make dates to spend time with the children doing activities they enjoy.

5.   Don't promise the children you'll spend time with them unless you are fairly sure you can follow through.

6.   Respect the children's right to confidentiality.

6.   Don't report back to the parent what the children tell you. Do so only if their health or well-being is seriously at stake.

Chapter 12

DANGER SIGNALS: WHEN IS PROFESSIONAL HELP NEEDED?

As you observe your children's reactions to your separation and divorce, it's important not to be on the lookout for the worst. If you are constantly hovering over your children, expecting problems to develop, you are surely going to find them, and maybe even cause a few. Most children adjust very well in time to their family's new circumstances under the conditions discussed throughout this book. When your children appear to be having problems, you need to remember that they may not be related at all to having divorced parents—they may just be part and parcel of growing up. Thus, your working presumption should always be that your child is normal. Nonetheless, it is helpful to be able to distinguish between reactions that are normal and expected in children after divorce and reactions that may signal a need for consultation with your pediatrician or a mental health professional.

As I discuss in Chapter 5, it is normal and healthy for children with divorced parents to miss the parent they are not with as well as the way the family used to be. They also may continue to pretend that the absent parent is there or fantasize what it would be like if the family were "whole" again. Talking about these memories and expressing their feelings are good therapy for children, not something that should be discouraged. Parents should join in these discussions and take care not to disparage the children's other parent or make them feel "bad" or childish because of their tears or fears.

It's reassuring to realize that all children are at times conniving little devils whose express mission seems to be driving their parents to distraction. I've found that a particularly sore spot among divorced parents is their children's skill at playing one parent off the other or expertise at pushing a parent's guilt button. These kinds of manipulative behaviors are normal and can be controlled. Some telltale remarks:

"Why won't you let me stay up till ten o'clock? Dad always lets me stay up late when I'm at his house."

"Mom buys me nicer things than you do."

"Daddy said you'd wouldn't take me to the zoo. He says you're always too busy to do fun stuff like that."

"It's a lot more fun to be at Mommy's house. Her new boyfriend has a convertible, and he takes us for rides all the time."

You'll get a lot more mileage out of reacting to such comments with a dose of good humor than with angry comebacks or a knotted stomach. Although parents don't have to ignore such comments, they should avoid getting caught up in answering what they believe to be the hidden message: that the parent the children prefer to be with or love more is the parent who gives them material things or who says yes all the time. By not responding in the way children expect—which is to get entangled in a discussion so that, weary at last, you give in to the children's demands—you'll take the wind out of their sails. They'll soon learn there's no sailing in calm seas.

When eight-year-old Seth tried to get his mother to buy him a video game system, he charged, "All the kids have one! I'm the only who doesn't. And it's just because you and Dad are divorced and we can't afford one."

Her reasoned reply was, "Maybe you and I can start saving up for one together. We'll make it a family project. For every dollar you save, I'll match it with a dollar. Perhaps we can figure out some extra chores for you to do around the house, and maybe Grandma has some for you to do, too, when you're at her house. We'll make up a chart to keep track of our progress. Then we'll watch the newspaper ads to see if we can get a good used one or one on sale."

Seth's anger and feelings of being cheated were turned around into a game that both mother and son went on to enjoy. A mother who had not taken the time to think through the situation and who was still upset with her ex-husband would probably have said, "I know it seems like you don't have as much as the other kids in the neighborhood, and I'm really sorry that we just can't afford one right now. Daddy doesn't give me enough money. . . ." Although these points may be true, placing blame on someone else does not solve anything and keeps an attitude of helplessness and victimization alive.

Threshold for the Abnormal

There's a point at which a child's normal reactions to the family's breakup cross the threshold to become abnormal and require intervention from your pediatrician or a mental health professional. Although it is difficult to say just how much time should elapse to see whether a problem will resolve, a good rule of thumb is this: If your instinct tells you that your child needs help, he or she probably does.

Here are some danger signals to be alert to:

> The normal reactions experienced on the heels of the separation and divorce (as described in Chapter 5) go on for a protracted period—about six months to a year, depending on the specific problem.
> The child seems overwhelmed and troubled by his feelings, unable to cope with them.
> The child cries a lot.
> The child frequently asks or hints for help with overwhelming feelings or with activities she was previously able to do on her own.
> The child's school performance declines and doesn't pick up again, and there is no evidence of a learning disability or social problems at school (such as other children making fun of the way the child dresses).
> The child's teachers, school administrators, or other authority figures in the child's life ask you what might be troubling your child.
> The child seems constantly preoccupied, worried, anxious, and intense. Some children develop a fear of a variety of things—rain, barking dogs, burglars, their parents' getting killed when out of sight, and so on. Other children simply wear their anxiety on their faces.
> The child has fears or phobias that are unreasonable or interfere with normal activities. One little boy refused to sit on the couch where he had been sitting when his mom told him about the divorce. He feared that if he broke this rule, other "bad things" would happen, too.
> The child can't seem to concentrate on schoolwork and other age-appropriate tasks.

➤ The child's play centers constantly on the family's breakup or getting back together.

➤ The child doesn't seem like a child anymore and loses interest in playing. One six-year-old boy, for example, talked in a grave, pseudo-adult manner, acting much older than a first-grader.

➤ The child tries to stimulate herself in various ways. Examples of this kind of behavior include excessive thumb sucking or hair pulling, rocking of the body, head banging to the point of hurting himself, and masturbating often or in public.

➤ The child has no friends and gets into fights with other youngsters. Teachers or others may report that "this is a very angry [or disruptive] kid."

➤ The child isolates himself from other people.

➤ The child regularly talks about death and dying.

➤ The child appears to have low self-esteem and little self-confidence. Over and over the child may make such comments as: "I can't do anything right." "I'm so stupid." "I don't see why anyone would love me." "I know you [or someone else] hates me." "Nobody likes me." "I'm ugly . . . too big . . . too small . . . too fat . . . too skinny . . . too tall . . . too short, etc."

➤ Sleep difficulties don't appear to be resolving. They include refusing to be separated from the parent at bedtime, inability to sleep, sleeping too much, sleeping on the parent's bed, nightmares, and night terrors.

➤ The child begins to act in a provocatively sexual manner. This is more common in girls as they approach puberty and thereafter, but even much younger girls may flirt with men in sexually suggestive ways.

Having only one or two of these problems is not necessarily cause for alarm. They may simply indicate that a practical solution is called for, such as more consistent discipline or a visit with the child's teachers or guidance counselor to see whether there is anything out of the ordinary going on. A group of symptoms, however, is a signal for professional intervention.

Indications for Immediate Help

Some symptoms or reactions are so serious that a pediatrician or a mental health professional should be consulted immediately:

➤ The child talks about suicide. Children don't talk idly about suicide to get attention. Once they have begun to talk about it, they may also have begun to plan a way to do it.

➤ The child appears to be accident-prone. In younger children a succession of accidents can become the equivalent of suicide attempts.

➤ The child mutilates herself in some way—cutting or scarring herself, pulling out her hair, or biting fingernails until nail beds bleed.

➤ The child mutilates or kills animals.

➤ The child's eating habits change to the point that his weight is affected. This can be caused by either overeating or undereating.

➤ The child adopts ritualistic behaviors. This is indicative of obsessive-compulsive disorder. A child may have to line up her toys in a certain way every night, for example, or get ready for bed following a routine that never varies. If she forgets one item in the routine, she must start all over again.

➤ The child beats up others—another child, a parent, or another adult.

A child who is violent or who has witnessed violence at home runs the risk of becoming homicidal. If guns are kept in the home, that youngster has both a model and a means for acting out of control. Although rare, the unfortunate truth is that a parent may not get much warning about it.

In one case in which I was involved, the estranged husband had been physically abusive to his wife and children. When he left the family home, he did not take his gun collection with him. The mother constantly told her children that she feared their father would return and hurt them, and she told them what to do if he came into the house. To her oldest son, the sum of these messages was "I wish your dad was out of the way." When the father came to the house one day, the son took one of the guns and killed him. This boy, who had never been in trouble before, had to serve a number of years in a detention home.

➤ The child is using alcohol or other drugs.

➤ The child is sexually active, or you fear he is on the verge of becoming so. Again, this is rare in children twelve and under but certainly not unheard of, especially because there is great pressure on kids today to become sexually active at progressively earlier ages. When children are depressed or their self-esteem is low, they may be more vulnerable to that pressure. Also, if they are still hurting from feelings of rejection and loneliness related to the divorce, they may be searching for love and affection and have a need to prove their lovability.

Boys Versus Girls

The problems I have just described occur in children of either gender, but there are slight variations in the degree to which they are experienced by girls and boys. For example, boys may be more apt to express their feelings through aggression and anger (known as *externalizing* or *acting-out* behaviors); girls are likely to experience more guilt, depression, and anxiety (known as *internalizing* behaviors). Girls approaching adolescence may become sexualized earlier than boys.

Girls in the custody of their mothers typically develop close relationships with them, and mothers and daughters may become quite dependent on each other. As I describe in Chapter 6, mothers must be careful not to allow overdependence (of either the mother on the daughter or vice versa) to develop. In contrast, boys and their mothers are more apt to get caught up in arguing with each other. As boys approach adolescence, they spend less time at home and more time alone or with their friends. Boys have a more difficult time talking about their feelings.

Generalities such as these, however, are of greater interest to researchers than to parents, because there is no predicting how any particular child will react to the breakup of his or her parents' marriage. Thus, parents need to be knowledgeable about the entire spectrum of problems that could possibly occur. Still, be assured that most children are exceedingly resilient and within a year or two of the divorce adjust fairly well to their new living arrangements.

Selecting a Therapist

The first line of defense when a child appears to be having problems is usually the family pediatrician. Since this physician has probably known the family for quite some time and is familiar with the family's history, parents may find it easier to talk over their concerns with him or her. The physician will be able to determine whether there is any physical cause associated with the problem. If the problem is not severe or debilitating, the pediatrician should also be able to give useful advice on how to deal with the situation or help the child resolve it. Examples of problems for which parents might want to get a pediatric consultation are bed-wetting, general complaints of not feeling well (without any apparent physical symptoms), refusal to go school, withdrawal from friends and family, and excessive complaints of stomachaches and headaches.

If the problem has gone on for a long time or appears to interfere with the child's ability to function or cope in general, a mental health professional who specializes in the treatment of children should be consulted.

The most common types of mental health professionals who provide psychotherapy are psychiatrists, psychologists, and social workers. A psychiatrist is a medical doctor who has studied the field of psychiatry for four or five years after graduating from medical school. Because of this medical training, a psychiatrist is able to determine whether an emotional or behavioral problem has a physical cause and to use any of a wide range of treatment methods now available, from psychotherapy (also known as talk therapy) to highly effective medication. A psychologist is trained in the science of psychology and applies psychological principles to the treatment of mental, emotional, and behavioral disorders and developmental disabilities through a broad range of psychotherapies. A social worker is also trained in psychotherapy and helps individuals deal effectively with a variety of mental health problems to improve overall functioning. Psychologists and social workers cannot prescribe medication.

Many pediatricians work closely with psychotherapists who specialize in the treatment of children and should be able to give parents a referral. Other sources of referrals are the local medical society and the local branches of associations to which psychiatrists, psychologists, and social workers belong, such as the American Psychiatric Association, the American Academy of Child and Adolescent Psychiatry, the American Psychological Association, and the National Association of Social Workers. The phone numbers of their local chapters can be found in the phone book or obtained from their national associations (also see Chapter 15).

Other good sources of referrals are friends and relatives who have seen a therapist themselves or know of someone who has. Whether the referral is right for you, however, depends on the type of problem for which the therapist was consulted.

Before proceeding further, it's a good idea to check with the company that insures your child to see what mental health benefits are provided. The plan may have no mental health provisions, or you may be responsible for a copayment or the balance of the bill not paid by the insurance company. Also, some plans limit your choice of therapist, requiring that you see one of its own therapists. Many plans have an annual limit on the number of sessions or days of hospitalization.

Although the cost of mental health services may seem high,

the cost of not getting treatment is far higher in the long run in terms of the child's emotional suffering, interrupted development, and associated medical problems. You and the child's other parent should split the cost or any copayments in proportion to your respective incomes. Don't put off seeking therapy, however, if the two of you can't reach a speedy agreement.

Once you have the names of potential therapists, you may want to talk to them or a staff member over the phone to choose the most appropriate one for your family. Here are some questions you might want to ask:

1. *Do you specialize in the treatment of children?*

    Many psychotherapists are considered generalists; others specialize in a particular area or population. You want someone who specializes in treating children or preadolescents. It is also helpful if the therapist has worked with children whose parents are divorced, but keep in mind that your child's problem may not be related to the divorce.

2. *What kind of therapy do you use?*

    There are many kinds of therapy used with children today—typically, play therapy, drawing, talk therapy (individual, group, and/or family), and behavioral therapy and, rarely, medication. The treatment plan should include the child and *both* parents, not just the parent who thinks the child needs therapy. Participation in peer-support groups may also be recommended.

3. *What will therapy cost?*

    Therapists charge by the session, typically forty-five or fifty minutes once a week. The cost varies from one part of the country to another—generally it's higher in urban areas and lower in rural areas. The initial evaluation, which may include psychological testing, costs extra.

    A therapist cannot tell you in a phone interview how many sessions will be necessary for treatment, but he or she should be willing to discuss with you his or her fee policies. Those who refuse to do so should be crossed off your list.

4. *Are you willing to accept payment directly from the insurance company instead of from me?*

   Many therapists are willing to file the necessary paperwork if they are eligible to receive payment for their services directly from the insurer. Other therapists expect payment in full from you for each session, leaving you to file the paperwork with the insurer to obtain reimbursement.

   If you or your child is covered under certain kinds of managed care plans (such as a health maintenance organization or preferred provider organization) and the therapist is a recognized provider in that plan, the plan will pay the therapist directly. You may be responsible for a copayment. Before seeing the therapist for the first time, it's a good idea to check with your plan to be sure that the therapist is still a recognized provider.

5. *What if we don't have insurance or mental health benefits under our plan?*

   If you don't have insurance and you can't afford the fees quoted to you, ask whether the therapist is willing to adjust his or her fees based on family income or can refer you to someone with such a policy.

   Also, you can check with your local government as well as your local medical or psychiatric societies about community mental health services for children or families. One drawback of community agencies, however, is that there is often a long wait because there are not enough mental health professionals to serve all comers.

These telephone interviews should help you select which therapist is best for you and your family. Chances are good that the person you select will work out, but if the first time you meet with him or her is disappointing, don't be discouraged. The first few appointments with any therapist are often upsetting, and it takes time to build up trust in someone with whom you are sharing highly personal information. If you continue to feel uneasy, however, you may need to try another therapist. Again, this is not uncommon. The more work you put into choosing a therapist, the greater the probability that your choice will work out.

Whether you are the custodial or noncustodial parent, you should (and in some cases *must*) get the other parent's permission before taking the child to a therapist. Most therapists will not see a child unless both parents agree to it and are willing to cooperate. If one parent won't agree, the other parent can go to court and petition for permission.

Evaluating the Child

To evaluate a child thoroughly, a therapist typically talks to the parents and the child alone and together, conducts or arranges for psychological testing, reviews the child's pediatric and school records, and gathers information from other relevant people in the child's life, such as teachers and grandparents. A medical examination also may be needed.

Parents who are embittered by their divorce, feel guilty about their child's problems, or are determined to pin blame on the other parent sometimes mislead the therapist or try to block the therapist's access to records and people important in the child's life. Full cooperation and total honesty are necessary for the therapist to help the child to the best of his or her ability.

In the first session the therapist will discuss the confidential nature of the material he or she is collecting. Parents need to understand that much of what takes place between the therapist and the child is confidential and thus will not be reported back to the parents. This is not intended to hide important information from them, but to create an atmosphere in which the child feels free to talk to the therapist about anything, without fear of parental disappointment or retribution. The therapist will, however, let the parents know if he or she thinks the child may harm himself or others or is doing something dangerous. The terms of this confidentiality agreement should be clearly spelled out so that it is understood by all parties before therapy begins.

Although parents may be eager to learn the outcome of the therapist's evaluation, some patience may be needed. Depending on the problem and the situation, it is not at all rare for the process to take anywhere from two to five sessions to gather all the information needed to make a diagnosis and devise a treatment plan.

When the therapist reports his or her findings and treatment recommendations, parents should not feel intimidated—they should ask as many questions as they want until they have a clear understanding. For some children and families, no treatment is recommended for the time being; for others, a limited number of visits may be recommended, say six or twelve.

Most people need some time to let the information from the evaluation sink in. At their next appointment, they can come prepared with a written list of questions to ask the therapist. Here's a sampling:

1. What is my child's problem?
2. What therapy do you recommend?
3. How long will it take? When will we know it's time to stop treatment?
4. Will you or someone else conduct the treatment? If someone else, does that person work for you, or would this be a referral? Will you continue to follow my child's therapy or supervise treatment?
5. If treatment is recommended in a residential facility, such as a hospital, why are you recommending it? What is the name of the facility and where is it? How far is it from here? How often can I visit? Call? Can brothers and sisters or other relatives and friends visit?
6. What are the alternative treatments?
7. What are the benefits and the risks associated with the recommended treatment? With the alternative treatments?
8. What role will I play in treatment? My child's other parent? Our other children? Other people?
9. What if the child doesn't want to participate in therapy?

10. What else can I do to help my child?
11. How often will you talk to me about my child's progress?

Sexual and Physical Abuse

Sexual and physical abuse of children becomes an issue usually through one of two routes in families of divorce: One parent seeks a psychiatric or medical evaluation because he or she charges that the other parent has abused the child, or the psychiatrist, other doctor, or other therapist, in the course of conducting an evaluation, suspects or learns of the abuse. All professionals who have responsibility for the care of children—from doctors to teachers—are required by state law to inform certain government agencies of suspected sexual and physical abuse of children. Exactly which agency varies by state.

Certainly parents who fear that a child has been sexually or physically abused should have the child evaluated by an expert in this area. The complicating problem, however, is that many parents use such allegations as a weapon against the former spouse to punish him or her for the divorce or deny visitation. Indeed, many of these parents are so filled with hatred and threatened by sharing the children's allegiance with the other parent that they truly believe the abuse occurred. Often their allegations are triggered by a child's innocent remarks, such as "Daddy came into bed with me until I fell asleep the other night." These parents jump on any sign that the other parent is bad or unfit, and they are unwilling to consider any other possibilities. The child is the ultimate loser—she may be denied visits with the accused parent and is exposed to more conflict between the parents. The child will be forced to go through an emotionally wrenching legal process in which she will be asked extremely explicit questions. This is bound to affect the child's development and relationship with each parent for many months, even years, to come.

One study found that the proportion of false allegations is

highest when the allegations are made in the context of custody and visitation disputes. Many allegations of abuse are well founded, however, and therefore professionals involved in child welfare take them all very seriously.

What To Do

Parents who suspect sexual or other physical abuse of a child should not act on their own. They should neither interrogate the child in depth nor ask him leading questions that could contaminate or undermine the evaluation process later. Instead, they should confer with a lawyer and go by the book.

The doctor who examines the child should be an expert in sexual or physical abuse. If the doctor does not find evidence of abuse, parents should not go doctor shopping to find one willing to back their position.

To protect the child, judges' working assumption is that abuse did occur, and an evaluation by a psychiatrist or psychologist (often called the impartial examiner because the individual does not represent either parent) will be ordered. If the accused is the noncustodial parent, unsupervised visitation is suspended; if the accused is the custodial parent, most often the children are removed from the home and placed with someone else, such as the noncustodial parent, grandparents, or foster parents. Sometimes the children are permitted to stay in the home and the alleged offender is required to leave.

In conducting the evaluation, the therapist interviews the parents, the child, and other people as determined relevant. The child's suggestibility, ability to lie, memory, and intellectual and language levels are assessed, as well as the child's possible motives for lying about the abuse. If sexual abuse is being investigated, the therapist also will assess the child's level of sexual knowledge. Generally, children who are telling the truth are able to describe what happened to them in response to open-ended questions, and they use words typical of their age group or intellectual level. The therapist may videotape the child during the interview. In play therapy, abused children may change the story over time to give them control over the perpetrator or to reverse the outcome of the experience. For example, one little girl I treated took a boy doll and threw it against the wall of a playhouse bedroom. "You can't do that to me or I'll hurt you!" she screamed as she removed the doll representing herself from the same room. In reality, she could never have overpowered her attacker.

Depending on the complexity of the case, other therapists may be brought in to support the mother's or father's position or serve as consultants in the case.

Although the court relies heavily on the examiner's report, it is the judge who determines whether abuse has occurred and, if it did, what remedial steps need to be taken. One goal of treatment may be for parent and child to resume their relationship at some future time.

How to Avoid Charges of Sexual Abuse

Lee Ann, the mother of nine-year-old Tracy, became very upset when her daughter came home after a weekend with her father, Richard, and talked about another extensive wrestling session he had had with her. "He wouldn't let me go!" she said, "and my blouse wouldn't stay down!" Lee Ann felt that Tracy was too old for her dad to be wrestling with her in that way and tried to get Richard to stop. Richard, however, thought that Lee Ann was overreacting and that a little roughhousing was good for their reserved daughter.

At this point, Lee Ann involved me in the case. Although she did not want to bring sexual abuse charges against Richard, she clearly wanted the wrestling to stop. To discuss whether Lee Ann was being reasonable, the family came to my office together one day, and what they described did not surprise me. Richard's wrestling was sexually stimulating to Tracy and obviously made her uncomfortable. There was no question that the wrestling had to stop, although Richard had a hard time understanding how it could be a sexual stimulant to a nine-year-old.

Of course, this case should never have gotten as far as my office. When Tracy first asked her dad to stop wrestling with her, he should have respected her wishes. Tracy should have been permitted to exercise control over her own body.

Most charges of sexual abuse are made by the custodial parent, usually the mother, against the noncustodial parent, usually the father. To avoid such charges or place them above any suspicion, parents can take a few commonsense steps to protect themselves:

1. Don't take baths or showers with the children.
2. Let the children bathe themselves. By the age of four, most children can wash themselves quite adequately, or at least well enough, until they return to their custodial parent. Perhaps an older sibling of the same gender can be enlisted to help.
3. Don't sleep with the children.
4. Don't permit the children to watch sexually explicit movies or television shows.
5. Don't keep pornographic or sexually explicit material in your house.
6. Don't make sexual jokes or crude or erotic references around the children.
7. Don't wrestle with or tickle the children or otherwise use your body to make them feel helpless.
8. Avoid touching the children in their private areas unless it's necessary, such as changing a baby's diaper or wiping a toddler after a bowel movement. If a child complains continually of a "hurt" in the genital area, check with a doctor after conferring with the child's other parent.
9. Don't engage in behavior that can be construed as sexual with another adult in front of the children. For example, such activities as holding hands or kissing hello or goodbye are reasonable, but deep kissing, sitting on someone's lap, fondling, and so on should occur only in private.

Chapter 13

ADJUSTING TO
LIFE IN A STEPFAMILY

After your divorce is final, the custody and visitation arrangements made and tested, and the new living situation settled into, you and your children may find yourselves at yet another crossroads: What happens now?

Within one to three years of divorce, most adults have adjusted well to their reconstructed lives and recovered their inner sense of equilibrium. Part of that adjustment usually involves a serious love relationship. More and more divorced adults are living with another partner before committing themselves to marriage again, and eventually two-thirds of divorced women and three-fourths of divorced men remarry. Obviously, divorce has not changed the value they place on this institution.

Although adults may view remarriage as a happy and welcome development, its meaning to children can be vastly different. To many it represents just another in a long line of losses stemming from their parents' divorce. First, remarriage may extinguish any hope the children may have had of their parents' getting back together again (but not always, much to the astonishment of many parents who have been remarried for years). Also, remarriage formally signals that their parent is sharing his or her life with another person, which in effect reduces the amount of time and attention available for the children. Instead of gaining a stepparent, they feel as though they have lost a parent for a second time. On top of that, with two adults now heading the family once again, the children may lose some of the autonomy and independence they gained or were forced to assume in a household run by a single parent.

Remarriage usually entails another wave of upheavals in children's lives. An unrelated adult whom they are expected to love joins their family. Another new house, new school, new neighborhood, and new friends may be in order. Living arrangements may become complicated and crowded—at least for part of the time—if the new stepparent has children, too. And then there's a whole new contingent of aunts and uncles and grandparents to get to know.

The sum of all these losses and changes in children's lives underscores their feeling, first awakened at the time of their parents' divorce, that they lack much control over their lives. This perception is not far from the truth. Today divorce is just one in a series of transitions within many families—25 percent of children can count on living in a stepfamily before they reach adulthood. Many, too, will live in families rocked by a second divorce. About 37 percent of remarriages undertaken by divorced women end in separation or divorce within ten years, versus 30 percent of first marriages.

Marriage is a contract between two adults, not between the adults and whatever children may already belong to either one of them. Yet when there are children involved, the contract appears to include a clause requiring the new spouse to parent the children in every sense of the word. Not only does this set up the stepparent for certain frustration and perhaps rejection, but it is also an offense to the children's attachment to their other parent. No matter how good the step-relationship turns out to be, the stepparent is not a replacement for the natural parent of the same gender in the children's lives and hearts.

There is no denying that remarriage presents some somber challenges for all family members, but the transition will be smoother and the outcome more promising when adults anticipate the children's reactions and are clear about the stepparent's role in the family.

Children's Reactions to Remarriage

There is a great diversity of reactions to remarriage among children—as seen in these quotations—and there is, of course, no way to predict what those of a particular child will be. Many factors enter into the equation, among them age, gender, temperament, personality, developmental level, and intellectual ability.

"When my mom remarried, she changed. I felt like I didn't matter anymore."—*Six-year-old boy*

"My dad wants me to call my new stepmom Mom, but she's not my real mom."—*Eight-year-old girl*

"My mother thought that when she married my stepdad, we'd be a real family again. Well, we'll never be a real family again."—*Nine-year-old girl*

"I like my stepfather, but sometimes seeing him with my mom makes me miss my dad more."—*Seven-year-old boy*

"Before my mom got married again, we didn't have much money. Now when I see all the stuff my stepfather's children have, I want to have it all, too."—*Eleven-year-old boy*

Most children experience some stress when a parent remarries. As with any disruption to their lives, they may become angry, argumentative, and disobedient; get into fights with siblings and peers; and perform less well at school. Some children withdraw into themselves and become depressed or anxious. Some of the reactions they experienced at the time of the divorce may resurface.

Generally, the younger the children are at the time of remarriage, the more readily they appear to accept a caring stepparent in their lives and go on to enjoy a good relationship with him or her. Children who are on the verge of young adulthood and leaving home, too, seem to adjust well when a parent remarries, because they are in the process of separating from the family and building a life of their own. Some are relieved that Mom or Dad now has someone else to rely on for support and companionship. Others feel a mixture of resentment and relief.

The children who seem to have the most difficulty accepting a parent's remarriage and the stepparent who goes along with it are the ones who are entering or have just entered adolescence. Adolescence is in itself a stressful time for most youngsters. Their bodies are undergoing rapid changes. They begin to question their attractiveness and recognize their sexuality. Two powerful competing influences are tugging at them—their family and their friends. Although they are trying to identify less with their family and more with their peers, they are nonetheless dependent on the safe home base that the family provides. Anything that makes them feel different from most other youngsters—such as having a single mother or a new stepparent—adds to the stress they would normally feel at this age.

Mom's or Dad's remarriage forces these youngsters to deal with difficult, embarrassing feelings. They see that the parent has (surprise!) a life of his or her own having nothing to do with them. They also become aware that the parent is sexually active. When it is Mom who is remarrying, a young girl often feels threatened by the dawning recognition of her mother as a woman and may begin to think of her as a competitor. With a strange man moving into the house, she also may be anxious about her stirring sexual feelings and his reaction to her. A young boy may feel uneasy about his mother's showing affection for someone other than his father and confused by the knowledge that his mother is behaving in ways that are the subject of his fantasies and crude talk among his friends. All this is occurring at a time when the youngsters are learning how to rechannel sexual feelings toward their parents in acceptable ways—a peck on the cheek, for example, replaces sitting on Daddy's lap or cuddling up close to Mom.

Problems in other areas also may become apparent. Many divorced mothers rely inappropriately on their daughters as confidantes and advisers. When daughters are replaced by long-term partners or husbands, daughters become jealous and resentful of their demoted status. Sons who have been considered the man of the house may react similarly after the divorce when it becomes clear that a new husband is now in charge. Both boys and girls accustomed to making their own decisions may chafe at the prospect of having to check in with someone they view as little more than an intruder. They know they are no less capable of taking care of themselves just because they now have two adults supervising them instead of one.

In contrast, some children lose parenting attention instead of gaining it. The new couple need time to themselves, and they probably have to carve this time out of hours that before the wedding were allotted to the children—after work, on weekends. Not only do the children grow to resent the newcomer; they also may step up efforts to get the parent's attention. Unfortunately, they may do this in a way that the parent labels misbehavior. When conflict ensues, the parent has a tendency to ally with the new spouse. Eventually the children get the message that they are outsiders.

For many children, accepting a stepparent is equivalent to turning their backs on the parent they feel is being "replaced" or "left out." It is a question of loyalty: they worry that loving, even liking, the new stepparent will hurt their other parent's feelings. Some parents play into this by being openly hostile to the new person in their ex-spouse's life or trying to get the children to take their side. Loyalty conflicts are particularly common among older children, who have had more time to establish a close relationship with the parent being "replaced." Lining up behind this parent, the children try to harden themselves against any positive feelings they have toward the stepparent. The situation may be doomed from the start if the stepparent was involved in the breakup of the parents' marriage. Even if, despite all, the children like the stepparent, some act as though they don't. A double life is born out of conflict and guilt.

Even when the children have been truly fond of the stepparent before the marriage, it is not unusual for their relationship to sour after the wedding, at least initially. The remarriage creates a new playing field—one that is no longer level. Everyone had started out as friends, but when they discover that the "family friend" is enjoying a new and private intimacy with Mom or Dad separate from them, they may feel betrayed. Also, the person is no longer a visitor in their lives, but a permanent family member who now holds some authority over them, at least theoretically.

Although the road to creating a happy, workable stepfamily may indeed be bumpy, stepparents should not be poised to expect the worst. Many children are eager to have a stepparent come into their lives. Girls in the custody of their fathers may miss having a woman with whom to talk and go shopping, for example, and boys in the custody of their mothers may miss having a man with whom to pal around. Both may miss the comfort of having a "normal" family life in which there are a mother and a father in charge, even if everyone is not related by blood. They may also yearn to be like their friends who live in two-parent families.

Ten-year-old Daphne put it this way: "My stepdad was one of the best things that ever happened to me." Daphne's parents had divorced when she was five, and a long custody battle ensued. Her father was a skilled attorney who knew how to work the legal system to his advantage. When he won custody of Daphne and her three-year-old brother, it soon became clear that he had cared more about winning than about the children. Rarely home, he hired a succession of babysitters to look after them. The children were lonely and unhappy; the only bright spot in their lives was that they could visit their mother regularly. When the mother remarried, she was able to afford another custody suit. This time, armed with the facts, she won. Daphne's new stepdad was supportive every step of the way and put a lot of effort into helping Daphne and her brother feel loved and wanted again. "I still love my dad, and I feel bad that he's all alone, but I like being part of a family again," Daphne said.

Stepmothers and Stepfathers: The Traps and Challenges

Most stepmothers face an uphill struggle. The label "stepmother" alone reawakens childhood images of the long-suffering Cinderella and Snow White, whose wicked stepmothers feigned affection for them until the fates permitted them to behave otherwise. Fairy tales notwithstanding, attitudes toward stepmothering today are often contradictory. On the one hand, many people assume that because the relationship is not biological, a stepmother cannot truly love the children or care for them well. On the other hand, a stepmother is expected to love her husband's children as if they were her own, and if she doesn't, there must be something wrong with her.

Since most children with divorced parents are in the custody of their mothers, the time they spend with a stepmother is limited. Thus, they are more likely to view her as "Dad's new wife" than as an additional parent for them. Upon marriage, however, many stepmothers feel compelled to jump in and assume the role of mother right away. Their intentions are good—they want to care for the children in a maternal way and earn the children's affection and eventual love. But approached in this manner, the children are more likely to draw back. They do not want a replacement for their mother; in their eyes, they have only one mother, who is irreplaceable.

Latisha's stepmom instinctively knew this fact. "My mom and dad still fight a lot, but my stepmom tries to sort of prevent trouble between them," Latisha said. "Like, for instance, she's the one who always takes me to my mom's house and picks me up again when it's time to come home. And I've noticed how she tries to answer the phone before my dad in case it's my mom calling. I don't even think Dad knows what she's up to—she's pretty tricky! I like that."

In contrast, some stepmothers view the children as rivals for their husbands' attention and resent the time the husbands spend with their children. Stepmothers may also grumble about the child support payments and the extra work created by the children during visits. Conflict between the spouses over these issues is inevitable, and the children soon surmise that they are the cause. To preserve harmony in the new family, fathers often begin to drift out of the first family's lives.

Stepmothers whose husbands have custody of the children face other problems. Unlike fathers in many divorced families, mothers are less likely to disappear from their children's lives. They continue to have a great deal of contact with them, making it more difficult for stepmothers to chisel out a workable role for themselves. Also, children often come into the custody of their fathers when their mothers can no longer handle them. Stepmothers have their hands full trying to deal with these troubled children.

The challenges for stepfathers are no less daunting. Since stepfathers most often become part of a household in which mothers have custody of the children, stepfathers live with the children full time, except when they are visiting their other parent.

Just what is a stepfather getting himself into? That question is sure to elicit different sets of answers and expectations from the stepfather, his new wife, and her children. From his perspective, he may already be fond of the children and eager to become a parent to them. Or he may figure that he has little or no responsibility for these children; after all, he is marrying their mother, not them. Whatever role he plays, he's probably hoping that he'll outshine the ex-husband about whom he has heard so many horrendous tales from his wife. The children see things differently. They know their stepfather can never replace their own father. They are uncertain about how he fits into their lives, even what to call him. They may be concerned about their father's reaction to the marriage, since in their minds Mom and Dad are still one entity. The children also may look on this man as potentially one more person in their lives who ultimately will let them down.

Most often a mother takes for granted that the children will be as thrilled as she is to have a man in their lives again on a presumedly permanent basis—someone to lighten their loads, make them a "complete" family again, provide a strong shoulder on which to lean. If she loves this man, she reasons, the children will certainly love him, too. When the children's enthusiasm doesn't match her own, which is more often the case than not, she may be surprised, even hurt, and so may the stepfather. Too many mothers who find themselves in this situation position themselves with their husbands and distance themselves from the children. This only serves to escalate the new family's problems.

Discipline is a common source of contention in many stepfamilies. Many mothers look to their new husbands to share or take over the role of disciplinarian. At the same time, they find it difficult to forfeit the control they had over the children as single parents. Before discipline can be effective, however, certain conditions must be met. Until the stepfather has earned the children's trust and respect, they will not regard him as an authority figure. This takes a heavy investment of time, patience, and persistence. The mother should remain the children's prime disciplinarian while being clear with the children about the stepfather's authority and backing up his efforts. Disagreements about discipline should be settled privately, not discussed in front of the children. The appearance of a united front is essential for children to learn that they cannot play one parent off the other to get what they want, or to prove that no one is in charge.

As time goes on, differences between the reactions of older boys and older girls to their stepfathers may become apparent.

A boy who is on the verge of adolescence or has just entered it at the time of his mother's remarriage is likely to come around eventually and warm up to a stepfather who has tried to be supportive without assuming the roles of parent and disciplinarian. E. Mavis Hetherington, a noted researcher on children and divorce, postulates that this may be because many boys are caught up in an unproductive contest of wills with their mother after divorce.

The case of Gida and her son, Omar, illustrates this point. Gida would tell Omar to pick up the clothes he had left on the bathroom floor and to put away his schoolbooks. When Omar didn't listen, Gida found it easier to do these and others tasks for him rather than confront him. This would go on night after night until she would reach the boiling point. Frustrated, Gida would yell at Omar, and although he would yell back at her, he'd finally do what was asked of him. For the next week or two, there'd be a truce, but the cycle was eventually repeated. When Gida sought professional help, it was clear that she viewed Omar as the problem. She didn't realize that her inconsistent discipline and mixed messages had little effect on her son.

When their mother remarries, sons appear to benefit from the presence of a man who is able to divert the mother's negative attention away from them and become a role model, companion, and source of emotional support.

In contrast, girls can be tougher. Since many girls enjoy an extremely close mother-daughter relationship after divorce, it is difficult for some to overcome their image of the stepfather as a competitor for their mother's affection and attention. Another complicating factor may be the possibility of sexual tension between a stepfather and a maturing stepdaughter. The presence of such feelings may cause a stepfather to put his guard up and behave coolly toward his stepdaughter rather than trying to forge a warm, responsive relationship with her. Alternatively, he may act on these feelings—for example, through flirting or overt sexual passes. This undermines the mother's authority and most often frightens the child.

Building a Cohesive Stepfamily

If stepparents are willing to put in the hard work necessary to build a two-way relationship with their stepchildren, many of the problems I just described can be avoided or successfully worked through. Indeed, stepchildren can benefit immensely from the presence of a stepparent who can act as a friend, sympathetic listener, booster, and additional source of advice.

One of a stepparent's strongest assets may indeed be the fact that he or she is *not* the children's parent. Many children find it easier to talk to someone other than a parent about troubling or delicate matters or problems with their biological parents. For example, an eight-year-old boy, not wanting to cause a showdown between his mother and father, may be more comfortable talking to his stepfather about the hurt and disappointment he feels because his biological father rarely visits him.

Whether children realize it or not, the success of a parent's remarriage is important to them for a number of reasons. It shows them that a happy, successful marriage is possible, and this gives them hope for their own future. I've often been struck by the degree to which children with divorced parents worry about having a happy family life when they become adults. Since they know all too well the devastation wrought by divorce, they are determined not do that to their own children. Seeing one or both of their parents in a fulfilling marriage shows them that an alternative model for marriage is possible. Sometimes it's the little things that mean a lot. One boy once told me, "The other day I heard my stepfather tell my mother that he really appreciated all the hard work she does taking care of us six kids. That made me feel really good. I could tell he really likes her."

Another almost universal characteristic of children of divorced parents is that they are absolutely terrified when they hear their parent and stepparent fight. Even when the two of them get along well for the most part, disagreements have a dangerous connotation to these children—that they are a prelude to divorce. The children may be reminded of the angry words traded between their own parents, perhaps for years, before the divorce. This doesn't mean that disagreements should be avoided at all costs; what's important is that they be handled in a calm, rational manner. This demonstrates that differences between people can be acknowledged in a way that yields useful solutions while respecting everyone's rights and needs. With this model, children learn not only how to handle conflicts themselves but also that disagreements don't signal the end of a relationship.

A good start to the remarriage helps everyone get off on the right foot. For one, it should not be sprung on the children. If it looks as though a dating relationship is headed for marriage, a parent should gradually introduce the person into the children's lives. Perhaps a trip to a museum can be planned one weekend, dinner at the local pizza joint the next. The children should also be introduced to prospective relatives, including future stepbrothers and stepsisters.

In most cases it is best for the parent to tell the children about the impending marriage alone. This way, the children will feel freer to talk about their reactions to the news. The parent, however, should not ask the children's permission to remarry. This invests the children with an authority over the parent's life to which they are not entitled. It is the parent's ultimate decision, not theirs.

Many of the suggestions that I outlined earlier in this book about preparing the children for their new lives are useful at this time, too. Since children are ego-centered and want stability and predictability in their lives, they have a great need to know how the remarriage will affect them. They will need answers to such questions as When are you getting married? Where will we live? Will the stepparent's kids live with us, too? Can the dog come? Where will we go to school? What about my other parent? Can I still see him or her as often? Can Grandma and Grandpa come visit us? Will I get a room of my own? If not, who will I share a room with? Will I ever see my old friends again? What do I call my new stepparent?

Parents should be prepared for these kinds of questions and comments as well: What will my other parent say about your getting married again? How can you turn your back on him or her? If you go through with this, I'll go live with my other parent! Now that you love someone else, you won't have time for me. If children don't say these kinds of things, parents should address the issues they raise anyway.

The children's concerns should not be ignored. Just as after the divorce, they'll probably be upset and feeling stressed in direct proportion to the number of changes they must face in their lives. And just as after the divorce, they need to hear that they are still loved and wanted. They'll feel less inclined to dig in their heels if they know that they are not being replaced in their parent's affection, that they figure heavily in the family decisions, and that their access to the other parent is not being cut off.

After the wedding ceremony, time is the family's best ally. Since the children have no real history with this new person in their midst, a happy bank of memories—a new family history—must be created.

It takes roughly two years for everyone to adjust to each other and create a truly blended family. During that time, the parent and stepparent both need to be generous with their patience, tolerance, perseverance, and sense of humor. It also helps if the stepparent has a thick skin against rejection. Many children try their hardest to reject a stepparent's friendly overtures to prove that he or she doesn't really care about them. When their efforts fail and the stepparent sticks by them no matter what, they are surprised and secretly pleased. But this won't happen overnight, and it may not happen with each stepchild at the same time.

Trust, too, takes time to develop. When the stepparent is able to form a relationship with a stepchild apart from the parent, the child feels like a valued human being, not just an extension of the parent or one of a brood. Such a relationship is born out of the experiences they share together through ordinary, everyday events and time alone getting to know each other. It is in such an atmosphere—one the child perceives as safe—that the seeds of trust are planted and the child's self-esteem gets a boost.

The more people in a stepfamily, the more chaos and confusion there will be. There are the two adults, the parent's children, and perhaps the stepparent's children as well—all of whom have different personalities, habits, and routines. These can be taken into account as the new couple create new routines and house rules that will work for the entire family (see Chapters 9 and 10). Encouraging everyone to have some say in setting these rules will increase the likelihood of their success.

Still, it is often in the area of discipline that trouble erupts between adults and children in stepfamilies. As I pointed out earlier, the job of disciplinarian falls to the parent, not to the stepparent. An agreement needs to be reached by the parent and the stepparent on the limits of the stepparent's authority. When the parent is not present, the children should understand that they are expected to respect the stepparent's authority. They need to know that such statements as "If my mom were here, I wouldn't have to wash the dishes" or "You're not my real dad, so I don't have to listen to you" will not be tolerated as excuses to disobey. When a stepparent is confronted by an emotional outburst of this kind, empathy and understanding will help defuse the moment: "You're right—I'm not your real dad. You only have one dad, and I'm sure you love him and miss him a lot. It must be awfully hard on you that your parents are not together anymore."

If the stepparent hasn't come into the family like Attila the Hun but instead is working diligently at getting to know the stepchildren as unique individuals, the likelihood that the children will respect the stepparent's authority is far greater. To respond to adults' authority, children must feel connected to them in some way and must genuinely want to please them and win their praise. If the connection isn't there, no amount of threats or punishments will do the trick. Love and respect cannot be forced; they must be earned.

Many second marriages fail because the spouses permit the

children to shove a wedge between them. According to John S. Visher, M.D., and Emily B. Visher, Ph.D., prominent researchers who have written extensively about stepfamilies, some remarried parents become confused about their different and sometimes overlapping roles in the family and wonder whether they should stick with their children or with their new spouse. Taking sides, however, is not the solution. Remarried parents need to learn a balancing act in which they are supportive of their children and their spouse without aligning themselves with one or the other. Stepparents in turn should respect and support the new spouse in his or her role as parent and work on forging a relationship with the children.

As I've said, children benefit from the success of a parent's remarriage, and they don't really want to have the kind of power that would make their lives crash around them for a second time. However, being children, they lack the insight and maturity to stop themselves from doing whatever it takes to get whatever they want whenever they want. Thus, from the start of their marriage, the couple need to recognize that although the children have a valid claim to their time and attention, they must put the marital relationship first. Most of all, they need to concentrate on building a supportive, two-way partnership. They also need to commit themselves to its success and believe in the ability of this partnership to last. That one or both of them experienced a first marriage that ended in divorce does not mean that this marriage is doomed as well. With a strong union and positive attitude in place, the children will soon learn they cannot cause trouble between the spouses. Although the children may be frustrated initially by the firmness of this bond and try all the harder to test it, they will feel more secure and protected when it doesn't give.

As teammates, the spouses should discuss the major issues in the household and agree on how to handle them before problems develop. These issues include discipline of the children, household duties, and resolving disagreements between themselves and between them and the children. When problems do develop, the spouses should try to solve them together, involving the children in matters pertaining to them as much as possible. Such consultation and cooperation may be difficult at first for adults who are accustomed to making decisions without having to confer with anyone else.

Another complication with which stepparents have to deal is the children's other parent, who is also the new spouse's ex-spouse. Again, it is a matter of attitude: framing the person as the children's other parent rather than their husband's or wife's former spouse will help set a positive tone for future interaction. Cooperating with the other parent, accepting the children's love for him or her, and recognizing the parent's rights and needs ultimately enhance a stepparent's relationship with the children. There is no room for competition or jealousy, although these are natural emotions. The children will benefit from having as many loving and supportive adults in their lives as possible.

Most children are capable of realistically assessing their lives, sometimes far beyond what adults give them credit for. Over and over again, I've talked to children who are settled in stepfamilies and who have reached peace with the fact that their parents' decision to divorce was probably best for all concerned. Their minds and bodies are relaxed now, not on guard as they were when Mom and Dad shouted ugly names at each other—or didn't talk at all. Although these children still wish their parents' marriage could have worked out, they'll tell you in their own words that the price was just too high.

Not long ago I was talking with a young girl, now fifteen, whose family was in counseling with me for about a year when she was eight. Her parents divorced when she was six. "I still hate the fact that my parents don't live together anymore," said Bonnie, an outgoing girl with a quick mind, "but they just couldn't. They fought all the time." Unfortunately, their battles continued after the divorce. The breaking point came when Bonnie, who was in her mother's custody, ran away from home and showed up at her grandmother's house. When Bonnie demanded that she be left there, the parents realized they needed professional help. That they were willing to make major changes and put

Bonnie's interests first was a big step forward for them. Within a few months they began to make progress in resolving their differences, and Bonnie moved back in with her mother.

Three years later, Bonnie's mother remarried. "At first, things were real tough again," she told me, "but not for the same reasons. Mom and Bill—that's my stepdad—don't fight. They get along pretty well. I realized later that I was the one who was doing all the fighting. After all the awful times following Mom and Dad's divorce, and before Bill came into Mom's life, everything was finally going pretty well. Mom and I were living together, and I spent lots of time with Dad. When he moved to a house only a few blocks from where we lived, I was really happy. It was like I had two houses.

"When Mom said she and Bill were going to get married, all that changed. They told me we would have to move to a bigger house. Bill had three kids, and their mother had died when they were little. We ended up moving to the town where Bill already lived, about an hour away from our old house and my dad. I had to go to a new school, where I had to make new friends.

"I hated my room in the new house. I had to share it with Eileen. She's two years younger than me. Eileen was always getting into my private stuff, like my rock collection and old jewelry that Mom didn't want anymore. Even though I didn't want to, Mom made me share my stuff with her. Bill's other two kids are Scott and Bruce. At the time Mom and Bill got married, Scott was eleven and Bruce was thirteen. They picked on me all the time. It got so bad I started taking a different route to school just so I wouldn't have to walk with them, but then I got into trouble for being late. That made me even madder."

At the time, Bonnie said, her mother was adjusting to the demands of a new job and had to work late a lot. "When she was home, she had four kids and a husband to take care of, so there was less time for me. Bill had his office at home, so he was with me more than Mom. Being together so much, I fought with him a lot."

I asked her whether Bill fought back. "No, that's the amazing thing. Oh, don't get me wrong—he was strict, at least stricter than Mom had been when we lived alone. I couldn't watch TV or call my friends until I had my homework done, for instance. Mom had made it clear that I had to listen to Bill, and so most of the time I did. I fought back in little ways, though, like not putting away my coat when I came home from school, leaving my dishes on the table after a snack, making life as miserable for Eileen as Scott and Bruce had made it for me. When I didn't do something I was supposed to do, Bill didn't yell at me or give me lectures or punish me. He just reminded me of what had to be done.

"Well, one day after school, Scott's dog chased my cat into the street, and she got hit by a car. I thought I was going to die. Dad had given me the cat right after the divorce. She was kind of like my lifeline to him. Whenever I missed Dad, I'd play with Angel and she'd remind me of him. When Bill heard me scream, he came running out of the house, scooped Angel up, and rushed us all to the vet's. The whole time the vet was operating on Angel, Bill held my hand. He called Mom and even asked me if I wanted to call Dad and have him come, too.

"Angel stayed in the hospital for a few days, and when it was time for her to come home, Bill and I picked her up. Since Mom was still working so much, it was Bill who really nursed Angel back to health and drove her for her checkups with the vet.

"For the first time, with Angel being so sick, I began thinking of someone other than myself. That's when a funny thing happened. I noticed I didn't feel so angry anymore. And because I didn't feel so mad all the time, I began to notice other things. Like how Mom seemed pretty happy most of the time, even with all the extra work. And that maybe Eileen, Scott, and Bruce weren't so bad after all. Eileen was just lonely and wanted someone to be her friend, and Scott and Bruce were really not that much different from the other boys at school. I realized how lucky I was that both of my parents were alive and how hard it must be for them to know they'll never see their mom again. I also thought about Bill, like how many times he had taken me to see my dad on weekends, how he had made special snacks for me after school—not just celery and carrots like Mom had done—and how he took me back and forth to see my friends in our old town. He even bought us a computer and helped me send messages to my dad on disks. I had to admit that he treated me the same way he treated his own kids. And best of all, Mom and Bill didn't fight."

I asked Bonnie how her life was now. It was almost ten years since her parents' divorce and five years since her mother had remarried. "Well, life isn't perfect, but it's pretty good, and a whole lot better than it was. Mom and Dad get along better now. He remarried last year, and he and his new wife come watch my soccer games whenever they can. Sometimes they sit with Mom and Bill. That seemed kind of strange at first, but it made me feel really good that all these people were there just because they cared about *me*.

"Bruce is going off to college next year, and I'm going to miss him. He and Scott both have helped me become a better soccer player. Eileen makes me feel needed—she looks to me for advice about her friends and clothes. But sometimes, deep down in my heart, I really wish that Mom and Dad could have stayed together. I always wanted our family to be like one of those television families where there's a mom and dad and a couple of happy kids, and nobody gets divorced. Life would have been so much simpler. But if it couldn't be, I'm glad that things worked out the way they did."

Guidelines for Stepfamilies

■ The marital relationship must come first. Spouses should act as a team in making the major decisions that affect the running of the household. Spending time by themselves on a regular basis will help strengthen their relationship and make them both feel that they are first in each other's priorities. Spouses who are happy with each other are more likely to be effective parents.

■ The parent and the stepparent should spend time *alone* regularly with *each child* in the family. The stepparent's goal is to get to know each child better and to create a warm, responsive relationship. The parent's goal is to show the children that they have not been replaced by the new spouse and do not have to compete with him or her for time and attention.

■ It is the parent's responsibility to discipline his or her children. Both spouses, however, should discuss and agree on the limits of the stepparent's authority. When the stepparent exercises that authority in the parent's absence, the parent should later back up the stepparent's actions in front of the children. If the parent disagrees with the stepparent, they should discuss it privately.

■ Just as in the period during and after the divorce, the children should be encouraged to discuss their feelings about the marriage and the new stepfamily.

■ The children should not be pushed to love and accept the stepparent or call the stepparent Mom or Dad. Each child should be permitted to address the stepparent in a way that's comfortable for the child. Likewise, the children should not be forced to participate in the parent's wedding.

■ Respect the children's feelings. If a child says something to a stepparent like "I don't love you, so I don't care what you

(continued)

say," the parent or stepparent should not dismiss those feelings by responding, "What a hateful thing to say!" The stepparent can grant the child his right to his feelings by saying, "I know you don't love me. But I care a lot about you, and maybe you'll love me eventually." The parent's response: "I don't expect you to love Susan yet. After all, you haven't known her all that long. I hope that someday you will like her a lot and maybe even love her, but in the meantime, I expect you to treat her with respect."

■ Many children experience a loyalty conflict that interferes with their ability to respond to the stepparent. They may fear that letting their guard down and liking the stepparent may be taken as a sign that they don't love the parent they feel is being replaced by the stepparent. Some children may find themselves having fun with a stepparent when they suddenly spoil it in some way. Only patience and understanding will prove to the children that the stepparent has their best interests at heart and is not trying to replace the biological parent. A sensitive stepparent may want to remark from time to time, "I'm not trying to replace your parent. I just want to help you."

■ Custodial parents who remarry should remember that the children's need to spend time with the noncustodial parent has not changed. The compassionate stepparent encourages and supports the children's relationship with the noncustodial parent. The truly exceptional stepparent acts as a mediator and facilitator when the two biological parents lock horns.

■ The stepfamily can adopt or create its own traditions and rituals. This helps the stepfamily create its own special memories. Still, old family traditions shouldn't be dropped. Keeping some of them alive comforts children and gives their lives a sense of continuity. These traditions

(continued)

also serve as another way they can share their family history with the stepparent and stepsiblings.

■ If both of the spouses have children, they can expect family life to be all the more complicated. More personalities and temperaments must be taken into account. The children may compete with each other for attention from the adults. Each child will still need some place that belongs only to him or her. A youngster who has been an only child previously may feel overwhelmed by all the comings and goings of so many family members. The new pecking order among the children may cause resentment. For example, a child who has been the oldest in the single-parent family may feel he has lost something special by now becoming the middle child. None of these problems is insurmountable; it just takes an investment of time and work to integrate two families successfully.

■ All children in the family should be treated fairly, and discipline should be applied to all equally. No matter how good stepparents are at carrying this out, however, they are bound to hear the taunt "You love your child better than me." Since the statement is probably true, denying it may reinforce the child's view that the stepparent is not to be trusted. A better response is, "Yes, I do love Robin more. I've known her since she was a baby, but I've only known you for a little while. I hope, however, that someday you and I will love each other, too."

■ Don't put off getting professional help if problems persist and relationships don't improve. A therapist can help stepfamilies learn how to share their feelings, negotiate solutions to problems, and improve their ability to communicate with one another.

Chapter 14

QUESTIONS AND

ANSWERS

Q: **What should I tell my seven-year-old daughter when her father doesn't show up for visits when he's supposed to? She's so upset she cries herself to sleep.**

A : Children whose parents don't keep visitation dates can be expected to experience a variety of emotional reactions, from sadness and withdrawal to anger and fighting. The frustration of being disappointed (perhaps over and over) by one of the most important people in their lives is more than most children can handle. It often reawakens some of the turmoil they felt at the time of their parents' separation. Making matters worse, some custodial parents secretly hope that the other parent won't show up, and when it happens, they have evidence to support their view that the other parent is somehow "bad" or inadequate.

First, you can try calling her dad. There may be a good reason why he didn't arrive when he said he would, and it's best to give him the benefit of the doubt. If he still plans on coming, you can reassure your daughter; if he isn't coming, perhaps he can talk to her directly to explain why.

Whether or not he can be reached, you should help your daughter deal with her feelings by empathizing with her disappointment while supporting her love for her dad. This means that you shouldn't make disparaging remarks about him. In addition, don't force her to "cheer up" or come out of her room if she doesn't feel like it. Instead, try to give her some options on how she—or better, you and she—can fill the time she would have spent with her dad. Here's a sample conversation:

"Honey, I know you must be terribly disappointed that Daddy isn't coming today. I know he loves you very much, but sometimes things come up that no one can predict. . . . When you feel a little better, let me know, and maybe we can find something else to do. We could take a walk and get an ice cream cone, or maybe we could read that new book from the library we got yesterday. I'll be in the kitchen." End with a hug and an expression of love.

Also, encourage her to talk to her dad about how she feels when he lets her down. If the problem persists, you should talk directly with her father at a time when she is not present.

Q: **My former wife tells my children lies about me when the children are with her. What can I do?**

A: Even though your wife may be determined to get the kids on "her side," it's important that you don't get caught up in the same game. Try to rise above her unfair antics and refrain from pushing the kids to choose between the two of you. Be assured that your children do indeed love you. As they grow older, they will see through your ex-wife's accusations and may end up resenting her for trying to turn them against you.

At a time when the two of you are alone or the children are

out of earshot, talk to your ex-wife in terms of how her actions are affecting the children, not you. Emphasize that they love and need both of you, and that saying disparaging things about you makes them distrust their own feelings and harms their sense of self-worth. Avoid an accusatory tone; it helps if you keep in mind that her actions may be prompted by her own pain and emotional needs, not necessarily vindictiveness. Keeping the conversation focused in this way will indeed be tough, because you'll be tempted to get your own feelings out, too.

If she refuses to listen—and don't be surprised if she doesn't listen—it may be necessary to enlist the assistance of a mental health professional in joint or family counseling. Oftentimes one parent is more likely to accept a message delivered by a neutral third party than by the other parent.

Q: **What should I do if my ex starts a scene in front of the children?**

A: A parent who starts a scene in front of the children, like the parent in the above question, undermines the children's feelings for their other parent for his or her own gain.

It may take only one parent to start a scene, but it takes two to keep it going. There is no need to respond point by point to whatever accusations or unpleasant words are being hurled at you. If you don't become engaged in the scene, it will soon sputter out.

For example, say your former husband comes to pick up the kids some Saturday morning and says, "Tom said he saw you out with that guy again the other night. He says it was really late. Why weren't you home with the kids? Who was home with them? Did you bring that guy home with you?"

You reply, "I believe the kids are ready to go with you now. Here's their bags. Kelly has an ear infection again, and I put her medicine in this bag. It needs to be refrigerated again as soon as possible."

"Why don't you answer me? I want to know if he came home with you the other night, when the kids were here."

"I heard you. How I spend my time is my business, and this is not a subject to discuss in front of the children."

"Well, I guess if you won't talk, it means you did bring him home. I figured as much. How could you?"

"This is not the time to talk. If you want to talk about other matters that concern the kids, let me know and we'll pick a time when the kids aren't around."

And just continue to stand firm. He will soon tire when he sees that he can't engage you in a fight and that you intend to shield the children from conflict between the two of you. This should help establish a model for future behavior.

Q**: The children's mother never has them ready when I arrive to pick them up for weekends. How can I get her to be more cooperative?**

A: First, discuss the problem with her. Perhaps she is unaware that not having the children ready on time presents a problem for you. If that doesn't help, try renegotiating the time you pick them up. Perhaps the current time interferes with some other activity, such as after-school chores. Be sure to talk to her when the children aren't present, and use a tone that doesn't put her on the defensive. For example, instead of "Why don't you ever have the kids ready when I come to pick them up?" say: "The kids never seem to be ready when I come to pick them up. What can we do about this problem?" She is more likely to stick to a solution if she helps determine it. Another good approach is to phrase your concern in a way that recognizes her feelings: "It must be a real problem for you that it takes so long to get the kids out of the house and into the car when I come to pick them up. What can we do to speed things up?"

Q : **My ex-wife never returns the children on time at the end of their weekends together. Should I insist that they return at the agreed-on time?**

A : Is there one time by which your ex-wife always returns the children home, or does the time vary? For example, if she always returns them at about 8:00 P.M. instead of 6:00 P.M., perhaps you could change the return time to 8:00 P.M. if certain conditions are met—for example, the children do their homework while at her house.

However, if the time varies greatly from weekend to weekend, so that you never know what time the children will be home, some understanding between the two of you must be reached. As in the answer above, start by examining the issue as a problem shared by the two of you. She may be having some difficulty that you may not know about. For example, maybe visits to Grandma's house stretch longer into the evening than she had planned. Once all the information is in, come up with a list of possible solutions. It may be that different circumstances require different solutions and that you can offer some flexibility and compromise. Explain that the children have a great need for constancy and routine in their lives.

Q : **What should I tell my four-year-old, who constantly wants to know when my wife and I will get back together? There is no hope of a reconciliation.**

A : First, be sure that you are not sending her mixed signals. Have any recent actions been suggestive of reconciliation? In their ardor to see their parents reunited, many children misread parental cooperation as a sign of their getting back together: "Mommy and Daddy must love each other again or else they'd be fighting."

Don't be afraid to tell your daughter that there is no hope that you and your ex-wife will get back together again. You may think that such direct language will hurt her, but the greater hurt will arise from allowing her to nurse unrealistic expectations.

Q: **My twelve-year-old daughter wants to know whether I have sex with my boyfriend. I hate to lie, but I don't think it's any of her business.**

A: Children with divorced parents often become aware of a parent's sexual nature at a younger age than children in traditional two-parent families. This fact, combined with the emphasis on early sexuality in our society and the risk of AIDS, makes it imperative that parents don't put off discussing sex with their children even though it's an uncomfortable topic.

You should not discuss the details of your sex life with your daughter. Instead, use her questions as a springboard for discussing sex in general, as well as her sexuality. Be explicit about your expectations of her with regard to sex, but realize that today most teenagers become sexually active while still in high school, and many before. She should learn to appreciate that some information is private and personal, both yours and hers.

Q: **Sometimes my son seems to be so angry with me since the divorce and says terrible things to me. What should I do when he is in a rage?**

A: In the short run, you need to acknowledge and accept his feelings. Many parents make the mistake of denying their children's feelings, perhaps out of a well-intended notion that doing so will alleviate their children's pain or because they feel defensive and guilty. Additionally, don't force your son to talk about his feelings. He may be worried that he'll alienate you or lose your love if he tells you what's on his mind, and this worry may translate into anger. Instead, reassure him that when he's ready to talk about what's on his mind, you'll be happy to listen and you'll still love him no matter what.

At the same time, however, you should not permit him to

use bad language, call you names, break things, or hit you. Explain to him that it's OK to talk about his feelings, but it's not OK to take out those feelings on you or anyone else. Be sure to be consistent in your approach to him. Don't assume that if you leave him alone, the problem will take care of itself.

If his rage persists, you may need a consultation from a mental health professional. Your son needs to understand why he is so angry and learn more effective ways to handle his emotions.

Q: **My ex-husband has custody of our two children, and lately they've been refusing to spend time with me. I'm afraid he's brainwashing them against me. What should I do?**

A: Your ex-husband has not resolved his feelings toward you, and he is using the children as a weapon against you. He has the advantage, since they live with him and depend on him for most of their day-to-day security.

If the children say they don't want to visit with you, insist that they come. Most children, once they are away from the influence of their other parent, come around and warm up in very little time. In all likelihood, talking to your husband about his behavior will not help, so encourage him to seek counseling with you to resolve your differences.

If the situation has deteriorated to the point where the children absolutely refuse to leave their other parent, you may have to sue your ex-spouse for enforcement of your visitation rights. In the meantime, don't stop communicating through letters, phone calls, or gifts to your children. Let the court know you are going to be doing this. If you suspect that your ex-husband is intercepting the mail, you can enlist the aid of a neutral friend or relative to deliver it in person.

Once lawyers are involved, cases such as these can drag on for a long time, and in the end, the judge may rule that it is not in the children's best interests to visit with you. Still, don't stop trying to communicate with the children. This leaves the door open for them to approach you when they are older and have developed an understanding of their father's actions.

Q: **Is it all right if I send my son to summer camp or boarding school?**

A: The answer is a qualified yes. If your children are emotionally ready for a protracted separation and appear to be handling their feelings about the divorce well, they will probably benefit from the special experiences that summer camp or boarding school make possible. Use common sense in making these decisions. Still, regular visits with your children remain important, whether you go there or they come home.

Also, discuss this question with the children's other parent, who I presume has visitation rights. Summer camp might interfere little with the visitation schedule, but boarding school could present a problem. If going to boarding school means that your son could not see his other parent much, it is probably not a good idea.

Q: **I'm afraid I was one of those parents who tried to turn the kids against their other parent. I'm really sorry that I did that, but I was just so upset when my husband walked out on us. I've been trying to explain to the kids that their dad is really a good man, but so far they won't listen. Is it too late?**

A: Probably not, but there's no way to predict how long it will take for your message to get through to your children. The important point is to continue to talk favorably about your ex-husband, regardless of the children's reactions. You also can encourage your ex-husband to continue showing the children himself that he loves and cares about them. Don't give up hope—most children come to their own conclusions about both their parents by the time they reach adulthood. In the long run you will be held in higher esteem by your children with your new attitude than had you continued to be embittered.

Q: **My former husband has been refusing to spend time with our son. When I press him about it, he says that now that he's remarried and he and his wife have a new baby, he's just too busy. Should I insist that he spend time with our son?**

A: "Insisting," as you put it, probably won't be very successful. Putting pressure on him may further alienate him. Instead, try to negotiate a solution that emphasizes how he and his son will benefit from contact with each other. Don't put it in terms that emphasize your feelings. In the meantime, try to adopt a neutral attitude and continue to keep your ex-husband informed about your son's activities and progress. Send him photos, videos, letters, and cards. If your son is old enough, he can take the initiative. Keep the door open—although your former husband may be preoccupied with his new family now, his interest in his son may resume at some later time.

You also may want to consider professional counseling, perhaps with your ex-husband participating. He may not realize the damage he is doing to his son, and he may be more receptive to such information when delivered by a professional. If he won't participate, counseling may still be useful to help your son handle his father's apparent rejection.

Q: **My ex-husband and I have very different values, and maybe that's why our marriage didn't work out. When we were married, he was a workaholic and had no outside interests. He didn't even like socializing with other people. I don't like the idea of our daughter spending much time with him because I think he'll mostly ignore her. Isn't she better off with me?**

A : Your daughter has the right to know both her parents, no matter how different the two of you are. In fact, exposing her to different kinds of people and lifestyles will enlarge her world view. Right now one of your main concerns is to keep your judgments about your former husband to yourself and let her form her own. If she has problems with her father, listen empathically by using the active listening techniques described in Chapter 9.

Q : **The hardest part of the day is in the evenings, after I pick up my daughters (ages five and seven) from their after-school program. Once we get home, they always seem to be fighting, and I don't have the energy to deal with it. Do you have any suggestions on how we can make the evenings go more smoothly?**

A : First, let everyone take a breather when you walk in the door at night. All three of you probably had a busy, tiring day. Experiment a little—do the girls prefer that you put off starting dinner and spend a little time with them, or do they seem to do better if they are separated? Perhaps the seven-year-old could do her homework while the younger one colors or pages through a book.

Another idea is to let one or both of them help you prepare dinner. It may be faster if you do it yourself, but they'll appreciate the chance to contribute and feel needed while interacting with you. They can also help you clean up. Helping out in this way keeps their attention focused, making it less likely they'll fight with each other.

The evenings will go more smoothly, too, if you devise a schedule so everyone knows what she is supposed to be doing and when. They both can be assigned a chore or two to do, which will lessen the demands on you. Set a different bedtime for each girl, maybe 8:00 P.M. for the younger one and 8:30 P.M. for the older. Try to include time when each girl gets your undivided attention, even if it's only for ten minutes. You can also plan a family activity, such as playing a game or taking a walk.

If your girls feel secure in the knowledge that they can get your attention when they need it, they'll probably reduce behaving in ways that try your patience.

Q: **I have custody of our son, but my wife has refused to pay child support for three years now, even though she makes more money than I do. I have to keep taking her to court, but it doesn't seem to make much of a difference. She's now moved out of state. Should I keep on trying?**

A: Yes, you probably should. Child support is a behavioral way of showing a child that the parent cares and also has followed a court order. Letting someone off the hook may be easier, but it does not provide good role modeling for creating a sense of responsibility in your son.

The hard part is not necessarily keeping up the legal pressure; it's the way in which you do it. Try to protect your son from your anger at your ex-wife. As much as possible, refrain from talking about all the legal activity and its associated costs of time and money. Don't disparage your wife in front of your son. Depending on your son's age, he probably knows about the child support problem, so it is impossible to shield him from it completely. When you do discuss it, talk about the actions you are taking and your feelings: "You know, I am very upset that I have to take time off from work to see our lawyer again."

Also—and I know this may be hard, especially if money is very short—don't focus your lives around the missing support payments. When you can't afford something your son wants or needs, it only makes it more painful for him when he hears, "You know your mother hasn't sent us a check in months. We just can't afford it."

Q: **My child's father is gay. In fact, it's the reason our marriage broke up. I believe that homosexuality is** morally wrong, and so I don't want my six-year-old son spending time with his father unless someone else is present. But the court granted him full visitation rights anyway. Is there anything I can do to prevent their spending time alone together?

A : You are making certain assumptions about your former husband that are not backed up by scientific data. I suspect that your real concern is not that your son is being exposed to an immoral way of life but that exposure to his father will cause him to become homosexual or that your former husband will sexually abuse him.

There is no evidence supporting the idea that a parent can cause a child to become homosexual. The latest research shows that homosexuality has a strong genetic predisposition, suggesting that people can no more choose or change their sexual orientation than they can their eye color. Psychological and social influences alone cannot cause homosexuality. Further, a parent's sexual orientation is not an important factor in the development of a child's sexuality. Data indicate that gay fathers do not have a higher percentage of gay and lesbian children than do heterosexual fathers. What is far more important is the parent's reinforcement of behavior appropriate to the child's gender.

Likewise, there is no evidence that homosexual parents are likely to abuse their children sexually. In fact, sexual abuse by parents appears to occur disproportionately more often among heterosexuals.

Whether homosexual or heterosexual, a person's sexual orientation has nothing to do with his or her ability to parent. Researchers have found that most homosexual parents' commitment to parenting is more important than living a gay or lesbian lifestyle. Children old enough to understand homosexuality are usually very accepting and supportive of their gay or lesbian parent. The fact that the parent has been able to share such a difficult and intensely personal piece of information with his or her children often indicates an honest and open relationship.

As in any family touched by divorce, the children's successful adjustment to their new circumstances hinges on the parents' postdivorce relationship. If the heterosexual parent criticizes and censures the gay or lesbian parent, the children are bound to be confused and upset—not because of the homosexuality per se but because of the continued conflict between the parents and the attacks on someone to whom the children are still very much attached.

If your ex-husband has been a responsible father up to this point, there is no reason to expect that he will change. Let your son judge his father for himself—as he will you—as he grows up.

Q: **My former wife has manic depression, and I'm uncomfortable about having our two children spend time with her alone. Because of her mental disorder, should I have our visitation agreement amended so that another adult must be present during visits?**

A: No, not necessarily. The germane issue is one of safety, not whether a parent has a mental illness. If the children's safety is compromised in some way when they are with her, it will have to be proved to the court before the visitation agreement can be amended. If the person is in treatment and continues as the doctor or therapist recommends, supervised visits are usually not necessary, assuming there are no other complicating factors.

Q: **Some kids at school are continually teasing my six-year-old daughter because of the divorce. The remarks often get quite cruel, like telling her she doesn't have a daddy anymore because he doesn't live at our house. What can I do to make the kids leave her alone?**

A: As you probably remember from your own elementary school days, the more a parent interferes in this kind of situation, the worse such teasing can sometimes get. Some youngsters thrive on knowing that their words or actions have great power over other children. They tend to seek out the weak and vulnerable. Once the child stands up to them, they often back down. Thus, as a first step, try explaining to your daughter the dynamics of bullies. Role-play responses with her, such as not crying, ignoring them, and walking away. You can pretend you're the bully, and she can practice what she would do in the real situation.

In most cases, the taunters give up and find someone else to pick on. If the teasing worsens, however, you may have to alert the teacher or principal to the problem. He or she can explain to the youngsters that your daughter needs the support of her classmates right now. Another possible solution is to separate her from the other children at times when they'd all be together, but I don't recommend this unless absolutely necessary, because it will only single her out more.

Q: **At one time or another my children have all asked me to explain to them why their mother and I divorced. Just saying "We don't love each other anymore" only leads them to ask more questions. Should I tell them everything?**

A: You don't have to tell them everything. Why you and your wife divorced is a personal matter between the two of you. However, if the reason was obvious to them—say one of you had a serious drinking problem or was having an affair— don't deny that it played a role in your eventual breakup if they ask you. Such problems as alcoholism or a spouse's infidelity have an impact on their lives as well, and they may have a need to talk about it for their own understanding. Besides, the older they are, the more they may suspect or know that this kind of history played a large role in the divorce.

Q: **I've been divorced for two years now, and my two children don't seem to have gotten over it yet. How**

do I know if they need to see a mental health professional?

A: Because it's been two years since your divorce and you
believe your children are still having difficulties, you
should consult a mental health professional. Many people mistakenly think of a visit to a mental health professional as some
kind of moral judgment on their ability as a parent. This is simply
not true. At the least, a mental health professional can reassure
you that your children are fine and help you address specific
parenting problems. If therapy is needed, you will know that
you made the best possible decision for them. For more information, see Chapter 12.

Q: My ex-wife has accused me of sexually abusing
our four-year-old daughter during visits with her. I
love my daughter very much and I would never harm
her in any way. What should I do?

A: Get a good lawyer immediately. You must defend yourself for your sake and your daughter's. In the meantime,
don't stop visitation with your child. While she is with you, have
someone else there, too, such as a mutual friend or the child's
day-care teacher. A grandparent or lover is not a good choice,
since that person may be dragged into the case as well.

If your ex-wife's lawyer tries to have your visitation rights
ended, at the very least fight for supervised visitation.

Also offer to see a mental health professional and have a
psychological evaluation performed. Don't take a lie detector
test, however, since its results are not always reliable.

Admittedly you are in a very difficult position, but don't
give up. Your cooperation and cool-headedness at this time will
be on your side—in direct proportion to the degree your ex-
wife is acting irrationally.

Q: My ex-wife, who has custody of our son and daughter, is relocating to another state because of a job promotion. I have been able to maintain a close relationship with my children since the divorce two years ago, and I spend time with them regularly three or four times a week. Of course I don't want them to move. Shall I try to stop my ex from moving? Won't another major upheaval in the kids' lives hurt them?

A: In most states, you would not be successful in a legal action to prevent your ex-wife from moving to a new location or to gain custody. In cases like this, the court generally assesses the former spouse's motivation to move, and if it determines that the person will benefit in some way—say, through education or higher pay—the court wil permit the move.

You are right, however, to be sensitive to the effect of the move on your children. They are used to seeing you, as you are them, on a regular basis, and they will certainly miss the regularity of your visits. Still, there are certain steps you can take to make the move easier on all of you. First, let the children know you will miss seeing them as frequently as you had in the past, but reassure them that you will contact them regularly through a variety of means—telephone calls, letters, videos, electronic mail—and invite them to communicate with you (see Chapter 7). Also, work out a generous visitation schedule with your ex. Then give the kids a calendar and mark the days when you will visit with them or, depending on their ages, when they will be visiting with you.

When it's time for the move, you might suggest to your ex-wife that you keep the kids while she sets up their new home and then deliver the kids to her when most of the commotion of the move has died down. This will help minimize the normal upset that results whether one moves across town or across country. If this is not possible, visit the children in their new home as soon as possible and share the excitement of exploring thier new turf with them.

Although you are apprehensive about the move, and perhaps about your own reaction to the loss in your life, try to put your children's feelings first and help them make a smooth transition to their new home. They need to know that no matter where they live, you will be a constant presence in their lives.

If you have a question that is not addressed here, please send it to Catherine F. Brown, American Psychiatric Association, 1400 K Street, N.W., Washington, D.C. 20005. The authors will consider including it in a subsequent edition of this book.

Chapter 15

Additional Resources

Helpful Organizations for Divorced Parents

Information or sample membership materials from each organization listed here were reviewed by the authors. Inclusion of an organization in this list, however, does not indicate endorsement. Information on additional organizations can be found in the *Encyclopedia of Associations*, available in the reference section at most libraries.

With the unbridled growth and popularity of the Internet, many of these organizations now sponsor informative and user-friendly sites on the World Wide Web. Among the services they provide are member forums, where members can chat and exchange information; lists of additional resources, including articles and pamphlets that can be downloaded for later reference and links to related organizations; online membership forms; and information on legislation and other news of interest. These sites are a good way to get information and help you decide whether you are interested in joining their sponsoring organizations.

There are also numerous other Web sites of interest to divorced parents, as well as news groups where you will find other people with informational needs and concerns similar to your own. Two such news groups are alt.support.divorce and alt.support.stepparents.

Parents Without Partners Inc.
401 N. Michigan Avenue
Chicago, IL 60611-4267
Telephone: (312) 644-6610
(800) 637-7974
World Wide Web:
   http://www.parentsplace.com/readroom/pwp/

Parents Without Partners (PWP) is an international network of approximately 400 local chapters for single parents, both custodial and noncustodial. Of its 63,000 members in the United States and Canada, about 85 percent are separated or divorced. PWP offers a variety of other helpful publications through its Single Parent Clearinghouse. Chapters serve as support groups and sponsor social and educational events for members. Many events include children, giving them opportunities to meet other children living in divorced families. College and trade school scholarships are available for dependents of single parents who are members. The Web site sponsors members-only forums where members from around the world can chat and exchange

ideas. Its also gives information on additional resources and re-
produces articles of interest to single parents. To find the chapter
closest to you, look in your phone book under Parents Without
Partners, call PWP's headquarters, or check the Web site.

Joint Custody Association
10606 Wilkins Avenue
Los Angeles, CA 90024
Telephone: (310) 475-5352
Fax: (310) 475-6541

This association provides information on joint custody and
other divorce-related issues. It also assists children, parents, attorneys, counselors, and jurists with implementing joint-custody
practices. It has produced a 700-page information kit of about
180 items and a bibliography that costs about $40. The associa-
tion has approximately 3,000 members in 43 states.

North American Conference of Separated and Divorced Catholics
P.O. Box 1301
La Grande, OR 97850
Telephone: (541) 893-6089
Fax: (541) 893-6089*51
E-mail: nacsdc@eoni.com
World Wide Web:
    http://www.eoni.com/nacsdc

This is a network of regional groups that sponsor workshops,
support groups, leadership training, resources, and liaisons with
church and civic organizations. The organization addresses the
religious, emotional, financial, and parenting issues related to
separation, divorce, and remarriage. Membership includes a

free subscription to the organization's quarterly newsletter, *Jacob's Well*, involvement in chapter activities, and discounts on regional and international conferences.

American Divorce Association of Men (ADAM)
1519 South Arlington Heights Road
Arlington Heights, IL 60005
Telephone: (847) 364-1555
Fax: (847) 364-7273

This association, which has about 24,000 members, provides educational services and meetings, legal information, lawyer referral lists, and divorce counseling and mediation. The association aims to help men understand their legal rights with regard to child custody and visitation and the operation of the American court system.

Academy of Family Mediators
4 Militia Drive
Lexington, MA 02173
Telephone: (617) 674-2663
Fax: (617) 674-2690
E-mail: afmoffice@igc.apc.org
World Wide Web:
    http://www.mediators.org

The academy promotes mediation as an alternative to the adversarial system in family and divorce disputes. It maintains a referral list of about 2,600 mediation professionals who work with couples facing decisions involving divorce, child custody, visitation, property division, alimony, child support, and related matters. An information packet describing mediation is available at no charge.

Association for Children for Enforcement of Support Inc.
2260 Upton Avenue
Toledo, OH 43606
Telephone: (800) 537-7072
Fax: (419) 472-6295
World Wide Web:
   http://www.childsupport-aces.org/

The goal of this membership organization, which has 35,000 members in 350 local groups, is improved child support enforcement. It provides members with information on parents' legal rights and remedies, government agencies to contact for help, local and interstate methods of collecting current and back child support, and methods of resolving visitation problems. The association has filed lawsuits against state governments that have not provided adequate child support enforcement services and has lobbied Congress for passage of laws strengthening parents' ability to collect child support. The association sponsors an annual conference and workshops and publishes the handbook *How to Collect Child Support*. Dues include a subscription to its semiannual newsletter.

Stepfamily Association of America
650 J Street
Suite 205
Lincoln, NE 68508
Telephone: (402) 477-STEP
(800) 735-0329
E-mail: stepfamfs@aol.com
World Wide Web:
   http://www.stepfam.org

This association sponsors a network of support groups throughout the country. The membership fee entitles members to involvement in chapter activities, a free subscription to its 16-page quarterly newsletter, a catalog of additional resources, and discounts on its conference fees and books, including *Stepfamily Stepping Ahead,* which describes its eight-step program for successful stepfamily living.

Stepfamily Foundation Inc.
333 West End Avenue
New York, NY 10023
Telephone: (212) 877-3244
E-mail: stepfamily@aol.com
World Wide Web:
    http://www.stepfamily.org/

This organization educates and counsels those who live in stepfamilies and conducts seminars and training programs for stepparents and counselors. The membership fee entitles members to an assortment of books and booklets, a subscription to a quarterly newsletter, and the audiotape *The Dynamics of Step.* Its Web site contains helpful information and provides links to related organizations.

Children's Rights Council
220 I Street, N.E.
Suite 220
Washington, DC 20002
Telephone: (202) 547-6227
(800) 787-KIDS
Fax: (202) 546-4272
E-mail: crcdc@erols.com
World Wide Web:
    http://www.vix.com/crc/aboutcrc.htm

The philosophy of this organization is that children have a right to have access to both parents. The council sponsors a variety of services and programs for its 2,500 members, including a national conference, to help divorced parents put their children's welfare first. The council seeks to strengthen families through divorce and custody reform, equitable child support, and the use of alternative methods of dispute resolution. Members receive a variety of free items, including a subscription to the quarterly newsletter *Speak Out for Children* and a catalog of useful books, audiocassettes, and other items that can be purchased at discount. The council's Web site provides information on membership, local chapters, and relevant legislation.

National Coalition Against Domestic Violence
P.O. Box 18749
Denver, CO 80218
Telephone: (303) 839-1852
Fax: (303) 831-9251

This is a grass-roots coalition of service organizations for battered women. The coalition sponsors a phone referral service for battered women in the United States and Canada and assists those who feel uncertain about their options. Information packets on domestic violence are available.

Parents, Families, and Friends of Lesbians and Gays
1101 14th Street, N.W.
Suite 1030
Washington, DC 20005
Telephone: (202) 638-4200
Fax: (202) 638-0243
E-mail: info@pflag.org
World Wide Web:
   http://www.pflag.org

Parents, Families, and Friends of Lesbians and Gays is a network of about 70,000 members in 30 chapters offering contacts and sponsoring support groups and specialized support networks (such as the Straight Spouse Support Network) in the United States, Canada, and 11 other countries. PFLAG offers a variety of publications, reading lists, regional conferences, and national conventions for families with problems or questions related to homosexuality. It also sponsors the Family AIDS Support Project.

American Academy of Child and Adolescent Psychiatry
Public Information
P.O. Box 96106
Washington, DC 20090
Telephone: (202) 966-7300
Fax: (202) 466-2891
E-mail: mbell@aacap.org
World Wide Web:
  http://www.aacap.org

This is a professional association representing approximately 6,300 psychiatrists who specialize in the treatment of children and adolescents. The academy produces *Facts for Families*, a series of brief publications on 59 topics. Titles include *Children and Divorce, Making Day Care a Good Experience, Bedwetting, Stepfamily Problems, Child Sexual Abuse,* and those on specific childhood mental disorders. Much of this information is now available at its excellent Web site. Parents may call the academy to obtain referrals to child or adolescent psychiatrists in their local area.

American Psychiatric Association (APA)
Division of Public Affairs
1400 K Street, N.W.
Washington, DC 20005
Telephone: (202) 682-6000
Fax: (202) 682-6114
E-mail: apa@psych.org
World Wide Web:
http://www.psych.org

This is a professional association of approximately 42,000 psychiatrists in the United States and Canada. Its membership includes general psychiatrists as well as specialists in such areas as child and adolescent psychiatry, adult psychiatry, and forensic psychiatry. APA produces a number of fact sheets on specific adult and childhood disorders, including *Eating Disorders* and *Teen Suicide*, and most of these can be accessed at its Web site. APA also assists callers in obtaining referrals to appropriate psychiatrists in their local area and provides the pamphlet *Let's Talk Facts About Choosing a Psychiatrist* (also available on the Web site) to assist in the process.

American Psychological Association
750 First Street, N.E.
Washington, DC 20002-4242
Telephone: (202) 336-5700
World Wide Web:
http://www.apa.org

This professional association represents approximately 151,000 psychologists and psychology students in research, educational, and clinical settings. The association offers informational brochures of interest to parents, such as selecting a day-care center, the link between violence and television, and teaching self-discipline. The association also helps callers obtain referrals to appropriate psychologists in their local area.

National Alliance for the Mentally Ill (NAMI)
200 North Glebe Road, No. 1015
Arlington, VA 22203-3728
Telephone: (703) 524-7600
(800) 950-NAMI
Fax: (703) 524-9094
World Wide Web:
   http://www.nami.org/namihome.htm

This organization of 130,000 members is made up of family members, friends, and advocates of mentally ill people as well as patients and former patients in 50 state groups. It has a contact person in each state, and local chapters serve as support groups. NAMI provides information on specific mental and neurobiological disorders in both adults and children.

National Mental Health Association
1021 Prince Street
Alexandria, VA 22314
Telephone: (703) 684-7722
(800) 969-NMHA (National Mental Health
   Information Center)
Fax: (703) 684-5968
World Wide Web:
   http://www.nmha.org

This organization works to meet the mental health needs of communities through 350 state support groups, community outreach and education, information and referral programs, patient advocacy, and other services. Its membership numbers 416,000, and it serves approximately 2 million Americans. Among the information pamphlets it makes available for families of divorce are *When the Family Breaks Up, Growing Up With One Parent,* and *Coping With Separation and Divorce.* Pamphlets are also available on childhood mental and emotional disorders.

American Bar Association (ABA)
750 North Lake Shore Drive
Chicago, IL 60611
Telephone: (312) 988-5000
World Wide Web:
http://www.abanet.org

The ABA provides numerous publications related to divorce and referrals to attorneys in callers' local areas. Its Web site includes a list of publications and other resources related to family law, divorce, and child custody.

For Further Reading

These books should be available through your local library or quality bookstore. Most can also be ordered online through such cyberbookstores as Amazon (http://www.amazon.com) and Barnes & Noble (http://www.barnesandnoble.com/).

Books for Parents

Books Related to Divorce

Child Custody: Building Agreements That Work, 2nd edition, by Mimi E. Lyster. Berkeley, CA, Nolo Press, 1996.

Child Support: How to Get What Your Child Needs and Deserves, by Carole A. Chambers. New York, Summit Books, 1991.

Crazy Time: Surviving Divorce and Building a New Life, by Abigail Trafford. New York, HarperCollins, 1993.

Divorce and Your Child: Practical Suggestions for Parents, by Sonja Goldstein and Albert Solnit. New Haven, CT, Yale University Press, 1984.

For the Sake of the Children, by Kris Kline and Stephen Pew, Ph.D. Rocklin, CA, Prima Publishing, 1992.

Growing Up With Divorce: Helping Your Child Avoid Immediate and Later Emotional Problems, by Neil Kalter. New York, Free Press, 1990.

How to Win as a Stepfamily, 2nd edition, by Emily Visher, Ph.D., and John Visher, M.D. New York, Brunner/Mazel, 1991.

The Joint Custody Handbook: Creating Arrangements That Work, by Miriam Galper Cohen. Philadelphia, PA, Running Press, 1991.

Long-Distance Parenting, by Miriam Galper Cohen. New York, Signet, 1991.

Marriage, Divorce, and Children's Readjustment, by Robert Emery. Newbury Park, CA, Sage Publications, 1988.

Martindale-Hubbell Dispute Resolution Directory, 1996 edition, published in cooperation with the American Arbitration Association. New Providence, NJ, Martindale-Hubbell, 1996. This comprehensive reference book provides U.S. dispute resolution practitioners, such as mediators and arbitrators; federal legislation pertaining to dispute resolution; the family mediation rules of the American Arbitration Association, including confidentiality guidelines; and sample dispute resolution forms. This directory should be available at most public libraries.

Mister Rogers Talks With Families About Divorce, by Fred Rogers and Clare O'Brien. New York, Berkley Books, 1987.

My Kids Don't Live With Me Anymore, by Doreen Virtue. Minneapolis, MN, CompCare Publishers, 1988.

The Parents' Book About Divorce, by Richard Gardner, M.D. New York, Bantam Books, 1991.

Psychotherapy With Children of Divorce, by Richard Gardner, M.D. Northvale, NJ, Jason Aronson, 1991.

Second Chances: Men, Women, and Children a Decade After Divorce, by Judith Wallerstein and Sandra Blakeslee. Boston, MA, Houghton Mifflin Company, 1996.

Talking About Stepfamilies, by Maxine B. Rosenberg. New York, Bradbury Press, a Division of Macmillan Publishing, 1990.

Books on Parenting

Bringing Up Kids American Style, by Joseph Novello, M.D. New York, A and W Publishers, 1981.

Bringing Up Kids Without Tearing Them Down, by Keven Leman. New York, Delacorte Press, 1993.

How to Survive Your Kids: From Prebirth to Preteen, by Joseph Novello, M.D. New York, McGraw-Hill, 1988.

How to Talk So Kids Will Listen and Listen So Kids Will Talk, by Adele Faber and Elaine Mazlish. New York, Avon Books, 1991.

Raising Self-Reliant Children in a Self-Indulgent World, by H. Stephen Glenn and Jane Nelson. Rocklin, CA, Prima Publishing and Communications, 1988.

Teaching Your Child to Be Home Alone, by Earl A. Grollman and Gerri L. Sweder. New York, Lexington Books, a division of Macmillan Publishing, 1992.

Teaching Your Children Values, by Linda and Richard Eyre. New York, Fireside Books, Simon and Schuster, 1993.

The Time-Out Solution, by Lynn Clark, Ph.D. Chicago, IL, Contemporary Books Inc., 1989.

Touchpoints: Your Child's Emotional and Behavioral Development: The Essential Reference, by T. Berry Brazelton, M.D. Reading, MA, Addison-Wesley, 1992.

The Trouble With Boys: A Wise and Sympathetic Guide to the Risky Business of Raising Sons, by Angela Phillips. New York, Basic Books, 1994.

Also:

What Kids Want to Know About Sex and Growing Up, by the Children's Television Workshop. This is a video program aimed at children between the ages of 8 and 12 and includes a parent's guide. 1992.

Books for Children

Changing Families: A Guide for Kids and Grownups, by David Fassler, Michele Lash, and Sally Blakeslee Ives. Burlington, VT, Waterfront Books, 1988.

The Choice Is Yours: A Teenager's Guide to Self-Discovery, Relationships, Values, and Spiritual Growth, by Bonnie M. Parsley. New York, Simon & Schuster, 1992.

The Dinosaurs Divorce: A Guide for Changing Families, by Laurene Krasny Brown and Marc Brown. Boston, MA, Atlantic Monthly Press, 1986.

The Divorce Workbook: A Guide for Kids and Families, by Sally Blakeslee Ives, David Fassler, and Michele Lash. Burlington, VT, Waterfront Books, 1988.

How It Feels When Parents Divorce, by Jill Krementz. New York, Knopf, 1984.

Please Come Home: A Child's Book About Divorce, by Doris Sanford. Sisters, OR, Multnomah Press, 1985.

What Am I Doing in a Stepfamily? by Claire Berman. New York, Carol Publishing Group, 1992.

What Would You Do? A Child's Book About Divorce, by Barbara Cain, M.S.W., and Elissa Benedek, M.D. Washington, DC, American Psychiatric Association, 1986.

Why Are We Getting a Divorce? by Peter Mayle. New York, Harmony Books, 1988.

BIBLIOGRAPHY

Beal EW, Hochman G: *Adult Children of Divorce*. New York, Delacort Press, 1991

Brooks R: *The Self-Esteem Teacher.* Circle Pines, MN, American Guidance Service, 1991

Caplan G: Parental divorce without harm. *Sexual and Marital Therapy*, vol 4, 1989, pp 125–126

Cherlin AJ: *Marriage, Divorce, Remarriage*. Cambridge, MA, Harvard University Press, 1992

Cherlin AJ, Furstenberg FF, Chase-Lansdale PL, et al: Longitudinal studies of effects of divorce on children in Great Britain and the United States. *Science*, vol 252, 1991, pp 1386–1389

Cramer D: Gay parents and their children: a review of research and practical implications. *Journal of Counseling and Development*, vol 64, 1986, pp 504–507

Dixon SD, Stein MT (ed): *Encounters With Children: Pediatric Behavior and Development*, 2nd Edition. St. Louis, MO, Mosby Year Book, 1992

Doherty WJ, Needle RH: Psychological adjustment and substance use among adolescents before and after a parental divorce. *Child Development*, vol 62, 1991, pp 328–337

Emery RE: Children in the divorce process. *Journal of Family Psychology*, vol 2, 1988, pp 141–144

Fauber R, Forehand R, Thomas AM, Wierson M: A mediational model of the impact of marital conflict on adolescent adjustment in intact and divorced families: the role of disrupted parenting. *Child Development*, vol 61, 1990, pp 1112–1123

Forehand R, Wierson M, Thomas AM, et al: A short-term longitudinal examination of young adolescent functioning following divorce: the role of family factors. *Journal of Abnormal Child Psychology*, vol 19, 1991, pp 97–111

Gardner RA: *Child Custody Litigation*. Crosskill, NJ, Creative Therapeutics, 1986

Glover RJ, Steele C: Comparing the effects on the child of post-divorce parenting arrangements. *Journal of Divorce*, vol 12 (special issue), 1988–89, pp 185–201

Hetherington EM: Coping with family transitions: winners, losers, and survivors. *Child Development*, vol 60, 1989, pp 1–14

Hetherington EM: Families, lies, and videotapes. *Journal of Research on Adolescence*, vol 1, 1991, pp 323–348

Hetherington EM, Stanley-Hagan M, Anderson ER: Marital transitions: a child's perspective. *American Psychologist*, vol 44 (special issue), 1989, pp 303–312

Hetherington EM, Cox M, Cox R: Long-term effects of divorce and remarriage on the adjustment of children. *Journal of the American Academy of Child and Adolescent Psychiatry*, vol 30, 1991, pp 349–360

Hodges WF, London J, Colwell JB: Stress in parents and late elementary age children in divorced and intact families and child adjustment. *Journal of Divorce and Remarriage*, vol 14, 1990, pp 63–79

Jenny C, Roesler TA, Poyer KL: Are children at risk for sexual abuse by homosexuals? *Pediatrics*, vol 94, 1994, pp 41–44

Kalter N, Kloner A, Schreier S, Okla K: Predictors of children's postdivorce adjustment. *American Journal of Orthopsychiatry,* vol 59, 1989, pp 605–618

Kelly JB: Longer-term adjustment in children of divorce: converging findings and implications for practice. *Journal of Family Psychology,* vol 2, 1988, pp 119–140

Kelly JB: Parent interaction after divorce: comparison of mediated and adversarial divorce processes. *Behavioral Sciences and the Law,* vol 9, 1991, pp 387–398

Kennelly J: Ways going on-line can change your life. *Fast Forward* (magazine), *Washington Post,* September 1994, pp 8–13

Kline K, Pew S: *For the Sake of the Children.* Rocklin, CA, Prima Publishing, 1992

Kurdek LA: Issues in the study of children and divorce. *Journal of Family Psychology,* vol 2, 1988, pp 150–153

McKinnon R, Wallerstein JS: Joint custody and the preschool child. *Behavioral Sciences and the Law,* vol 4, 1986, pp 169–184

McKinnon R, Wallerstein JS: A preventive intervention program for parents and young children in joint custody arrangements. *American Journal of Orthopsychiatry,* vol 58, 1988, pp 168–178

Novello JR: *Bringing Up Kids American Style.* New York, A and W Publishers, 1981

Portes PR, Howel SC, Brown JH, et al: Family functions and children's postdivorce adjustment. *American Journal of Orthopsychiatry,* vol 62, 1992, pp 613–617

Robbins NN (ed): Visitation: there is a better way. *Michigan Family Law Journal* (special issue), 1992

Saluter AF: Marital status and living arrangements: March 1993. U.S. Bureau of the Census, *Current Population Reports,* Series P20-478. Washington, DC, U.S. Government Printing Office, 1994

Schetky DH, Benedek EP: *Clinical Handbook of Child Psychiatry and the Law.* Baltimore, MD, Williams and Wilkins, 1992

Schwartzberg AZ: The impact of divorce on adolescents. *Hospital and Community Psychiatry*, vol 43, 1992, pp 634–637

Tschann JM, Johnston JR, Kline M, Wallerstein JS: Conflict, loss, change and parent-child relationships: predicting children's adjustment during divorce. *Journal of Divorce*, vol 13, 1990, pp 1–22

U.S. Bureau of the Census: *Child Support and Alimony: 1989. Current Population Reports*, Series P-60, No. 173. Washington, DC, U.S. Government Printing Office, 1991

U.S. General Accounting Office: *Interstate Child Support: Wage Withholding not Fulfilling Expectations* (GAO/HRD-92-65BR). Washington, DC, U.S. Government Printing Office, February 1992

Wakefield H, Underwager R: Sexual abuse allegations in divorce and custody disputes. *Behavioral Sciences and the Law*, vol 9, 1991, pp 451–468

Wallerstein JS: Children of divorce: preliminary report of a ten-year follow-up of older children and adolescents. *Journal of the American Academy of Child Psychiatry*, vol 24, 1985, pp 545–553

Wallerstein JS: The long-term effects of divorce on children: a review. *Journal of the American Academy of Child and Adolescent Psychiatry*, vol 30, 1991, pp 349–360

Wallerstein JS, Blakeslee S: *Second Chances*. New York, Ticknor and Fields, 1990

Wallerstein JS, Corbin SB: Daughters of divorce: report from a ten-year follow-up. *American Journal of Orthopsychiatry*, vol 59, 1989, pp 593–604

Wallerstein JS, Kelly JB: *Surviving the Breakup*. New York, Basic Books, 1980

Wallerstein JS, Kelly JB: Effects of divorce on the visiting father-child relationship. *American Journal of Psychiatry*, vol 137, 1988, pp 1534–1539

Weiss RS: *Marital Separation*. New York, Basic Books, 1975

Weissman HN: Child custody evaluations: fair and unfair professional practices. *Behavioral Sciences and the Law,* vol 9, 1991, pp 469–476

Wolfe DA: *Preventing Physical and Emotional Abuse of Children.* New York, Guilford Press, 1991

Wolman R, Taylor K: Psychological effects of custody disputes on children. *Behavioral Sciences and the Law,* vol 9, 1991, pp 399–417

Index

About the Authors

ELISSA P. BENEDEK, M.D., is a leading child psychiatrist and forensic expert. She is the Director of Research and Training at the Center for Forensic Psychiatry in Ann Arbor, Michigan, and Clinical Professor of Psychiatry at the University of Michigan, Michigan State University, and Wayne State University. Benedek has held some of the most prestigious positions in her profession, including a term as only the second woman president of the American Psychiatric Association in its 153-year history. She has also worked tirelessly for many years as an advocate of the mental needs of American children to policymakers and legislators. She lives in Ann Arbor, Michigan.

CATHERINE F. BROWN, M.ED., has been with *Psychiatric News,* the newspaper of the American Psychiatric Association, since 1982.

ABOUT THE AUTHOR

Parenting and Childcare Books from Newmarket Press

Baby Massage
Parent-Child Bonding Through Touching
Amelia D. Auckett; Introduction by Dr. Tiffany Field

A fully-illustrated, practical, time-tested approach to the ancient art of baby massage. Topics include bonding and body contact; baby massage as an alternative to drugs, healing the effects of birth trauma; and massage as an expression of love. Includes 34 photographs and drawings, a bibliography, and an index. (128 pages; 5 ½" x 8 ¼"; paperback)

How Do We Tell the Children?
A Step-by-Step Guide for Helping Children Two to Teen Cope When Someone Dies—Updated Edition
Dan Schaefer and Christine Lyons; Foreword by David Peretz, M.D.

This invaluable book provides straightforward language to help parents explain death to children from age two through teens. It includes insights from psychologists, educators, and clergy. Special features include a 16-page crisis-intervention guide to deal with situations such as accidents, AIDS, terminal illness, and suicide. "Parents need this clear, extremely readable guide...highly recommended." *(Library Journal)* (192 pages; 5 ½" x 8 ¼"; hardcover & paperback)

Inner Beauty, Inner Light
Yoga for Pregnant Women
Frederick Leboyer, M.D.

In matchless prose and stunning photographs, Frederick Leboyer discusses the importance and beauty of yoga for pregnant women. He shows how they can use yoga to move toward healthy and joyous childbearing, and how the health benefits will far outlast the birthing process for both mother and child. "Frederick Leboyer is that rare modern combination of scientist, mystic and poet." *(Newsweek)* (276 pages; 8" x 10"; paperback)

In Time and With Love
Caring for the Special Needs Baby
Marily Segal, Ph.D.

Sensitive, practical advice on play and care for the preterm and handicapped child. Includes information about daily care, interacting with siblings, coping with doctors, discipline, social skills, and tough decision making. Also included is a special section on activities to promote emotional development and encourage motor and language skills. "This book accomplishes its goal of presenting an honest picture of what it's like to live with a difficult baby." *(Journal of the Association for Persons with Severe Handicaps)* (208 pages; 7 ¼" x 9"; hardcover & paperback)

Loving Hands
The Traditional Art of Baby Massage
Frederick Leboyer, M.D.

In *Loving Hands*, Frederick Leboyer uses his deep insight into childcare, as well as knowledge gleaned from his travels in India, to show us how, in the weeks and months following birth, we can use the flowing rhythms of the art of baby massage to communicate our love and strength to our babies. "Leboyer puts the baby into psychological focus. He conveys his message with superb photography and poetic language." *(Psychology Today)* (144 pages; 8" x 10"; paperback)

Mothering the New Mother
Your Postpartum Resource Companion
Sally Placksin

This all-in-one resource guide covers everything from homecare options, help for breastfeeding problems, and workplace negotiation strategies, to adjusting to full-time motherhood, postpartum depression, and hiring a doula. Each chapter is filled with practical suggestions, hands-on solutions;,and an invaluable listing of the newsletters, books, hotlines, videocassettes, support groups, services, and caregivers available to the new mother. Includes checklists, planning sheets, an index, and resource guides. (352 pages; 7 ¼" x 9"; paperback)

My Body, My Self for Boys
The What's Happening to My Body? Workbook for Boys
Lynda Madaras and Area Madaras
Packed with drawings, cartoons, games, checklists, quizzes, and innovative exercises, this book encourages boys to address head on their concerns with their body, body image, height, weight, growth, hair, voice changes, reproductive organs, sexuality, emotional problems of puberty, diet, and health. Winner of the *American Library Association* "Best Books of the Year" Award. (128 pages; 7 ¼" x 9"; paperback)

My Body, My Self for Girls
The What's Happening to My Body? Workbook for Girls
Lynda Madaras and Area Madaras
The companion book to *The What's Happening to My Body? Book for Girls*, this workbook/diary encourages girls ages 9 to 15 to explore their feelings about their changing bodies. Everything affected by the onset of puberty is covered, from body image, pimples, and cramps, to first periods, first bras, and first impressions. Includes quizzes, checklists, exercises, and illustrations. (128 pages; 7 ¼" x 9"; paperback)

My Feelings, My Self
Lynda Madaras' Growing-Up Guide for Girls
Lynda Madaras with Area Madaras
For preteens and teens, a workbook/journal to help girls explore their changing relationships with parents and friends; complete with quizzes, exercises, letters, and space to record personal experiences. Includes drawings and a bibliography. (160 pages; 7 ¼" x 9"; paperback)

Raising Your Jewish/Christian Child
How Interfaith Parents Can Give Children the Best of Both Their Heritages
Lee F. Gruzen, Forewords by Rabbi Lavey Derby and the Reverend Canon Joel A. Gibson
This pioneering guide details how people have found their own paths in Jewish/Christian marriages, and how they have given their children a solid foundation to seek their own identity. Includes a bibliography and an index. (288 pages; 5 ⁵⁄₁₆" x 8"; paperback)

The Ready-to-Read, Ready-to-Count Handbook
How to Best Prepare Your Child for School—A Parent's Guide
Teresa Savage
A step-by-step guide that shows how to teach preschoolers basic phonics and numbers. Over 60 phonetic learning exercises, 35 games, homemade flashcards, 24 assignments, and a series of cartoons encourage a tension-free, fun-filled environment while your child develops skills in motor ability, logic, listening, and comprehension. Includes a biblography, an index, and reference lists. (272 pages; 5 ⁵⁄₁₆" x 8"; paperback)

Saying No Is Not Enough
Helping Your Kids Make Wise Decisions About Alcohol, Tobacco, and Other Drugs—A Guide for Parents of Children Ages 3 Through 19
Robert Schwebel, Ph.D.; Introduction by Benjamin Spock, M.D.
This acclaimed book is the most recommended guide for parents to help them meet the growing problem of "kids and pot" as well as other drug prevention issues. Since its initial publication in 1989, health education and parenting experts have recommended the book for its wisdom and practical advice. "Wise and wondrously specific: a solid parenting manual." (*Kirkus Reviews*) Includes a bibliography and an index. (304 pages; 6" x 9"; paperback)

The Totally Awesome Business Book for Kids (and Their Parents)
Adriane G. Berg and Arthur Berg Bochner
Everything kids need to know about business with special attention to jobs that help the environment. Introduces vital business skills such as research, telephoning, negotiating, complaining when appropriate, making contracts, filing, and record keeping. Includes illustrations, a bibliography, and a glossary. (160 pages; 5 ⁵⁄₁₆" x 8"; paperback)

The Totally Awesome Money Book for Kids (and Their Parents)
Adriane G. Berg and Arthur Berg Bochner

For young readers from ten to seventeen, this fun, fact-filled guide uses quizzes, games, riddles, stories, and drawings to teach the basics of saving, investing, borrowing, working, taxes, and more. Includes illustrations, a bibliography, and a glossary. An *American Library Association* "Best Book of the Year" finalist. (160 pages; 5 ⁵⁄₁₆" x 8"; hardcover & paperback)

The What's Happening to My Body? Book for Boys
Growing Up Guide for Parents and Sons—New Edition
Lynda Madaras with Dane Saavedra

Written with candor, humor, and clarity, here is much-needed but hard-to-find information on the special problems boys face during puberty. It includes chapters on the body's changing size and shape, hair, perspiration, pimples, and voice changes; the reproductive organs; sexuality; and more. "Down-to-earth, conversational treatment of a topic that remains taboo in many families." *(The Washington Post)* Includes drawings, charts, diagrams, a bibliography, and an index. (288 pages; 5 ½" x 8 ¼"; hardcover & paperback)

The What's Happening to My Body? Book for Girls
Growing Up Guide for Parents and Daughters—New Edition
Lynda Madaras with Area Madaras

Selected as a "Best Book for Young Adults" by the *American Library Association*, this bestselling book provides explains what takes place in a girl's body as she grows up. Includes chapters on the body's changing size and shape, the reproductive organs, menstruation,; and much more. Includes drawings, charts, diagrams, a bibliography, and an index. (304 pages; 5 ½" x 8 ¼"; hardcover & paperback)

Your Child at Play: Birth to One Year
Discovering the Senses and Learning About the World
Marilyn Segal, Ph.D.

Focuses on the subtle developmental changes that take place in each of the first twelve months of life and features over 400 activities that parent and child can enjoy together during day-to-day routines. "Insightful, warm, and practical . . . expert knowledge that's a must for every parent." (T. Berry Brazelton, M.D.) Includes more than 250 photographs and a bibliography. (352 pages; ¼" x 9"; hardcover & paperback)

Your Child at Play: One to Two Years
Exploring, Daily Living, Learning, and Making Friends
Marilyn Segal, Ph.D.

Hundreds of suggestions for creative play and for coping with everyday life with a toddler, including situations such as going out in public, toilet training, and sibling rivalry. "An excellent guide to the hows, whys, and what-to-dos of play." *(Publishers Weekly)* Includes more than 300 photographs, a bibliography, and an index. (288 pages; 7 ¼" x 9"; hardcover & paperback)

Your Child at Play: Two to Three Years
Growing Up, Language, and the Imagination
Marilyn Segal, Ph.D.

Provides vivid descriptions of how two-year-olds see themselves, learn language, play imaginatively, get along with others, make friends, and explore what's around them. It give specific advice on routine problems and concerns common to this age group. Includes more than 175 photographs, a bibliography, and an index. (272 pages; 7 ¼" x 9"; hardcover & paperback)

Your Child at Play: Three to Five Years
Conversation, Creativity, and Learning Letters, Words, and Numbers
Marilyn Segal, Ph.D.

Hundreds of practical ideas for exploring the world of the preschooler, with sections devoted to conversation, creative play, learning letters and numbers, and making friends. Includes more than 300 photographs, a bibliography, and an index. (288 pages; 7 ¼" x 9"; hardcover & paperback)

PARENTING/CHILDCARE BOOKS FROM NEWMARKET PRESS

Ask for these titles at your local bookstore or use this coupon and enclose a check or money order payable to: **Newmarket Press**, 18 E. 48th St., NY, NY 10017.

Baby Massage
____ $11.95 pb (1-55704-022-2)
How to Help Your Child
Overcome Your Divorce
____ $14.95 pb (1-55704-329-9)
How Do We Tell the Children?
____ $18.95 hc (1-55704-189-X)
____ $11.95 pb (1-55704-181-4)
Inner Beauty, Inner Light:
Yoga for Pregnant Women
____ $18.95 pb (1-55704-315-9)
In Time and With Love
____ $21.95 hc (0-937858-95-1)
____ $12.95 pb (0-937858-96-X)
Loving Hands: Traditional Baby Massage
____ $15.95 pb (1-55704-314-0)
Mothering the New Mother, Rev. Ed.
____ $16.95 pb (1-55704-317-5)
My Body, My Self for Boys
____ $11.95 pb (1-55704-230-6)
My Body, My Self for Girls
____ $11.95 pb (1-55704-150-4)
My Feelings, My Self
____ $11.95 pb (1-55704-157-1)
Raising Your Jewish/Christian Child
____ $12.95 pb (1-55704-059-1)
The Ready-to-Read,
Ready-to-Count Handbook
____ $11.95 pb (1-55704-093-1)

Saying No Is Not Enough, Rev. Ed.
____ $14.95 pb (1-55704-318-3)
The Totally Awesome Business Book
for Kids (and Their Parents)
____ $10.95 pb (1-55704-226-8)
The Totally Awesome Money Book
for Kids (and Their Parents)
____ $18.95 hc (1-55704-183-0)
____ $10.95 pb (1-55704-176-8)
The What's Happening to My Body?
Book for Boys
____$18.95 hc (1-55704-002-8)
____$11.95 pb (0-937858-99-4)
The What's Happening to My Body?
Book for Girls
____ $18.95 hc (1-55704-001-X)
____ $11.95 pb (0-937858-98-6)
Your Child at Play: Birth to One Year, Rev.
____ $24.95 hc (1-55704-334-5)
____ $15.95 pb (1-55704-330-2)
Your Child at Play: One to Two Years, Rev.
____ $24.95 hc (1-55704-335-3)
____ $15.95 pb (1-55704-331-0)
Your Child at Play: Two to Three Years, Re
____ $24.95 hc (1-55704-336-15)
____ $15.95 pb (1-55704-332-9)
Your Child at Play: Three to Five Years, Re
____ $24.95 hc (1-55704-337-X)
____ $15.95 pb (1-55704-333-7)

For postage and handling, please add $3.00 for the first book, plus $1.00 for each additional book. Prices and availability are subject to change.

I enclose a check or money order payable to **Newmarket Press** in the amount of _____

Name _____

Address _____

City/State/Zip _____

For discounts on orders of five or more copies or to get a catalog,
contact Newmarket Press, Special Sales Department, 18 East 48th Street, NY, NY 10017;
Tel.: 212-832-3575 or 800-669-3903; Fax: 212-832-3629.